Electrician

and

Electrician's Helper

9th Edition

Edited by
Dr. Rex Miller
Professor Emeritus of Industrial Technology
State University College
Buffalo, NY

and

Dr. Mark R. Miller
Chairman and Associate Professor of Industrial Technology
Texas A & M University-Kingsville

THOMSON
ARCO

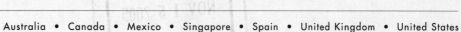
Australia • Canada • Mexico • Singapore • Spain • United Kingdom • United States

An ARCO Book

ARCO is a registered trademark of Thomson Learning, Inc., and is used herein under license by Peterson's.

About The Thomson Corporation and Peterson's

With revenues of US$7.2 billion, The Thomson Corporation (www.thomson.com) is a leading global provider of integrated information solutions for business, education, and professional customers. Its Learning businesses and brands (www.thomsonlearning.com) serve the needs of individuals, learning institutions, and corporations with products and services for both traditional and distributed learning.

Peterson's, part of The Thomson Corporation, is one of the nation's most respected providers of lifelong learning online resources, software, reference guides, and books. The Education Supersite[SM] at www.petersons.com—the Internet's most heavily traveled education resource—has searchable databases and interactive tools for contacting U.S.-accredited institutions and programs. In addition, Peterson's serves more than 105 million education consumers annually.

For more information, contact Peterson's, 2000 Lenox Drive, Lawrenceville, NJ 08648;
800-338-3282; or find us on the World Wide Web at www.petersons.com/about.

ISBN 0-7689-0854-X

Printed in the United States of America

10 9 8 7 6 5 4 3   06 05 04

CONTENTS

PART 3: PREVIOUS EXAMINATIONS FOR PRACTICE

APPENDIX

WHAT THIS BOOK WILL DO FOR YOU

ARCO has followed testing trends and methods ever since the line was created. We specialize in books that prepare people for tests. Based on this experience, we have prepared the best possible book to help you score high.

To write this book, we carefully analyzed every detail surrounding electrician examinations, including

- the job itself;

- official and unofficial announcements concerning electrician examinations;

- previous examinations, many not available to the public;

- related examinations; and

- technical literature that explains and forecasts the examination.

CAN YOU PREPARE YOURSELF FOR YOUR TEST?

You want to pass this test. That's why you bought this book. Used correctly, your "self-tutor" will show you what to expect and will give you a speedy brush-up on the subjects tested on your exam. Even if your study time is very limited, you should

- become familiar with the type of examination you will have.

- improve your general test-taking skills.

- improve your skill in analyzing and answering questions involving reasoning, judgment, comparison, and evaluation.

- improve your speed and skill in reading and understanding what you read—an important part of your ability to learn and an important part of most tests.

This book will do the following:

Present the type of questions you will see on the actual test—This will help you feel at ease with the test format.

Pinpoint your weaknesses—Once you know the subjects in which you're weak, you can get right to work and concentrate on those areas. This kind of selective study yields maximum test results.

Supply practice with sample tests—Almost all our sample and practice questions are taken from actual previous exams. On the day of the exam, you'll see how closely this book follows the format of the real test.

Give you confidence *now*, while you are preparing for the test. It will build your self-confidence as you proceed and will prevent the kind of test anxiety that can cause low test scores.

Focus on the multiple-choice type of question because that's the kind you'll encounter on your test. You must not be satisfied with merely knowing the correct answer for each question. You must find out why the other choices are incorrect. This will help you remember information you thought you had forgotten.

After testing yourself, you may find that you are weak in a particular area. You should concentrate on improving your skills by using the specific practice sections in this book that apply to you.

PART ONE

The Kind of Work You Will Be Doing

THE KIND OF WORK YOU WILL BE DOING

Electricity is essential for light, power, air-conditioning, and refrigeration. Electricians install and maintain electrical systems for a variety of purposes, including climate control, security, and communications. They also may install and maintain the electronic controls for machines in business and industry. Although most electricians specialize in either *construction* or *maintenance*, a growing number do both.

NATURE OF THE WORK

Electricians work with blueprints when they install electrical systems in factories, office buildings, homes, and other structures. Blueprints indicate the location of circuits, outlets, load centers, panel boards, and other equipment. Electricians must follow the National Electric Code and comply with state and local building codes when they install these systems. In factories and offices, they first place conduit (pipe or tubing) inside designated partitions, walls, or other concealed areas. They also fasten to the wall small metal or plastic boxes that will house electrical switches and outlets. They then pull insulated wires or cables through the conduit to complete circuits between these boxes. In lighter construction, such as residential, plastic-covered wire usually is used rather than conduit.

Regardless of the type of wire being used, electricians connect it to circuit breakers, transformers, or other components. Wires are joined by twisting ends together with pliers and covering the ends with special plastic connectors. For additional strength, electricians may use an electric "soldering gun" to melt solder onto the twisted wires, which they then cover with durable electrical tape. When the wiring is finished, they test the circuits for proper connections.

In addition to wiring a building's electrical system, electricians may install coaxial or fiber optic cable for computers and other telecommunications equipment. A growing number of electricians install telephone and computer wiring and equipment. They also may connect motors to electrical power and install electronic controls for industrial equipment.

Maintenance work varies greatly, depending on where the electrician is employed. Electricians who specialize in residential work may rewire a home and replace an old fuse box with a new circuit breaker to accommodate additional appliances. Those who work in large factories may repair motors, transformers, generators, and electronic controllers on machine tools and industrial robots. Those in office buildings and small plants may repair all kinds of electrical equipment. Maintenance electricians spend much of their time in preventive maintenance. They periodically inspect equipment and locate and correct problems before breakdowns occur. When breakdowns occur, they must make the necessary repairs as quickly as possible in order to minimize the inconvenience to the customer. Electricians may replace items such as circuit breakers, fuses, switches, electrical and electronic components, or wire. When working with complex electronic devices, they may work with engineers, engineering technicians, or industrial machinery repairers. Electricians also may advise management whether continued operation of equipment could be hazardous. When needed, they install new electrical equipment.

Electricians use handtools such as screwdrivers, pliers, knives, and hacksaws. They also use power tools and testing equipment such as oscilloscopes, ammeters, and test lamps.

WORKING CONDITIONS

Electricians' work is sometimes strenuous. They may stand for long periods and frequently work on ladders and scaffolds. They often work in awkward or cramped positions. Electricians risk injury from electrical shock, falls, and cuts; to avoid injuries, they must follow strict safety procedures. Most electricians work a standard 40-hour week, although overtime may be required. Those in maintenance work may have to work nights or on weekends, and may have to be on call.

EMPLOYMENT

Electricians held about 570,000 jobs in the late 1990s. Slightly more than half were employed in the construction industry. Others worked as maintenance electricians and were employed in virtually every industry. In addition, about one out of eleven electricians was self-employed.

Because of the widespread need for electrical services, jobs for electricians are found in all parts of the country.

TRAINING

The best way to learn the electrical trade is by completing a four-year apprenticeship program. Apprenticeship gives trainees a thorough knowledge of all aspects of the trade and generally improves their ability to find a job. Although more electricians are trained through apprenticeship than workers in other construction trades, some still learn their skills informally on the job.

Large apprenticeship programs are usually sponsored by joint committees made up of local unions of the International Brotherhood of Electrical Workers and local chapters of the National Electrical Contractors Association, by company management committees of individual electrical contracting companies, and by local chapters of the Associated Builders and Contractors. Because of the comprehensive training received, those who complete apprenticeship programs qualify to do both maintenance and construction work. The typical program provides at least 150 hours of classroom instruction each year and 8,000 hours of on-the-job training over the course of the apprenticeship. In the classroom, apprentices learn blueprint reading, electrical theory, electronics, mathematics, electrical code requirements, and safety and first aid practices. On the job, under the supervision of experienced electricians, apprentices must demonstrate mastery of the electrician's work. At first, they drill holes, set anchors, and set up conduit. Later, they measure, bend, and install conduit, as well as install, connect, and test wiring, outlets, and switches. They also learn to set up and draw diagrams for entire electrical systems.

Those who do not enter a formal apprenticeship program can begin to learn the trade informally by working as helpers for experienced electricians. While they are learning to install conduit, connect wires, and test circuits, helpers also are taught safety practices. Many helpers supplement this training with trade school or correspondence courses.

Regardless of how one learns the trade, previous training is very helpful. High school courses in mathematics, electricity, electronics, mechanical drawing, science, and industrial arts/technology education provide a good background. Special training offered in the Armed Forces and by postsecondary technical schools also is beneficial.

QUALIFICATIONS

All applicants should be in good health and have at least average physical strength. Agility and dexterity also are important. Good color vision is needed because workers frequently must identify electrical wires by color.

Most apprenticeship sponsors require applicants for apprentice positions to be at least 18 years old and to have a high school diploma or its equivalent. High school equivalency certificates are not accepted by joint union-management programs. For those interested in becoming maintenance electricians, a background in electronics is increasingly important because of the growing use of complex electronic controls on manufacturing equipment.

Although licensing requirements vary from area to area, electricians generally must pass an examination that tests their knowledge of electrical theory, the National Electrical Code, and local electric and building codes. Note that most localities require electricians to be licensed.

Experienced electricians periodically take courses offered by their employer or union to keep abreast of changes in the National Electrical Code and in new materials and methods of installation.

ADVANCEMENT

Experienced electricians can become supervisors. Those with sufficient capital and management skills may start their own contracting business. In many areas, however, a contractor must have an electrical contractor's license. Courses offered by employers or unions can also help speed up the advancement process.

JOB OUTLOOK

Employment of electricians is expected to increase about as fast as the average for all occupations through the year 2005. As the population and the economy grow, more electricians will be needed to install and maintain electrical devices and wiring in homes, factories, offices, and other structures. New technologies also are expected to continue to stimulate the demand for these workers. Buildings will be prewired during construction to accommodate use of computers and telecommunications equipment. More and more factories will be using robots and automated manufacturing systems. Installation of this equipment, which is expected to increase sharply, should generate many job opportunities.

Although the employment outlook for electricians is expected to be good over the long run, people wishing to become construction electricians should be prepared to experience periods of unemployment. These result from the limited duration of construction projects and the cyclical nature of the construction industry. During economic downturns, job openings for electricians are reduced as the level of construction declines. Apprenticeship opportunities also are less plentiful during these periods.

Employment of maintenance electricians is steadier than that of construction electricians, those working in the automotive, metalworking, and other industries that are sensitive to cyclical swings in the economy, but they may be laid off during recessions. Also, efforts to reduce operating costs and increase productivity through the increased use of contracting out for electrical services may limit opportunities for maintenance electricians in many industries. However, this should be partially offset by increased demand by electrical contracting firms.

Job opportunities for electricians also vary by geographic area. Employment opportunities follow the movement of people and businesses among states and local areas and reflect differences in local economic conditions. The number of job opportunities in a given year may fluctuate widely from area to area. Some parts of the country may experience an oversupply of electricians, for example, while others may have a severe shortage. Civil service employment provides job stability and career growth for many qualified electricians.

In addition to jobs created by increased demand for electrical work, many openings will occur each year as electricians transfer to other occupations, retire, or leave the labor force for other reasons. Because of their lengthy training and relatively high earnings, a smaller proportion of electricians than other craft workers leave their occupation each year. The number of retirements is expected to rise, however, as more electricians reach retirement age. Young adults have traditionally filled apprenticeship and other training slots; this group is expected to shrink through the year 2005. If employers and unions aren't successful in attracting more applicants to training programs, widespread shortages of qualified electricians could develop.

Women are now looking at the electrician's trade as an opportunity for them to enter a once men only occupation. For more information, contact:

The National Association of Women in Construction
327 South Adams Street
Ft. Worth, Texas 76104
817-877-5551
www.nawic.org

EARNINGS

Median weekly earnings for full-time electricians who were not self-employed were $21.00 per hour in the late 1990s. The middle 50 percent earned between $12.69 and $22.34 per hour. The lowest 10 percent earned less than $10.07 per hour, while the highest 10 percent earned more than $30.99 per hour.

Maintenance electricians in metropolitan areas earned about $16.68 an hour in 1998. The middle half earned between $13.10 and $19.15 an hour. Annual earnings of electricians also tend to be higher than those of workers in other building trades because electricians are less affected by the seasonal nature of construction. Those who work in the Midwest and West generally earn more than those in the Northeast and South. Annual earnings of electricians also tend to be higher than those of other building trades workers because electricians are less affected by the seasonal nature of construction.

Depending on experience, apprentices usually start at 30 to 50 percent of the rate paid to experienced electricians. As they become more skilled, they receive periodic increases throughout the course of the apprenticeship program.

Electricians receive a variety of employer-provided benefits. Although benefits for unionized electricians usually are more generous, most electricians receive health insurance. Many employers also provide training opportunities for experienced electricians to improve their skills.

Many construction electricians are members of the International Brotherhood of Electrical Workers. Among unions organizing maintenance electricians are the International Brotherhood of Electrical Workers; the International Union of Electronic, Electrical, Salaried, Machine, and Furniture Workers; the International Association of Machinists and Aerospace Workers; the International Union, United Automobile, Aerospace, and Agricultural Implement Workers of America; and the United Steelworkers of America.

Related Occupations

To install and maintain electrical systems, electricians combine manual skill and a knowledge of electrical materials and concepts. Workers in other occupations involving similar skills include:

- air-conditioning mechanics
- cable installers and repairers
- electronics mechanics
- elevator constructors

Sources of Additional Information

For details about apprenticeships or other work opportunities in this trade, contact local electrical contractors; local chapters of the Independent Electrical Contractors, Inc., the National

Electrical Contractors Association, or the Associated Builders and Contractors; a local union of the International Brotherhood of Electrical Workers; a local union-management electrician apprenticeship committee; local firms that employ maintenance electricians; or the nearest office of the state employment service or state apprenticeship agency.

For general information about the work of electricians, contact:

Independent Electrical Contractors, Inc.
2010-A Eisenhower Ave.
Alexandria, VA 22314
Telephone: 800-456-4324 (toll-free)
703-549-7351
www.ieci.org

International Brotherhood of Electrical Workers (IBEW)
1125 15th St. N.W.
Washington, D.C. 20005
Telephone: 202-833-7000
www.ibew.org

National Electrical Contractors Association (NECA)
3 Bethesda Metro Center, Ste. 1100
Bethesda, MD 20814
Telephone: 301-657-3310
www.necanet.org

Associated Builders and Contractors
1300 N. 17th St.
Rosslyn, VA 22209
Telephone: 703-812-2000
www.abc.org

Home Builders Institute
1201 15th St. NW
Washington, D.C. 20005
Telephone: 202-371-0600
www.hbi.org

National Joint Apprenticeship Training Committee
301 Prince George's Blvd., Suite F
Upper Marlboro, MD 20814
Telephone: 301-715-2300
www.njatc.org

SAMPLE NOTICE OF EXAMINATION FOR APPRENTICE ELECTRICIAN/ELECTRICIAN'S HELPER

Qualifications Requirements

MINIMUM REQUIREMENTS

To apply for an *apprenticeship* to become an electrician, you should contact your local committee for apprenticeships. They are usually found in the Electrician's Union Headquarters, and in most instances, they are in the local telephone book. This book also gives the phone numbers and Web sites for the national headquarters for the International Brotherhood of Electrical Workers (IBEW) and the National Joint Apprenticeship Training Committee. They can direct you to your local Union representative and the proper person to speak with to obtain an *application* for an apprenticeship program.

1. Three years of full-time paid experience acquired within the last fifteen years as an Electrician's Helper; or

2. Not less than one and one-half years of such experience acquired within the last ten years plus sufficient full-time paid experience as a helper or apprentice or training of a relevant nature acquired in an approved trade or vocational high school to make up the equivalent of three years of acceptable experience. Six months of acceptable experience will be credited for each year of helper or apprentice experience or approved trade or vocational high school; or

3. A satisfactory equivalent.

The minimum requirements must be met by the last date for the receipt of applications.

Experience Paper Form A Must Be Filed With the Application: The experience paper must be filled out completely and in detail.

At the time of appointment and at the time of investigation, eligibles must present all the official documents and proof required to qualify. Failure to present required documents and proof of education or experience requirement will result in disqualification for appointment or a direction to terminate services.

All candidates who file an application will be summoned for the written test prior to the determination of whether they meet the above requirements. Only the experience papers of passing candidates will be examined with respect to meeting these requirements.

JOB DESCRIPTION

Duties and Responsibilities: Under direct supervision, assists an electrician in installing, repairing, replacing, and maintaining of electric wiring systems, appliances, apparatus, and equipment according to the provisions of the Electrical Code and approved plans and specifications; performs related work.

Examples of Typical Tasks: Assists electricians in the erection and placing of components of electrical systems. Helps electricians in pulling wires and testing electrical systems. Replaces defective light switches, plugs, lighting fixtures, and checks signal systems. Keeps electricians supplied with materials, tools, and supplies. Cleans working areas, machines, tools, and equipment. Performs routine machine operations.

TEST INFORMATION

This information is for those cities with a large population (such as New York City) and that have the Electrician's Helper job title as part of the city's employee roster. The passing score, of course, is subject to local interpretation.

Tests: Written test, weight 100. Passing score 70 percent. The written test will be multiple choice and will include questions on the materials, tools, and equipment used in electrical work; safe working practices; basic electrical skills; good housekeeping practices; maintaining and cleaning machines, tools, and equipment; basic principles of electricity; and electrical calculations, diagrams, schematics, and plans.

Eligibles will be required to pass a medical test prior to appointment. An eligible will be rejected for any current medical and/or psychiatric impairment that impairs his or her ability to perform the duties of the class or positions.

PROMOTION OPPORTUNITIES

Employees in the title of Electrician's Helper are accorded promotional opportunities, when eligible, to the title of Electrician.

APPRENTICESHIP

This is a **FOUR-YEAR** program in most places. It requires the apprentice to be a high school graduate with an interest in the electrical field and some work experience or mechanical ability. High school industrial arts, vocational education, or industrial technology courses aid in getting the application approved for the program.

SAMPLE NOTICE OF EXAMINATION—ELECTRICIAN

In conjunction with the holding of this examination, a promotion examination will be held. The names appearing on the promotion list will receive prior consideration in filling vacancies. However, it is expected that there will be sufficient vacancies so that the open-competitive list will be used as well.

It is expected that the list resulting from this examination will be used to fill vacancies in the various city departments and in the health and hospitals departments.

Promotion Opportunities: Employees in the title of Electrician are accorded promotion opportunities when eligible to the title of Foreman Electrician.

Minimum Requirements:

Five years of full-time paid experience in or on buildings as an electrician working on the installation, repair, or maintenance of high or low potential electrical systems for light, heat, and power

Not less than three years of experience as specified in (A) plus sufficient helper or apprentice experience, or educational training in an approved trade or vocational school to make a total of five years of acceptable experience. Six months of acceptable experience will be credited for each year of helper or apprentice experience or for each school year of approved educational training.

All candidates who file an application will be summoned for the written test prior to the determination of whether they meet the above requirements. Only the experience papers of passing candidates will be evaluated with respect to meeting these requirements.

The minimum requirements must be met by the last date for the receipt of applications.

Experience Paper Form A **must be filed with the application:** Applicants must print their Social Security Number in the box labeled Application Number on the Experience Paper Form A.

At the time of appointment and at the time of investigation, candidates must present all the official documents and proof required to qualify as stated in this Notice of Examination. Failure to do so will result in a refusal to qualify for appointment or a direction to terminate services.

Duties and Responsibilities: Under direction, works as an electrician on the installation, repair, and maintenance of high- or low-tension electrical systems for light, heat, and power in or on buildings and/or on highways; performs related work.

Examples of Typical Tasks: Installs, repairs, replaces, and maintains electric wiring systems and components, equipment and apparatus in or on buildings or structures in accordance with the provisions of the Electrical Code, pertinent plans, and specifications or job orders. Installs, repairs, replaces, and maintains electric wiring systems and components and traffic signals and controllers. Installs conduit, raceway, and electrical conductors. Makes tests on existing installations to determine faults and makes necessary repairs. Keeps job and other records. May supervise assigned personnel.

Tests: Written test, weight 100. Passing score 70 percent. The written test will be multiple choice and will include questions on AC and DC circuits; machinery; applied electronics; the New York City Electrical Code; electrical diagrams and specifications; electrical calculations; methods and procedures for installation, alteration, maintenance, and repair of electrical wiring and equipment; installation of conduit; tools, fittings, materials, measuring instruments, and meters used in the electrician's trade; supervision; record keeping; report writing; and safety.

Eligibles will be required to pass a qualifying medical test prior to appointment. An eligible will be rejected for any current medical and/or psychiatric impairment that impairs his or her ability to perform the duties of the class or position.

TECHNIQUES OF STUDY AND TEST-TAKING

PREPARING FOR THE EXAM

1. **Make a study schedule.** Assign yourself a period of time each day to devote to preparation for your exam. A regular time is best, but the important thing is daily study.

2. **Study alone.** You will concentrate better when you work by yourself. Keep a list of questions you find puzzling and points you are unsure of to talk over with a friend who is preparing for the same exam. Plan to exchange ideas at a joint review session just before the test.

3. **Eliminate distractions.** Choose a quiet, well-lit spot as far as possible from telephone, television, and family activities. Try to arrange not to be interrupted.

4. **Begin at the beginning.** Read. Underline points that you consider significant. Make marginal notes. Flag the pages that you think are especially important with little Post-it™ Notes.

5. **Concentrate on the information and instruction chapters.** Study the Electrical Code Definitions, the Dictionary of Electrical Terms, and the Scrambled Dictionary of Equipment and Usage. Learn the language of the field. Focus on the technique of eliminating wrong answers. This information is important to answering all multiple-choice questions.

6. **Answer the practice questions chapter by chapter.** Take note of your weaknesses; use textbooks to brush up.

7. **Try the previous exams.** When you believe that you are well prepared, move on to the exams. If possible, answer an entire exam in one sitting. If you must divide your time, divide it into no more than two sessions per exam.

When you do take the practice exams, treat them with respect. Consider each as a dress rehearsal for the real thing. Time yourself accurately, and do not peek at the correct answers. Remember, you are taking these for practice; they will not be scored; they do not count. So learn from them.

IMPORTANT: Do not memorize questions and answers. Any question that has been released will not be used again. You may run into questions that are very similar, but you will not be tested with these exact questions. These questions will give you good practice, but they will not have the exact answers to any of the questions on your exam.

HOW TO TAKE AN EXAM

1. **Get to the examination room about 10 minutes ahead of time.** You'll get a better start when you are accustomed to the room. If the room is too cold, too warm, or not well ventilated, call these conditions to the attention of the person in charge.

2. **Make sure that you read the instructions carefully.** In many cases, test takers lose points because they misread some important part of the directions. (An example would be reading the *incorrect* choice instead of the *correct* choice.)

3. **Don't be afraid to guess.** The best policy is, of course, to pace yourself so that you can read and consider each question. Sometimes this does not work. Most civil service exam scores are based only on the number of questions answered correctly. This means that a wild guess is better than a blank space. There is no penalty for a wrong answer, and you just might

guess right. If you see that time is about to run out, mark all the remaining spaces with the same answer. According to the law of averages, some will be right.

However, you have bought this book for practice answering questions. Part of your preparation is learning to pace yourself so that you need not answer randomly at the end. Far better than a wild guess is an educated guess. You make this kind of guess not when you are pressed for time but when you are not sure of the correct answer. Usually, one or two of the choices are obviously wrong. Eliminate the obviously wrong answers and try to reason among those remaining. Then, if necessary, guess from the smaller field. The odds of choosing a right answer increase if you guess from a field of two instead of from a field of four. When you make an educated guess or a wild guess in the course of the exam, you might want to make a note next to the question number in the test booklet. Then, if there is time, you can go back for a second look.

4. **Reason your way through multiple-choice questions very carefully and methodically.**

MULTIPLE-CHOICE SAMPLES AND TEST-TAKING TIPS

Here are a few samples that we can "walk through" together:

I. On the job, your supervisor gives you a hurried set of directions. As you start your assigned task, you realize you are not quite clear on the directions given to you. The best action to take would be to

(A) continue with your work, hoping to remember the directions and do the best you can.

(B) ask a co-worker in a similar position what he or she would do.

(C) ask your supervisor to repeat or clarify certain directions.

(D) go on to another assignment.

In this question you are given four possible answers to the problem described. Though the four choices are all *possible* actions, it is up to you to choose the *best* course of action in this particular situation.

Choice (A) will likely lead to a poor result; given that you do not recall or understand the directions, you would not be able to perform the assigned task properly. Keep choice (A) in the back of your mind until you have examined the other alternatives. It could be the best of the four choices given.

Choice (B) is also a possible course of action, but is it the best? Consider that the co-worker you consult has not heard the directions. How could he or she know? Perhaps his or her degree of incompetence is greater than yours in this area. Of choices (A) and (B), the better of the two is still choice (A).

Choice (C) is an acceptable course of action. Your supervisor will welcome your questions and will not lose respect for you. At this point, you should hold choice (C) as the best answer and eliminate choice (A).

The course of action in choice (D) is decidedly incorrect because the job at hand would not be completed. Going on to something else does not clear up the problem; it simply postpones your having to make a necessary decision.

After careful consideration of all choices given, choice (C) stands out as the best possible course of action. You should select choice (C) as your answer.

Every question is written about a fact or an accepted concept. The question above indicates the concept that, in general, most supervisory personnel appreciate subordinates' questioning directions that may not have been fully understood. This type of clarification precludes subsequent errors on the part of the subordinates. On the other hand, many subordinates are reluctant to ask questions for fear that their lack of understanding will detract from their supervisor's evaluation of their abilities.

The supervisor, therefore, has the responsibility of issuing orders and directions in such a way that subordinates will not be discouraged from asking questions. This is the concept on which the sample question was based.

Of course, if you were familiar with this concept, you would have no trouble answering the question. However, if you were not familiar with it, the method outlined here of eliminating incorrect choices and selecting the correct one should prove successful for you.

We have now seen how important it is to identify the concept and the key phrase of the question. Equally, or perhaps even more important, is identifying and analyzing the key word— the qualifying word—in a question. This word is usually an adjective or adverb. Some of the most common key words are:

most	*least*	*best*	*highest*
lowest	*always*	*never*	*sometimes*
most likely	*greatest*	*smallest*	*tallest*
average	*easiest*	*most nearly*	*maximum*
minimum	*only*	*chiefly*	*mainly*
but	*or*		

Identifying these key words is usually half the battle in understanding and, consequently, answering all types of exam questions.

Now we will use the elimination method on some additional questions:

  II.   On the first day you report for work after being appointed as an electrician's helper, you are assigned to routine duties that seem to you to be very petty in scope. You should

  (A)   perform your assignment perfunctorily while conserving your energies for more important work in the future.
  (B)   explain to your superior that you are capable of greater responsibility.
  (C)   consider these duties an opportunity to become thoroughly familiar with the workplace.
  (D)   try to get someone to take care of your assignment until you have become thoroughly acquainted with your new associates.

Once again we are confronted with four possible answers from which we are to select the *best* one.

Choice (A) will not lead to getting your assigned work done in the best possible manner in the shortest possible time. This would be your responsibility as a newly appointed electrician's helper, and the likelihood of getting to do more important work in the future following the approach stated in this choice is remote. However, since this is only choice (A), we must hold it aside because it may turn out to be the best of the four choices given.

Choice (B) is better than choice (A) because your superior may not be familiar with your capabilities at this point. We therefore should drop choice (A) and retain choice (B) because, once again, it may be the best of the four choices.

The question clearly states that you are newly appointed. Therefore, would it not be wise to perform whatever duties you are assigned in the best possible manner? In this way, you would not only use the opportunity to become acquainted with procedures, but also to demonstrate your abilities. Choice (C) contains a course of action that will benefit you and the location in which you are working because it will get needed work done. At this point, we drop choice (B) and retain choice (C) because it is by far the better of the two.

The course of action in choice (D) is not likely to get the assignment completed, and it will not enhance your image to your fellow electrician's helpers. **Choice (C), when compared to choice (D), is far better and therefore should be selected as the *best* choice.**

Now let us take a question that appeared on a police officer examination:

III. An off-duty police officer in civilian clothes riding in the rear of a bus notices two teenage boys tampering with the rear emergency door. The most appropriate action for the officer to take is to

(A) tell the boys to discontinue their tampering, pointing out the dangers to life that their actions may create.

(B) report the boys' actions to the bus operator and let the bus operator take whatever action is deemed best.

(C) signal the bus operator to stop, show the boys the officer's badge, and then order them off the bus.

(D) show the boys the officer's badge, order them to stop their actions, and take down their names and addresses.

Before considering the answers to this question, we must accept that it is a well-known fact that a police officer is always on duty to uphold the law even though he or she may be technically off duty.

In choice (A), the course of action taken by the police officer will probably serve to educate the boys and get them to stop their unlawful activity. Since this is only the first choice, we will hold it aside.

In choice (B), we must realize that the authority of the bus operator in this instance is limited. He can ask the boys to stop tampering with the door, but that is all. The police officer can go beyond that point. Therefore, we drop choice (B) and continue to hold choice (A).

Choice (C) as a course of action will not have a lasting effect. What is to stop the boys from boarding the next bus and continuing their unlawful action? We therefore drop choice (C) and continue to hold choice (A).

Choice (D) may have some beneficial effect, but it would not deter the boys from continuing their actions in the future. **When we compare choice (A) with choice (D), we find that choice (A) is the better one overall, and therefore it is the correct answer.**

The next question illustrates a type of question that has gained popularity in recent examinations and that requires a two-step evaluation. First, the reader must evaluate the condition in the question as being "desirable" or "undesirable." Once the determination has been made, we are then left with making a selection from two choices instead of the usual four.

IV. A visitor to an office in a city agency tells one of the office aides that he has an appointment with the supervisor of the office who is expected shortly. The visitor asks for permission to wait in the supervisor's private office, which is unoccupied at the moment. For the office aide to allow the visitor to do so would be

(A) desirable; the visitor would be less likely to disturb the other employees or to be disturbed by them.

(B) undesirable; it is not courteous to permit a visitor to be left alone in an office.

    (C)   desirable; the supervisor may wish to speak to the visitor in private.

    (D)   undesirable; the supervisor may have left confidential papers on the desk.

First of all, we must evaluate the course of action on the part of the office aide of permitting the visitor to wait in the supervisor's office as being *very* undesirable. There is nothing said of the nature of the visit; it may be for a purpose that is not friendly or congenial. There may be papers on the supervisor's desk that he or she does not want the visitor to see or to have knowledge of. Therefore, at this point, we have to decide between choices (B) and (D).

This is definitely not a question of courtesy. Although all visitors should be treated with courtesy, permitting the visitor to wait in the supervisor's office in itself is not the only possible act of courtesy. Another comfortable place could be found for the visitor to wait.

Choice (D) contains the exact reason for evaluating this course of action as being undesirable, and when we compare it with choice (B), choice (D) is far better.

TEST DAY STRATEGY

On the examination day assigned to you, allow the test itself to be the main attraction of the day. Do not squeeze it in between other activities. Arrive rested, relaxed, and on time. In fact, plan to arrive a little bit early. Leave plenty of time for traffic tie-ups or other complications that might upset you and interfere with your test performance.

Here is a breakdown of what occurs on examination day and tips on starting off on the right foot and preparing to start your exam:

1. In the test room the examiner will hand out forms for you to fill out and will give you the instructions that you must follow in taking the examination. Note that you must follow instructions exactly.

2. The examiner will tell you how to fill in the grids on the forms.

3. Exam time limits and timing signals will be explained.

4. Be sure to ask questions if you do not understand any of the examiner's instructions. You need to be sure that you know exactly what to do.

5. Fill in the grids on the forms carefully and accurately. Filling in the wrong grid may lead to loss of veterans' credits to which you may be entitled or to an incorrect address for your test results.

6. Do not begin the exam until you are told to begin.

7. Stop as soon as the examiner tells you to stop.

8. Do not turn pages until you are told to.

9. Do not go back to parts you have already completed.

10. Any infraction of the rules is considered cheating. If you cheat, your test paper will not be scored, and you will not be eligible for appointment.

11. Once the signal has been given and you begin the exam, read every word of every question.

12. Be alert for exclusionary words that might affect your answer—words like "not," "most," and "least."

MARKING YOUR ANSWERS

Read all the choices before you mark your answer. It is statistically true that most errors are made when the last choice is the correct answer. Too many people mark the first answer that seems correct without reading through all the choices to find out which answer is *best*.

Be sure to read the suggestions below now and review them before you take the actual exam. Once you are familiar with the suggestions, you will feel more comfortable with the exam itself and find them all useful when you are marking your answer choices.

1. Mark your answers by completely blackening the answer space of your choice.

2. Mark only **ONE** answer for each question, even if you think that more than one answer is correct. You must choose only one. If you mark more than one answer, the scoring machine will consider you wrong even if one of your answers is correct.

3. If you change your mind, erase completely. Leave no doubt as to which answer you have chosen.

4. If you do any figuring on the test booklet or on scratch paper, be sure to mark your answer on the answer sheet.

5. Check often to be sure that the question number matches the answer space number and that you have not skipped a space by mistake. If you do skip a space, you must erase all the answers after the skip and answer all the questions again in the right places.

6. Answer every question in order, but do not spend too much time on any one question. If a question seems to be "impossible," do not take it as a personal challenge. Guess and move on. Remember that your task is to answer correctly as many questions as possible. You must apportion your time so as to give yourself a fair chance to read and answer all the questions. If you guess at an answer, mark the question in the test booklet so that you can find it easily if time allows.

7. Guess intelligently if you can. If you do not know the answer to a question, eliminate the answers that you know are wrong and guess from among the remaining choices. If you have no idea whatsoever of the answer to a question, guess anyway. Choose an answer other than the first. The first choice is generally the correct answer less often than the other choices. If your answer is a guess, either an educated guess or a wild one, mark the question in the question booklet so that you can give it a second try if time permits.

8. If you happen to finish before time is up, check to be sure that each question is answered in the right space and that there is only one answer for each question. Return to the difficult questions that you marked in the booklet and try them again. There is no bonus for finishing early so use all your time to perfect your exam paper.

With the combination of techniques for studying and test taking as well as the self-instructional course and sample examinations in this book, you are given the tools you need to score high on your exam.

PART TWO

A Self-Instructional Course to Help You Master the Work and Pass the Test

INTRODUCTION TO THE SELF-INSTRUCTIONAL COURSE

Many cities, some industries, and apprenticeship programs require prospective electricians or apprentices to pass a basic knowledge test that shows if he/she knows the basic elements of electricity and has the ability to assimilate the information that will be forthcoming on the job. There is, of course, much more to the job, and much will have to be learned before a master electrician emerges to take on the responsibility of an entire plant, factory, municipal office complex, school system, or housing project.

Take this preliminary basic electricity exam now, before you begin your study of this book. It will help you to assess your current knowledge and your grasp of the concepts and terms associated with the job. It will help you pinpoint your weakness and to focus your study in areas you need it most.

To help you understand exactly how to answer multiple-choice questions, we give you a sample item.

The unit for measuring electrical capacity is the
    (A) volt.
    (B) farad.
    (C) ohm.
    (D) watt.

The correct answer is (B). Since a volt is a measure of electromotive force, an ohm is a unit of electrical resistance, and a watt is a unit of electrical power. Mark this answer on the answer sheet:

On the actual exam, you will probably answer by darkening spaces on an answer sheet. In this book, we recommend that you write the letter of each answer you choose before the question number, or simply circle the letter of each correct answer.

When you have completed and corrected the preliminary basic electricity exam, move right on to the Electrical Self-Tutor, which is the heart of this book.

The following chapters on electrical work are an important contribution to the literature of the job. Every relevant topic is covered, from Kirchhoff's laws to the wiring and maintenance of complicated electrical equipment.

Note that each chapter is divided into sections and at times, the sections are divided into subsections. Key answers follow immediately after each section or after each subsection if it is particularly large. Concentrate upon one group of questions and answers at a time, check your answers, calculate if you are weak or strong, and brush up on your weaknesses before going on to the next section. Don't peek at the answers before answering all the questions in a section— the whole purpose of this book is to help you find out what you don't know. After you have finished using the study guide, go on to answer the questions on the actual previous exams.

PRELIMINARY BASIC ELECTRICITY EXAM

1. An atom is

   (A) an electron.
   (B) the smallest particle of an element that retains its characteristics.
   (C) a proton.
   (D) a neutron.

2. An electron is

   (A) a proton.
   (B) a neutron.
   (C) an orbiting particle.
   (D) the smallest part of an atom with a negative charge.

3. Current flow is

   (A) movement of electrons.
   (B) voltage.
   (C) resistance.
   (D) measured in ohms.

4. Current is measured in

   (A) ohms.
   (B) volts.
   (C) watts.
   (D) amperes.

5. Voltage is measured in

   (A) watts.
   (B) ohms.
   (C) amperes.
   (D) volts.

6. Resistance is measured in

   (A) ohms.
   (B) amperes.
   (C) watts.
   (D) volts.

7. Power is measured in

   (A) ohms.
   (B) amperes.
   (C) watts.
   (D) volts.

8. A coulomb is

   (A) a unit of power.
   (B) 6.25×10^{18} electrons.
   (C) a static charge.
   (D) a meter movement.

9. An emf is measured in

   (A) amperes.
   (B) volts.
   (C) ohms.
   (D) watts.

10. An insulator is a material

    (A) with free electrons.
    (B) with no free electrons.
    (C) with no protons.
    (D) with no neutrons.

11. A joule is a unit of

    (A) energy measurement.
    (B) voltage measurement.
    (C) resistance measurement.
    (D) power measurement.

12. A resistor is a device used to

    (A) add power to a circuit.
    (B) add energy to a circuit.
    (C) add resistance to a circuit.
    (D) add voltage to a circuit.

13. A carbon composition resistor has its value

    (A) printed on it.
    (B) color-coded on the body with dots of color.
    (C) color-coded on the body with rings of color.
    (D) written in color on the body.

14. A permanent magnet found in nature is called a

    (A) lodestone.
    (B) flux stone.
    (C) helix.
    (D) magnetic flux machine.

15. A flux field refers to

    (A) a magnetic field.
    (B) a field of a resistor.
    (C) a field of a capacitor.
    (D) a field of an inductor.

16. A solenoid is a coil of wire used to

    (A) operate valves and switches.
    (B) improve communications.
    (C) improve magnetic fields.
    (D) improve methods of operation.

17. An armature is usually found in a

    (A) motor.
    (B) motor and relay.
    (C) relay.
    (D) bell.

18. Parallax error refers to

    (A) a meter scale.
    (B) a unit of resistance.
    (C) a unit of inductance.
    (D) eddy currents.

19. A microampere is equal to

    (A) 0.001 ampere.
    (B) 0.0001 ampere.
    (C) 0.00001 ampere.
    (D) 0.000001 ampere.

20. A milliampere is equal to

    (A) 0.001 ampere.
    (B) 0.0001 ampere.
    (C) 0.00001 ampere.
    (D) 0.000001 ampere.

21. A shunt is used to extend the range of a

    (A) relay.
    (B) motor.
    (C) meter.
    (D) resistor.

22. A kilohm is equal to

    (A) 100 ohms.
    (B) 1,000 ohms.
    (C) 10,000 ohms.
    (D) 100,000 ohms.

23. Autoranging refers to

    (A) the range of resistances in a circuit.
    (B) the range of voltages in a circuit.
    (C) the ability of a meter to select a range.
    (D) the ability of a circuit to switch automatically.

24. An alternator is another name for a(n)

    (A) DC generator.
    (B) AC generator.
    (C) signal generator.
    (D) bar generator.

25. Root means square is another way of representing

    (A) effective current.
    (B) average current.
    (C) peak current.
    (D) Real Means Second.

26. Audio frequencies range from

    (A) 10 kHz to 100 kHz.
    (B) 16 Hz to 16 kHz.
    (C) 0 Hz to 100 kHz.
    (D) 100 kHz to 100 MHz.

27. An autotransformer has

    (A) one coil.
    (B) two coils.
    (C) three coils.
    (D) four coils.

28. An alternation is

    (A) one hertz.
    (B) one cycle.
    (C) one-half cycle.
    (D) one alternator.

29. Inductance is the ability of an inductor to

    (A) increase the flow of electrons.
    (B) oppose any change in circuit current.
    (C) oppose any change in circuit voltage.
    (D) amplify voltage.

30. Another name for an inductor is

    (A) a choke or coil.
    (B) a henry.
    (C) a farad.
    (D) a filter.

31. CEMF is found in a circuit with

    (A) capacitance.
    (B) resistance.
    (C) wattage.
    (D) inductance.

32. Inductive reactance is measured in

    (A) volts.
    (B) henrys.
    (C) farads.
    (D) ohms.

33. Permeability refers to

    (A) a permanent magnet.
    (B) the ability of a material to remain magnetized.
    (C) the ability of a material to lose its magnetism.
    (D) the ability of a coil to produce magnetism.

34. A filter is a circuit designed to

    (A) add resistance to a circuit.
    (B) add capacitance to a circuit.
    (C) smooth out voltage and current variations.
    (D) add variations to a DC circuit current.

35. The picofarad is

    (A) 0.001 farad.
    (B) 0.000000000001 farad.
    (C) 0.000001 farad.
    (D) 0.01 farad.

36. The letters WVDC on a capacitor mean

    (A) Working Volts Direct Current.
    (B) Working Volts Directional Current.
    (C) Wrong Voltage Direct Current.
    (D) Wrong Voltage Directional Current.

37. The dielectric of a capacitor is located

    (A) around the capacitor.
    (B) through the ends of the capacitor.
    (C) between the plates of the capacitor.
    (D) as part of the plates of the capacitor.

38. Capacitors in parallel

    (A) increase their capacitance.
    (B) reduce their capacitance.
    (C) increase their working voltage.
    (D) decrease their working voltage.

39. Capacitors in series

    (A) reduce their capacitance.
    (B) increase their capacitance.
    (C) decrease their working voltage.
    (D) keep the circuit value the same capacitance.

40. The time constant of a resistance-capacitance circuit can be found by the following formula:

    (A) $T = R \times C$
    (B) $T = R - C$
    (C) $T = R + C$
    (D) $T = R \times C \times S$

41. An electrolytic capacitor has

    (A) resistance.
    (B) polarity.
    (C) inductance.
    (D) reluctance.

42. Capacitive reactance is measured in

    (A) volts.
    (B) farads.
    (C) henrys.
    (D) ohms.

43. Impedance in a series RL circuit is found by

    (A) $Z = R + L$
    (B) $Z = \sqrt{R \times L}$
    (C) $Z = \sqrt{R^2 \times X_L^2}$
    (D) $Z = \sqrt{R - L}$

44. Power factor is the

    (A) $\cos \angle \theta$
    (B) $2 \times \sqrt{RL}$
    (C) $2 + RL$
    (D) $\sqrt{R + L}$

45. The flywheel effect is present in a

    (A) parallel LC tank circuit.
    (B) series LC tank circuit.
    (C) parallel RL circuit.
    (D) series RL circuit.

46. Resonance occurs in a series LC circuit when

    (A) $R = LC$
    (B) $X_L = X_C$
    (C) $R = X_C$
    (D) $R = X_L$

47. The Pythagorean theorem is used to

    (A) find the inductance in a circuit.
    (B) find the phase angle of a circuit.
    (C) find the capacitance of a circuit.
    (D) find the resistance of a circuit.

48. A tank circuit is composed of a

    (A) resistor and a capacitor.
    (B) capacitor and an inductor.
    (C) resistor and an inductor.
    (D) resistor, a capacitor, and an inductor.

49. A damped oscillation is one that

    (A) is strong and goes on indefinitely.
    (B) is gradually diminishing in height.
    (C) grows stronger with time.
    (D) dumps its energy into a capacitor.

50. The formula for finding resonant frequency is

    (A) $f_r = R \times C \times L$
    (B) $f_r = 2\pi\sqrt{LC}$
    (C) $f_r = \dfrac{1}{2\pi\sqrt{LC}}$
    (D) $f_r = R \times C \times L^2$

51. A wattmeter measures power consumed in

(A) one hour.
(B) one minute.
(C) one second.
(D) one day.

52. The proper way to write kilowatthour is

(A) kWh
(B) KWh
(C) kWHR
(D) kWH

53. Total resistance in a parallel circuit is

(A) more than the smallest resistor.
(B) less than the smallest resistor.
(C) sum of the resistances.
(D) difference between largest and smallest resistors.

54. Total resistance in a series circuit is

(A) more than the smallest resistor.
(B) less than the smallest resistor.
(C) sum of the resistances.
(D) difference between largest and smallest resistors.

ANSWER KEY

1. B	10. B	19. D	28. C	37. C	46. B
2. D	11. A	20. A	29. B	38. A	47. B
3. A	12. C	21. C	30. A	39. A	48. B
4. D	13. C	22. B	31. D	40. A	49. B
5. D	14. A	23. C	32. D	41. B	50. C
6. A	15. A	24. B	33. B	42. D	51. C
7. C	16. A	25. A	34. C	43. C	52. A
8. B	17. B	26. B	35. B	44. A	53. B
9. B	18. A	27. A	36. A	45. A	54. C

ELECTRICAL THEORY AND WORK

Definition of Electricity. Electricity is an invisible force that we know about only through the effects it produces. Although the exact nature of electricity is not known, the laws governing electrical phenomena are clearly understood and defined, just as the laws of gravitation are known, although we cannot define the nature of gravity.

The Movement of Electricity. In many ways electricity in motion is like flowing water, and electrical phenomena can be more easily understood if this analogy is borne in mind. In dealing with the flow of electricity and the flow of water, we consider three factors: (a) current (flow of electricity, usually along a conductor), (b) pressure (that which causes the current to flow), and (c) resistance (that which regulates the flow of current).

Electrical Current or Flow. If we wanted to know about the flow of water in a pipe, we would determine how many gallons of water flow through the pipe in a second. In exactly the same way, the electrician determines the number of *coulombs* of electricity that flow through a wire in a second. Just as the gallon is a measure of the quantity of water, the coulomb is a measure of the quantity of electricity. There is an abbreviated method of describing the flow of electrical current. The electrician speaks of the *ampere*, which means one coulomb per second, and is thus saved the trouble of saying "per second" every time he or she wants to describe the current flow.

Electrical Pressure. Water pressure is measured in pounds per square inch. There is also a measure of electrical pressure. This electrical pressure has a definite effect upon the number of amperes flowing along a wire. The electrical unit of pressure is the volt. A volt means the same thing in speaking of a current of electricity that a pound-per-square-inch pressure does in speaking of a current of water. Just as a higher pressure is required to force the same current of water through a small pipe than through a large pipe, so a higher electrical pressure is required to force the same current of electricity through a small wire than through a large wire. The voltage (pressure) between two points in an electric circuit is sometimes spoken of as the difference in potential, or the drop in potential, or merely the "drop" between those two points.

The distinction between amperes and volts should now be plain. The amperes represent the amount of current flowing through a circuit; the volts represent the pressure causing it to flow.

Electrical Resistance. The electrical unit of resistance is the ohm. We say a wire has one ohm resistance when a pressure of one volt forces a current of one ampere through it.

Ohm's Law. In any circuit through which a current is flowing, the three following factors are present: (1) The pressure or potential difference, expressed in volts, causing the current to flow. (2) The opposition or resistance of the circuit, expressed in ohms, which must be overcome. (3) The current strength, expressed in amperes, which is maintained in the circuit as a result of the pressure overcoming the resistance. A definite and exact relation exists between three factors: pressure, current strength, and resistance in any circuit, whereby the value of any one factor may always be calculated when the values of the other two factors are known. This relation, known as Ohm's Law, is very important, since it forms the basis for all calculations in electrical engineering, it may be summarized as follows:

The current in any electric circuit is equal to the electromotive force applied to the circuit, divided by the resistance of the circuit.

Let E = emf or available pressure, expressed in volts, applied to any circuit

R = resistance of the circuit, expressed in ohms

I = current strength, expressed in amperes, to be maintained through circuit

Then, by the above statement of Ohm's Law,

$$\text{Current} = \frac{(\text{Pressure})}{\text{Resistance}}$$

$$\text{or Amperes} = \frac{\text{volts}}{\text{ohms}} \text{ or } I = \frac{E}{R}$$

The Circuit. Electricity is not as simple as water in that it can not be piped from one point to another. In order to flow, electricity must be sent along a closed circuit. Except through a generator or a battery cell, electricity always flows from a higher to a lower level. The higher level, or positive, is marked + , and the lower level, or negative, is marked – , in order to indicate the direction in which the current is flowing. A given point is + to all points below its level, and – to all points above its level.

If any of the wires leading from the + to the – terminal is broken, the current cannot flow, for the circuit has been interrupted and is incomplete.

Measuring Electrical Current. In order to find out how much current is flowing through an electric circuit, we insert a current meter into the circuit so that all the current that we wish to measure flows through the meter. Since an instrument that measures an electric current must read in amperes, such a current meter is called an ammeter. The ammeter must be of very low resistance in order not to hinder the current. Such an instrument is very delicate and must be handled carefully.

Measurement of Electrical Pressure. When it is necessary to measure the pressure that is causing an electric current to flow through a circuit, the terminals of a *voltmeter* are tapped on to that circuit in such a way that the voltmeter is made to register not current, but pressure. The method of attaching a voltmeter is different from that used in attaching an ammeter. The ammeter becomes a part of the circuit. The voltmeter does not become a part of the circuit.

Measurement of Electrical Resistance. In order to find the resistance of an electrical piece, the voltmeter reading is divided by the ammeter reading.

Regulating and Controlling Electrical Current. The usual method of regulating and controlling the current required for various electrical purposes is by inserting or removing resistance from a circuit. An adjustable resistance, or any apparatus for changing the resistance without opening the circuit, is called a rheostat. The function of a rheostat is to absorb electrical energy; and this energy, which appears as heat, is wasted instead of performing any useful work. A rheostat may be constructed of coils of iron wire, iron plates, or strips; of carbon, either pulverized in tubes or in the form of solid rods or disks; of German silver, platinoid, or wires of other alloys wound on spools; or of columns of liquids, such as water and mercury, etc. The cross-sectional area of the material must be sufficient to carry the current without excessive heating. In rheostats used for regulating the current in commercial electrical circuits, no great degree of accuracy of the resistance coils is required, as is the case with laboratory rheostats.

The Effects of a Current. A current of electricity is believed to be a transfer of electrons through a circuit, and since these carriers are so minute, a direct measurement of them is impractical. Consequently, an electric current is measured by the effects it produces, all of which are commercially utilized. The effects manifested by a current of electricity are:

- Heating Effect
- Magnetic Effect
- Chemical Effect
- Physiological Effect

The effects are defined below.

Heating Effect. Every wire that conducts a current of electricity becomes heated to some extent as a result of the current, because even the best conductors offer some opposition (resistance) to the flow of the current, and it is in overcoming this resistance that the heat is developed. If the wire is large in cross-sectional area and the current small, the heat developed will be so small in amount as not to be recognized by the touch; nevertheless, the wire releases some heat energy. On the other hand, with a small wire and a large current, the wire becomes quite hot.

Magnetic Effect. A wire carrying a current of electricity deflects a magnetic needle. When the wire is insulated and coiled around an iron core, the current magnetizes the core.

Chemical Effect. Electrical current is capable of decomposing certain chemical compounds when it is passed through them, breaking up the compounds into their constituent parts. In the production of electrical energy by a simple primary cell, electrolytic decomposition takes place inside the cell when the current is flowing. Electroplating, or the art of depositing a coating of metal upon any object, is based upon the principles of electrolytic decomposition.

Physiological Effect. A current of electricity passed through the body produces muscular contractions that are due to the physiological effects of an electrical current. Electrotherapeutics deals with the study of this effect.

Direct and Alternating Current. A direct or continuous current flows always in the same direction. In many cases it has a constant strength for definite periods of time. A pulsating current has a uniform direction, but the current strength varies. Most direct current generators furnish pulsating current; but since the pulsations are very small, the current is practically constant.

An alternating current of electricity is one that changes its direction of flow at regular intervals of time. These intervals are usually much shorter than one second. During an interval, the current strength is capable of varying in any way. In practice, the strength rises and then falls smoothly. Most electricity today comes in the form of alternating current. This is so because high voltage can more easily be obtained with alternating current than with direct current. High voltages, of course, are much more cheaply transmitted over power lines than are low voltages.

Electromagnetic Induction. The electrical generator and the electric motor are intimately related. The term generator is applied to machines that convert mechanical energy into electrical energy. The motor converts energy into mechanical energy by utilizing the principle of electromagnetic induction.

The generator consists fundamentally of a number of loops of insulated wires revolving in a strong magnetic field in such a way that these wires cut across the lines of magnetic force. This cutting of the lines of force sets up an electromotive force along the wires.

We have shown that wherever there is an electric current present, there is also present a magnetic field. It is not true that wherever a magnetic field exists there also exists an electric current, in the ordinary sense; but we can say that wherever a conductor moves in a magnetic field in such a way as to cut lines of force, an electromotive force is set up. It is on this principle that the electric generator works.

Electrical Safety. Most fatal electrical shocks happen to people who should know better. Before working around motors, transformers and other electrical equipment operating on high voltages, there are a number of things you should become aware of first.

Electrical Shock. It is not the voltage but the current that kills. People have been killed with as little as 42 volts direct current (dc). The real measure of a shock's intensity lies in the amount of current forced through the body, not in the voltage. Any electrical device used on a house wiring circuit is capable of transmitting a fatal current.

Since you do not know how much current went through the body, it is necessary to perform artificial respiration to get the person breathing again, or if the heart is not beating, CPR.

NOTE: A heart that is in fibrillation cannot be restricted by closed-chest cardiac massage. A special device called a defibrillator is available in some medical facilities and is often carried by ambulance services.

Muscular contractions are so severe with 200 mA and above that the heart is forcibly clamped during the shock. Clamping prevents the heart from going into ventricular fibrillation, making the victim's chances for survival better.

GFCIs. Electricity can be safe if properly respected. Some dangerous situations have been minimized by using ground-fault circuit interrupters (GFCIs). Since 1975, the NEC (National Electrical Code) has required installation of GFCIs in outdoor, bathroom, and kitchen outlets in new construction, but most homes built before then have no GFCI protection. Ground-fault protection can also be installed in motor control centers. Other electrical safety devices include the fuse and the circuit breaker.

THE WORKING ELECTRICIAN

> **DIRECTIONS:** For each question read all choices carefully. Then select that answer that you consider correct or most nearly correct. Write the letter preceding your best choice next to the question number.

1. Alternating current voltages may be increased or decreased by means of a

   (A) generating machine.
   (B) dynamo.
   (C) transformer.
   (D) motor.

2. The best of the following conductors of electricity is

   (A) silver wire.
   (B) mica.
   (C) nickel and chromium wire.
   (D) gold.

3. Different amounts of resistance in a circuit may be introduced by means of

   (A) a voltmeter.
   (B) a rheostat.
   (C) an ammeter.
   (D) a good connection.

4. In sockets, the extension cord is protected by means of the _____ knot.

   (A) sheepshank
   (B) clove hitch
   (C) fire
   (D) underwriters'

5. The fuse plug contains a safety element composed of a piece of metal that has a

   (A) high resistance and a low melting point.
   (B) low resistance and a high melting point.
   (C) low resistance.
   (D) high melting point.

6. Storage battery electrolyte is formed by the dissolving of _____ acid in water.

   (A) hydrochloric
   (B) sulphuric
   (C) acetic
   (D) atric

7. The electric pressure of electromotive force is measured by the

   (A) volt.
   (B) electric meter.
   (C) watt.
   (D) kilowatt.

8. The unit of measurement for electrical resistance is the

   (A) ohm.
   (B) ampere.
   (C) volt.
   (D) watt.

9. Electricity is sold by the kilowatt, which equals _____ watts.

    (A) 1,000
    (B) 2,000
    (C) 10,000
    (D) 100

10. The unit for measuring electrical capacity is the

    (A) farad.
    (B) volt.
    (C) ohm.
    (D) watt.

11. The central terminal of a dry cell is said to be

    (A) positive.
    (B) negative.
    (C) neutral.
    (D) charged.

12. The spark plug used in automobiles produces electrical energy at _____ voltage.

    (A) high
    (B) low
    (C) medium
    (D) no

13. A DC series motor that has the current reversed turns in the _____ direction.

    (A) opposite
    (B) same
    (C) reverse
    (D) wrong

14. The current used for charging storage batteries is

    (A) direct.
    (B) alternating.
    (C) negative.
    (D) positive.

15. The starting motor of an automobile requires a high

    (A) amperage.
    (B) voltage.
    (C) capacity.
    (D) degree of insulation.

16. Receptacles in a house-lighting system are regularly connected in

    (A) parallel.
    (B) series.
    (C) diagonal.
    (D) perpendicular.

17. Wire connections should encircle binding posts in the _____ manner the nut turns to tighten.

    (A) opposite
    (B) same
    (C) reverse
    (D) different

18. The headlights to automobiles are found to be connected ordinarily in

    (A) parallel.
    (B) series.
    (C) diagonal.
    (D) perpendicular.

19. The average dry cell gives a voltage of approximately

    (A) 1.5
    (B) 1.3
    (C) 1.1
    (D) 1.7

20. Grounding the metallic cover of Greenfield, conduit or B.X. is for protection

    (A) against open field circuits.
    (B) against shock or injury.
    (C) against storms.
    (D) against change of rate of speed.

21. Placing a resistance in series with a series-wound motor

    (A) increases its starting torque.
    (B) decreases its starting torque.
    (C) causes it to start quickly.
    (D) produces quicker pickup under load.

22. A load is missing from a DC shunt-wound motor. If you happen to open the field circuit

    (A) the speed of the motor will slow down greatly.
    (B) the speed of the motor will be much greater.
    (C) the speed will be the same.
    (D) the motor will cease to operate.

23. The instrument that is used to determine electric current is

    (A) the scanner drum.
    (B) the constant-speed racket.
    (C) an ammeter.
    (D) a voltmeter.

24. In lights controlled by 3-way switches, the switches should be treated and put in as

    (A) flush switches.
    (B) single-pole switches.
    (C) three-double-pole switches.
    (D) three-pole switches.

25. A light needs to be controlled from two locations. This means a minimum of

    (A) one 3-way switch and one single-pole switch.
    (B) one 4-way switch and one 3-way switch.
    (C) two single-pole switches.
    (D) two 3-way switches.

26. Is it a sound principle to install direct current and alternating current conductors in one pull box?

    (A) Yes, if soldered
    (B) No
    (C) Yes, if covered with rubber
    (D) Yes, in dry places

27. Low Potential is a trade term that refers to

    (A) 700 volts.
    (B) 600 volts or less.
    (C) 1,200 volts.
    (D) 900 volts.

28. An electrical capacitor is best defined as

    (A) a coil of wire.
    (B) a coil of wire with layers of metal foil.
    (C) a wrapping of many layers of metal foil set apart by waxed paper.
    (D) a wrapping of layers of metal foil.

29. Stranded wire should be _____ before being spliced or placed under a screw head.

    (A) twisted together tightly
    (B) sanded lightly
    (C) checked for conductivity
    (D) allowed to free form

30. To speed up a DC compound-wound motor to more than its name plate rating, it is necessary to

    (A) connect resistance in the shunt-field circuit.
    (B) connect resistance in the armature circuit.
    (C) connect a shunt across the armature circuit.
    (D) connect resistance coil in line leads.

31. A megger is a tool used for the purpose of

    (A) polarizing the system.
    (B) shunting the system.
    (C) determining high resistances.
    (D) determining amperes.

32. The instruments used to connect electrical apparatus to lath and plastered ceilings are

    (A) meggers.
    (B) wood plugs.
    (C) wood screws.
    (D) toggle bolts.

33. The hot wire in a single-phase source can be determined by

    (A) using the touch method.
    (B) using a megger.
    (C) using a neon tester.
    (D) using an ohmmeter.

34. The instrument used in fastening electrical apparatus to terra-cotta walls is a(n)

    (A) megger.
    (B) ammeter.
    (C) toggle bolt.
    (D) lead shield.

35. Is it proper procedure to ground the frame of a portable motor?

    (A) No
    (B) No, if it is AC
    (C) Yes, unless the tool is specifically designed for use without a ground
    (D) Yes, if the operation takes place at less than 150 volts

36. Motors require a fuse to have a

    (A) slow-blow feature.
    (B) fuse element of copper.
    (C) safety factor of 10.
    (D) screw-in base.

37. Neutral wire can be quickly recognized by the

    (A) greenish color.
    (B) bluish color.
    (C) natural or whitish color.
    (D) black color.

38. The instrument by which electric power may be measured is a

    (A) rectifier.
    (B) scanner drum.
    (C) ammeter.
    (D) wattmeter.

39. To determine directly whether all finished wire installations possess resistance between conductors and between conductors and ground, use

    (A) clamps.
    (B) set screws.
    (C) shields.
    (D) a megger.

40. If no change were possible in the voltage and frequency of the supply or mains, to speed up a 3-phase synchronous motor it would be necessary to

    (A) connect a shunt across the field circuit.
    (B) connect a shunt against line leads.
    (C) do nothing as it is impossible to change the speed.
    (D) connect a shunt across the series field.

41. The instruments used to connect electrical apparatus to a concrete ceiling or wall are

    (A) toggle bolts.
    (B) toggle bolts and wooden screws.
    (C) screws and shields.
    (D) shields.

42. The most accurate method to employ in finding the circular mil area of a piece of stranded wire is to

    (A) multiply the number of strands by the circular mil area of one strand.
    (B) square the area of the number of strands.
    (C) use a footage meter.
    (D) use a micrometer.

43. The appropriate lighting fixture for a room used to keep gasoline and paints is a

    (A) vapor-proof fixture plus porcelain socket.
    (B) vapor-proof fixture plus mogul socket.
    (C) vapor-proof fixture plus vapor-proof globe.
    (D) porcelain fixture plus mogul socket.

44. The size of a wire of 600 MCM is

    (A) 1,000 circular mils.
    (B) larger than ever required.
    (C) 600,000 circular mils.
    (D) too large to bend even with a conduit bender.

45. A *mil* measures

    (A) an eighth of an inch.
    (B) a millionth of an inch.
    (C) a thousandth of an inch.
    (D) a ten-thousandth of an inch.

46. S_3 is a symbol used in wiring that indicates that the kind of switch required is a

    (A) flush switch.
    (B) 2-pole switch.
    (C) 4-pole switch.
    (D) 3-way switch.

47. An incandescent lamp of 1,000 watts type P.S. requires a base mainly of

    (A) rubber.
    (B) tie wire.

    (C) mogul.
    (D) metal.

48. The ground wire of the conduit system in a factory must have a connection with a

    (A) floor outlet.
    (B) ceiling outlet.
    (C) water main, located on the street side of the meter.
    (D) sewer main.

49. Incandescent lamps can have their brilliance controlled by a(n)

    (A) special ballast.
    (B) variable capacitor.
    (C) dashpot controller.
    (D) electronic dimmer.

50. Lamps that require a ballast are called

    (A) incandescent.
    (B) halogen.
    (C) fluorescent.
    (D) neon.

51. Cold temperature affects the light output of a

    (A) incandescent lamp.
    (B) fluorescent lamp.
    (C) halogen lamp.
    (D) mercury lamp.

52. An electric motor should have an on-off switch that is

    (A) marked for use with capacitors only.
    (B) marked for inductive use only.
    (C) marked for resistance use only.
    (D) marked for use with neon devices only.

53. The starter motor on an automobile is

    (A) a compound motor.
    (B) a series motor.
    (C) a capacitor start motor.
    (D) a cumulative-wound motor.

54. A light controlled from 5 locations will have

    (A) five four-way switches.
    (B) two three-way switches and three four-way switches.
    (C) three three-way and two four-way switches.
    (D) four three-way and a four-way switch.

55. Increasing the number of energized poles in a motor

    (A) increases the speed.
    (B) decreases the speed.

(C) does not affect the speed.
(D) causes it to stop.

56. The device used to connect and insulate two wires is called

(A) a wire splicer.
(B) a nut driver.
(C) a wire nut.
(D) a soldering iron.

57. The HOT wire in an AC home wiring circuit is colored

(A) white.
(B) green.
(C) gray.
(D) black.

58. One of the old standard frequencies for power line electricity was

(A) 120 Hz.
(B) 50 Hz.

(C) 60 Hz.
(D) 25 Hz.

59. The electric motors designed for 400 Hz power (usually found on airplanes) are

(A) the same size as 60 Hz motors.
(B) larger than 60 Hz motors.
(C) smaller than 60 Hz motors.
(D) the same size as DC motors.

60. Three-phase electric motors are rugged and long-lasting and require very little

(A) oil.
(B) water.
(C) electricity.
(D) maintenance.

ANSWER KEY

1. C	11. A	21. B	31. C	41. C	51. B
2. D	12. D	22. B	32. D	42. A	52. B
3. B	13. B	23. C	33. C	43. C	53. B
4. D	14. A	24. B	34. C	44. C	54. B
5. A	15. A	25. D	35. C	45. C	55. B
6. B	16. A	26. B	36. A	46. D	56. C
7. A	17. B	27. B	37. C	47. C	57. D
8. A	18. A	28. C	38. D	48. C	58. D
9. A	19. A	29. A	39. D	49. D	59. C
10. A	20. B	30. A	40. C	50. C	60. D

SYMBOL TEST IN ELECTRICITY

> **DIRECTIONS:** Symbols are an important part of the electrician's vocabulary. Column I consists of often-used symbols. Column II is a list of the instruments or conditions for which these symbols stand. Select the letter in Column II that correctly identifies the symbol in Column I. Write that letter next to the numbered symbol in Column I.

COLUMN I

COLUMN II

A. POTENTIOMETER

B. CONDENSER OR CAPACITOR } FIXED

C. CONDENSER OR CAPACITOR } VARIABLE

D. GROUND

E. ANTENNA, TRANSMITTING

F. FUSE

G. LAMP

H. DIODE

I. DIAC

J. TRIAC

K. ARMATURE ONLY (DC MOTOR GENERATOR)

L. DC GENERATOR

M. DC MOTOR

N. AC GENERATOR OR ALTERNATOR

O. AC MOTOR

P. TRANSFORMER, AIR CORE

Q. TRANSFORMER, IRON CORE

R. COIL, AIR CORE

S. COIL, IRON CORE

T. SPEAKER, PERMANENT MAGNET

U. PLUG

V. JACK, OPEN CIRCUIT

W. JACK, CLOSED CIRCUIT

X. CONTACTS { NORMALLY OPEN

Y. CONTACTS { NORMALLY CLOSED

Z. HEADPHONES

AA. SWITCH SINGLE-POLE SINGLE-THROW

BB. SWITCH DOUBLE-POLE SINGLE-THROW

CC. SWITCH DOUBLE-POLE DOUBLE-THROW

DD. SWITCH, ROTARY

EE. METER SHUNT

FF. GALVANOMETER

GG. AMMETER

HH. VOLTMETER

II. CELL

JJ. BATTERY

KK. CONNECTIONS

LL. NO CONNECTIONS

MM. RESISTOR OR RESISTANCE } FIXED

NN. RHEOSTAT

DIRECTIONS: The following symbols are used in **motor control relay circuits.** Column I consists of the symbols. Column II is a list of the conditions represented by relay contacts. Select the letter in Column II that correctly identifies the condition that the symbol represents in Column I. Write that letter next to the numbered symbol in Column I.

COLUMN I (symbols)

COLUMN II

OO. make SPSTNO

PP. break SPSTNC

QQ. break, make (transfer) SPDT

RR. make, break (continuity transfer)

SS. break, make, break

TT. make, make

UU. break, break

VV. break, break, make

WW. make, break, make

XX. make, make, break

YY. single pole, double, throw, center off SPDTNO

ZZ. break, make, make

AAA. double make contact on arm

BBB. double break, contact arm

CCC. double make, double break, contact on arm

DDD. double make SPSTNODB

EEE. double break SPSTNCDB

FFF. double make, double break SPDTDB

DIRECTIONS: Match the symbol in Column II to its name in Column I.

COLUMN I   COLUMN II

59. Single receptacle outlet   GGG. ⊖

60. Duplex receptacle outlet   HHH. ⊜

61. Triplex receptacle outlet   III. ⊕

62. Quadruplex receptacle outlet   JJJ. ⊕

63. Duplex receptacle outlet—split wired   KKK. ⊜

64. Triplex receptacle outlet—split wired   LLL. ⊕

65. Single special-purpose receptacle outlet   MMM. △

66. Duplex special-purpose receptacle outlet   NNN. ◁

67. Range outlet (typical)   OOO. ⊜ᴿ

68. Special purpose connection or provision   PPP. ●ᴰᵂ
    for connection (dishwasher)

69. Outside telephone   QQQ. ▷

70. Interconnecting telephone   RRR. Ⓣ

71. Bell ringing transformer   SSS. ◀

72. Floor outlet   TTT. ◉

ANSWER KEY

1. FF	9. NN	17. H	24. O	31. V	38. CC	45. SS	52. DDD	59. GGG	66. NNN
2. GG	10. A	18. I	25. P	32. W	39. DD	46. XX	53. EEE	60. HHH	67. OOO
3. HH	11. B	19. J	26. Q	33. Z	40. EE	47. YY	54. FFF	61. III	68. PPP
4. II	12. C	20. K	27. R	34. X	41. OO	48. ZZ	55. TT	62. JJJ	69. SSS
5. JJ	13. D	21. L	28. S	35. Y	42. PP	49. AAA	56. UU	63. KKK	70. QQQ
6. KK	14. E	22. M	29. T	36. AA	43. QQ	50. BBB	57. VV	64. LLL	71. RRR
7. LL	15. F	23. N	30. U	37. BB	44. RR	51. CCC	58. WW	65. MMM	72. TTT
8. MM	16. G								

ELECTRICAL CODE REVIEW

The words used in electrical work are derived from the vocabulary of science and from the vocabulary of tools and mechanics. Although their meaning is often determined by convention, for the most part they have been established by laws, such as the various electrical codes.

> **DIRECTIONS:** Use a separate, blank sheet to write out your answers to these questions. Try to write independently, without looking at our answers. After you have done your best on your own, you'll be able to go back and review, comparing your answers with ours. The answer for each question is given with the question. In addition to the answer, we have provided more extended explanations wherever we felt they would be helpful.

(The following questions are based on the electrical code generally used throughout the country. Although these questions may be typical, you should review the code for your particular area.)

Q. 1. Explain meanings of (A) low potential, (B) high potential, (C) extra high potential.

A. (A) 600 volts or less, (B) between 601 and 5,000 volts, (C) over 5,000 volts.

Q. 2. Give five factors to be considered in determining whether to use a device, fitting apparatus, or electrical appliance.

A. (1) Suitability for installation in conformity with the Electrical Code, (2) mechanical strength and durability, (3) electrical insulation, (4) heating effects under normal and abnormal conditions, (5) arcing effects.

Q. 3. Describe a satisfactory base on which live parts are to be mounted.

A. Base of insulating material, designed to withstand the most severe conditions liable to arise in service. Holes for supporting screws countersunk or located to allow 1/2 inch between the screw head and nearest live metal part. Nuts or screw heads on underside of the base countersunk and sealed with waterproof compound.

Q. 4. What compounds may be used as lubricants in inserting conductors in raceways?

A. Graphite, talc, or other approved compounds.

Q. 5. What general principles should be followed in laying out an installation?

A. Work should be started from the center of the distribution, and the switches and cutouts controlling and connected with the branches should be grouped together in a safe and easily accessible place where they can readily be reached for repairs or attention. The load should be divided as evenly as possible among the branches, and all complicated and unnecessary wiring should be avoided.

Q. 6. Overhead service conductors, at the point of attachment to a building, shall be not less than __ feet above ground.

A. 12′ residential; 18′ commercial and industrial

Q. 7. A wooden pole 35 feet long supporting overhead wires should be buried in the ground to a depth of __ feet.

A. six

Q. 8. Give the minimum clearance above ground of wires (A) above alleys and driveways on other than residential property, (B) supplying lights in automobile parking lots, (C) between buildings on residential property.

A. (A) eighteen feet, (B) twelve feet, (C) ten feet.

Q. 9. What precautions should be followed in preparing a string of lights for temporary festoon lighting?

A. The voltage between any two conductors should not be over 300 volts. Wiring must be arranged so that not more than 15 amperes will be placed on a branch circuit fuse. Socket sets and receptacles must be of approved moulded composition, waterproof type. All joints must be substantially soldered and covered with both rubber and friction tape and then painted with insulating paint. No. 14 or larger wire must be used with standard sockets, No. 18 or larger with intermediate and smaller size lamps. Lighting strings must not be supported from fire escapes or drainpipes and must be insulated from their supports by strain insulators.

Q. 10. How would you run service conductors from overhead supply wires underground to a building?

A. Should be run in approved metallic conduit.

Q. 11. What type of conduit must be used for wiring on the exterior of buildings?

A. Metallic conduit made of weatherproof material.

Q. 12. What size wire must be used in service entrance conductors?

A. Not smaller than No. 8.

Q. 13. Describe three ways in which a service switch may be installed.

A. (1) As an air-break or oil-immersed switch mounted on a switchboard or panelboard that is accessible to qualified persons only; (2) As an air-break or oil-immersed switch enclosed in a metal case. An enclosed service switch of 600 amperes or less must be externally operable and readily accessible; (3) Where the current of a circuit or group of circuits is separately metered, switch and cutout must be installed to control each separately: switch and cutout enclosed: switch externally operable.

Q. 14. How should wires be located in damp locations?

A. Open wires in damp places shall be located to permanently maintain an air space between them and pipes that they cross. Wires run in proximity to water pipes or tanks are considered exposed to moisture. Wires must be run over rather than under pipes on which moisture may gather or which may leak.

Q. 15. When may link fuses be used?

A. On switches of over 600 amperes capacity.

Q. 16. How are plug fuses of 15 amperes capacity or less distinguished from those of larger capacity?

A. By a hexagonal (eight-sided) opening in the cap through which the mica window shows, or a hexagonal recess in the cap, or some other prominent eight-sided feature of construction.

Q. 17. What is the general requirement for the use of overcurrent devices (automatic overcurrent protection)?

A. In general, overcurrent devices must be provided in all constant-potential interior wiring systems and so placed as to protect each ungrounded conductor and must be located at the point where the conductor receives its supply.

Q. 18. When is a conductor considered as properly protected?

A. By use of fuses or circuit breakers of the time-delay-thermal type with fixed settings or ratings not higher than the allowable carrying capacity of the wires, or when circuit breakers of the instantaneous or time-delay magnetic type are used with a setting not greater than 125 percent of the instantaneous or allowable capacity of the wires.

Q. 19. What is the maximum allowable rating of fuses or setting of over-current breakers or controllers when used as motor-running protective devices in terms of motor full-load current?

A. 125 percent of the motor full-load current.

Q. 20. Under what conditions may the controller for a DC motor serve as the motor-running protective device?

A. If it is equipped with a suitable number of over-current units (trip coils, relays, or thermal cutouts) and these over-current units are operative in both the starting and running positions.

Q. 21. Which conductor on a 3-wire, single-phase source is grounded?

A. The uninsulated or white wire is grounded. The black and red wires are hot or above ground potential.

Q. 22. Describe four ways in which to assure the electrical continuity of a raceway system containing a conductor at more than 150 volts to the ground.

A. (1) Threaded fittings with joints made up tight; (2) threadless fittings, made up tight, including fittings for rigid conduit, electrical metallic tubing, armored cable, and flexible conduit; (3) bonding jumpers of a size equal to that specified for the grounding conductor for interior conduit, with proper fittings; (4) two locknuts, one inside, one outside of boxes or cabinets.

Q. 23. Describe a satisfactory grounding electrode to be used where a continuous metallic underground water piping system is not available.

A. An electrode of plate copper at least .06 inch thick, or iron or steel plate at least 1/4 inch thick, presenting two square feet of surface to the soil and buried below permanent moisture level.

Q. 24. What information should appear on the nameplate of a generator or motor?

A. Maker's name, rating in kilowatts or kilovolts amperes, normal volts, and amperes corresponding to the rating and revolutions per minute, for generators. For motors, maker's name, rating in horsepower, volts, and amperes, including those for the secondary of a wound rotor-type motor, the normal full-load speed and the interval during which it can operate starting cold before reaching its rated temperature.

Q. 25. Under what conditions may a single disconnecting means serve a group of motors?

A. If the motors drive the different parts of a single machine or apparatus (metal or wood working machines for example) groups or motors under the protection of one set of automatic overcurrent protective devices; groups of motors in a single room and within sight of the disconnecting means.

Q. 26. What information should appear on the nameplate of a transformer?

A. Maker's name, rating in kilovolt amperes, primary and secondary voltage ratings, frequency and number of phases. If the liquid-filled type, the liquid capacity. Each capacitor for power correction must be provided with a plate carrying the maker's name, kVA voltage, frequency and number of phases.

Q. 27. What general principles should be followed in installing switches?

A. They should not be placed where exposed to mechanical injury or in the vicinity of easily ignitable material or where exposed to inflammable dust or flying or combustible materials, except those of the oil-immersed type, which should be enclosed in metal boxes and cabinets. All switches operating over 100 volts to the ground other than those mounted on switchboards, open control panels, and reversing switches must be enclosed in metal boxes or cabinets and must be of the externally operable type, if of 800 amperes or less, except oil switches, circuit breakers, and similar devices that have casings.

Q. 28. How should a 3-way switch be installed for proper on-off operation?

A. It can be mounted in either position because the on-off action of the switch is dependent on the other switch. Two 3-ways are needed for operation in two locations. 3-way switches do not have on-off marked on them because they can do either function in either position.

Q. 29. Give five rules that determine the location of switchboards.

A. (1) Should be so placed as to reduce danger of fire. Space behind the board must not be used for storage; (2) Leave three feet between the top of the board and the ceiling; (3) Must be accessible from all sides when the connections are on the back; (4) Should not be exposed to moisture; (5) Switchboard frame should be grounded.

Q. 30. Explain the regulations that control the installation of lighting fixtures.

A. Metal fixtures on circuits above 150 volts and metal electrical fixtures used with conduit, armored cable, or metal raceways must be grounded. Gas piping to which fixtures are attached must be grounded. Combination gas-electric fixtures may not be installed. Fixtures are considered grounded when mechanically connected permanently and effectively to a metal conduit, tubing, armored cable, or a metal raceway system. Fixtures and supports should have adequate mechanical strength, and supports should consist of suspension from the gas piping or special hangar support from the outlet box (ceiling or side wall fixtures) by means of a fixture stud or by metal straps fastened to studs or lugs in the outlet box. Fixtures weighing five pounds or less may be supported by straps and secured to strap by two machine screws. Fixtures weighing 50 pounds or more must be supported independent of the outlet box by a hangar. Gas pipes shall be covered with insulating tubing back of the blind hickey. Fixtures must be installed so that the connections between the fixtures and the branch circuit wires will be available for inspection without disconnecting any portion of the wiring, unless the fixture is attached by an approved plugging device.

Q. 31. What precautions should be taken in installing a lamp holder in a closet?

A. Flexible cord pendant lamps in closets (other than linen and clothes closets) should be of such length that the lamps cannot be left in contact with combustible material and should not be exposed to mechanical injury. Lamp holding devices in clothes or linen closets must be installed on the wall or ceiling and controlled by wall or door switch or pull-chain socket receptacle.

Q. 32. What precautions should be taken in installing a fixture in a bathroom?

A. It should be equipped with a wall switch. Metal pull chains of porcelain fixtures must be provided with insulating links.

Q. 33. What is a GFCI?

A. GFCI stands for ground fault circuit interrupter. These safety devices are now required by the Code to be placed in some kitchen outlets, in bathroom outlets, and in receptacles for operation of equipment outdoors.

Q. 34. What size wire must be used in a circuit containing a mogul lamp holder?

A. No. 12 or larger.

Q. 35. How much current can safely be drawn through a No. 14 Romex cable?

A. Most codes limit the current to no more than 15 amperes for No. 14 wire.

Q. 36. Describe Class I, Class II, and Class III hazardous locations.

A. Class I—Where inflammable, volatile liquids, gases, or mixtures are manufactured or used or handled outside of their original containers, such as work rooms in dry-cleaning plants, gasoline pumps and discharge pedestals at service stations, pump houses or gasoline storage tanks, varnish manufacturing plants, spray-paint shops, etc.

Class II—Where inflammable dust or flyers collect, such as flour mills, feed mills, grain elevators, sugar, cocoa or coal pulverizing plants, cotton and textile mills, clothing manufacturing plants, woodworking plants, etc.

Class III—Where combustible fibers are stored such as warehouses in which cotton, cotton linters, cotton waste, jute, baled waste, kapok, excelsior, etc., are stored.

Q. 37. How would you install a fuse in a Class I hazardous location? In a Class II hazardous location?

A. Class I—Must be mounted in an explosion-proof enclosure. Fuse cutout bases and enclosures must be of type approved for use in explosive atmosphere.

Class II—Must be enclosed in dust-tight metal cases or cabinets and circuit breakers must be of dust-tight or dust-tight oil-immersed type.

Q. 38. How would you provide service for a detached garage from a private house?

A. By conductors run in conduit or underground Romex and buried at least 18 inches below the surface of the ground; an approved switch (snap, flush, or externally operated knife switch) at the entrance of the service conductor, arranged to cut off all ungrounded conductors in the garage; service conductors protected by fuses or circuit breakers at cutout cabinet where conductors leave the house.

**(NOTE ON ELECTRICAL CODES. Electrical codes change. Code items in this section may be obsolete even as this book goes to print. Before taking your examination, review the latest edition of your local code and become familiar with the standards of the National Board of Fire Underwriters.) Most communities now use the National Electrical Code (NEC) as a basis for their own codes; some even adopt it verbatim.

ELECTRICAL CODE DEFINITIONS

> **DIRECTIONS:** Use a separate, blank sheet to write out your answers to these questions. Try to write independently, without looking at our answers. After you have done your best on your own, you'll be able to go back and review, comparing your answers with ours.

CAN YOU COMPLETE THESE DEFINITIONS?

1. Accessible; (A) as applied to wiring methods; (B) as applied to equipment means

2. Adjustable speed motor is one in which

3. Appliances are

4. An Automatic Door is one that

5. Automatic overcurrent protection means use of a device such as

6. Branch Circuit is

7. Cable is

8. Certificate of Inspection is

9. Circuit Breaker is

10. Concealed refers to wires that

11. Conductor is

12. Controller is

13. Cutout Box is an enclosure

14. Dead-front (as applied to switchboards and panel boards) means

15. Demand Factor of any system or part of a system is

16. Device is

17. Different Systems are those that

18. Dust-proof means

19. Dust-tight means

20. Continuous Duty is

21. Intermittent Duty is

22. Periodic Duty is

23. Short-time Duty is

24. Varying Duty is

25. Enclosed means

26. Equipment is a general term including

27. Explosion-proof means

28. Exposed means

29. An Externally Operable switch is one that

30. Factory Yard is

31. Feeder is

32. Fitting is an accessory such as

33. Flexible Conduit is

34. Flexible Cord is

35. General Use Switch is one

36. Grounding Conductor is

37. Guarded means

38. Hazardous Locations are

39. Hoistway is

40. Isolated means

41. Isolated Plant is

42. Isolating Switch is

43. Lighting Outlet is

44. License is

45. Main Distribution Board or Center consists of

46. Mains are

47. Manually Operable means

48. Master Electrician is

49. Master Service means

50. Motor Control Equipment includes

51. Motor Installation includes

52. Motor Room is

53. Service Conductors are

54. Service Conduit is

55. Service Drop is

56. Service Entrance Conductors are

57. Service Equipment consists of

58. Service Raceway is

59. Setting (of circuit breaker) is

60. Substation is

61. Switchboard is

62. System Ground Conductor is

63. Totally Enclosed Motor is a motor that is

64. Vapor-tight means

65. Ventilated means

66. Voltage (of a circuit) is

67. Voltage to Ground means

68. Weatherproof means

69. Class I hazardous locations are

70. Class II hazardous locations are

71. Class III hazardous locations are

72. Purging is

73. Inerting is

74. Sealing is

75. Encapsulation is

HERE'S WHAT THEY MEAN

Here are the official definitions of the terms you have just given your explanations for, according to the Electrical Code. Check your answers with these. Don't try to memorize these definitions, but you should understand the full meaning of each term.

1. (A) Not permanently closed in by the structure or finish of the building; capable of being removed without disturbing the building structure or finish.

   (B) Admitting close approach because not guarded by locked doors, elevation, or other effective means.

2. The speed can be varied gradually over a considerable range, but when once adjusted remains practically unaffected by the load, such as shunt motors designed for a variation of field strength.

3. Current-consuming equipment, fixed or portable.

4. Closes automatically by means of a device operated by heat.

5. A fuse or current breaker by which the electrical continuity of a circuit will be automatically broken by overcurrent or voltage.

6. That portion of a wiring system extending beyond the final overcurrent device protecting the circuit.

7. A stranded conductor (single-conductor cable) or a combination of conductors insulated from one another (multiple-conductor cable).

8. The certificate of the local inspection agency that the installation, alteration, or repair of electric wiring or appliances for light, heat, or power in or on a building specified in such certificate has been inspected and is approved by the department either temporarily or finally.

9. A device designed to open a current-carrying circuit without injury to itself only on the occurrence of abnormal conditions. The term, as used in the Code, applies only to the automatic type designed to trip on a predetermined overload of current.

10. Are rendered inaccessible by the structure or finish of the building. Wires in concealed raceways are considered concealed even though they may become accessible by withdrawing them.

11. A wire or cable or other form of metal suitable for carrying electrical energy.

12. A device or group of devices that serve to govern, in some predetermined manner, electric power delivered.

13. Designed for surface mounting and having swinging doors or covers secured directly to and telescoping with the walls of the box proper.

14. Boards that are so designed and constructed that current-carrying parts are not exposed in such manner that persons are liable to come into contact with them while operating the switches or renewing fuses and so that persons cannot come into contact with the current-carrying parts at any time without using special means to gain access to such parts.

15. The ratio of the maximum demand of the system, or part of the system, to the total connected load of the system or of the part of the system under consideration.

16. A unit of an electrical system other than a conductor that is intended to carry but not consume electrical energy.

17. Derive their supply from (1) different sources of current, from (2) transformers connected to separate primary circuits, or from (3) transformers having different maximum secondary voltages, or from (4) sources of different voltage where the voltage of one circuit is over three hundred percent greater than the other, or (5) where one circuit is protected by a different overcurrent protection device from another and the difference between these devices is more than 700 percent.

18. So constructed or protected that an accumulation of dust will not interfere with its successful operation.

19. So constructed that dust will not enter the enclosing case.

20. A requirement of service that demands operation at a substantially constant load for an indefinitely long time.

21. A requirement of service that demands operation for alternate intervals of (1) load and no load, or (2) load and rest, or (3) load, no load, and rest.

22. A type of intermittent duty in which the load conditions are regularly recurrent.

23. A requirement of service that demands operation at a substantially constant load for a short and definitely specified time.

24. A requirement of service that demands operation at loads, and for intervals of time, both of which may be subjected to wide variation.

25. Surrounded by a case that will prevent accidental contact with live parts.

26. Material, fittings, devices, appliances, fixtures, apparatus, and the like, used as a part of, or in connection with an electrical installation.

27. Enclosed in a case that is designed and constructed to withstand an explosion of a specified gas or dust that may occur within it and to prevent ignition of the specified gas or dust surrounding the enclosure by sparks, flashes, or explosions of the specified gas or dust that may occur within the enclosure.

28. Accessible; not concealed.

29. Capable of being operated without exposing the operator to contact with live parts. (This term is applied to equipment such as a switch that is enclosed in a case or cabinet.)

30. A plot containing an assemblage of buildings served by an isolated plant, or by a substation, or by a master service and permitting access from building to building within the yard.

31. Any conductor of a wiring system between the main switchboard or point of distribution and the branch circuit overcurrent device.

32. Such as a locknut, bushing, or other part of a wiring system that is intended primarily to perform a mechanical rather than an electrical function.

33. A flexible metal tube made up of strips of metal wound in a close spiral.

34. A small flexible cable consisting of two or more conductors, separately insulated, each made up of a number of strands of very small wire. The two or more separately insulated conductors are usually twisted together to form the cord (twisted cord); in some cases these are parallel to each other and are surrounded by an outer braid or covering (parallel cord).

35. Which is intended for use in a general distribution and branch circuit. It is rated in amperes and is capable of interrupting its rated voltage.

36. A conductor that is used to connect the equipment device or wiring system with a grounding electrode or electrodes.

37. Covered, shielded, fenced, enclosed, or otherwise protected by means of suitable covers or casings, barriers, rails or screens, mats or platforms to prevent dangerous contact or approach by persons or objects to a point of danger.

38. Premises, locations, rooms, or portions thereof in which (A) inflammable gases, inflammable volatile liquids, mixtures, or other inflammable substances are manufactured or used or are stored in other than original containers, or (B) where combustible dust or flyings are liable to be present in quantities sufficient to produce an explosive or combustible mixture, or (C) where easily ignitible fibers or materials producing combustible flyings are handled, manufactured, stored, or used.

39. Any shaftway, hatchway, well hole, or other vertical opening or space in which an elevator or dumbwaiter is designed to operate.

40. Not readily accessible to persons unless special means for access are used.

41. A private electrical installation deriving energy from its own generator driven by a prime mover.

42. A switch intended for isolating a circuit from its source of power. It is to be operated only when the circuit has been opened by some other means.

43. An outlet intended for the direct connection of a lampholder, a lighting fixture, or a pendant cord terminating in a lampholder.

44. The written authorization of the proper municipal agency to an individual, partnership, or corporation to engage in the business of installing, altering, or repairing electric wiring or appliances for light, heat, or power in or on any building or premises or lot in the city.

45. One or more cutouts or switches and cutouts supplied by service entrance conductors and controlling feeders, subfeeders, or branch circuits.

46. Conductors of a wiring system between the lines of the public utility company and other source of supply and the main switchboard or point of distribution.

47. Operated by a person or by personal intervention. A manual operation may be the initial operation of a certain series in which the subsequent operations may be automatic. Manually operated devices are of two classes—those that are operated directly by hand, such as an ordinary knife switch, and those that are auto-manual, in which the action is initiated by hand but carried out automatically, such as a magnetically

operated switch, the opening and closing of which is controlled by manually operated push buttons.

48. Any person, partnership, or corporation who engages in or carries on as his or its regular business of installing, erecting, altering, extending, maintaining or repairing electrical wiring, apparatus, fixtures, devices, appliances, or equipment utilized or designed for the utilization of electricity for light, heat, or power purposes or for signalling systems operating on fifty volts or more, exclusive of interior fire alarm systems and their attachments under the jurisdiction of the Fire Department, the Board of Standards and Appeals, or similar agency and who carries on such business as an independent contractor having the final determination and the full responsibility for the manner in which the work is done, for the materials used, and for the selection, supervision, and control of any persons employed on the work engaged in by said person, partnership, or corporation.

49. The service conductors and service equipment supplying a group of buildings under one management.

50. Apparatus and the devices immediately accessory thereto for starting, stopping, regulating, controlling, or protecting electrical motors. Switches or circuit breakers that are used, or intended to be used, for motor starting are to be considered as motor control equipment. Where the equipment mounted on switchboards, panelboards, etc., is used essentially or primarily for starting, stopping, regulating, and controlling motors, it is to be considered as motor control equipment.

51. The motor and its control equipment together with all necessary wiring.

52. A building, room, or separate space within which a motor installation is located and has such construction or arrangement as to prevent the entrance of unauthorized persons or interference by them with the equipment inside and has all entrances not under the observation of a qualified attendant kept locked, and has signs prohibiting entrance to unauthorized persons conspicuously displayed at entrance. An enclosure that is not of sufficient size to permit the entrance of attendants and to afford safe access and working space within the enclosure cannot be considered as a motor room.

53. That portion of the supply conductors that extends from the street main or duct to the service equipment of the building supplied. For overhead conductors, this includes the conductors from the last line pole to the service equipment.

54. The conduit or duct that contains underground service conductors and extends from the junction with outside supply wires into the consumer's premises.

55. That portion of overhead service conductors between the last line pole and the first point of attachment to the building.

56. That portion of service conductors between the terminals of service equipment and a point outside the building, clear of building walls, where joined by tap or splice to the service drop or to street mains or other source of supply.

57. The necessary equipment, usually consisting of circuit breaker or switch and fuses and their accessories, located near point of entrance of supply conductors to a building and intended to constitute the main control and means of cutoff for the supply to that building.

58. The conduit that encloses service entrance conductors.

59. The setting of an instantaneous-trip circuit breaker is the current value in amperes at which it will trip; the setting of a time-delay circuit breaker is the value of current in amperes that it will carry indefinitely and beyond which it will trip at specified values of overload and time.

60. A building, room, or enclosure in which transformers or generating equipment or other substation apparatus are installed. The term generally includes isolated generating stations on the premises of the consumers.

61. A single panel, frame, or assembly of panels on which are mounted on the face or back, or both, of switches, overcurrent and other protective devices, buses; and usual instruments. Switchboards are generally accessible from the rear as well as the front and are not intended to be installed in cabinets.

62. An auxiliary grounded conductor used for connecting the individual grounding conductors throughout a given area, but that is not part of a circuit wire.

63. So completely enclosed by integral or auxiliary covers as to practically prevent the circulation of air in the interior. Such a motor is not necessarily air-tight.

64. So enclosed that vapor will not enter the enclosure.

65. Provided with means to permit circulation of the air sufficiently to remove an excess of heat, fumes, or vapors.

66. The greatest effective difference of potential between any two conductors of the circuit concerned.

67. In grounded circuits, the voltage between the given conductor and that point of the conductor of the circuit that is grounded: in ungrounded circuits, the greatest voltage between the given conductor and any other conductor of the circuit.

68. So constructed or protected that exposure to the weather will not interfere with successful operation.

69. Where highly flammable gases or vapors are encountered. Division 1 is where hazardous concentrations are probable or where accidental occurrence should be simultaneous with failure of electrical equipment. Division 2 is where flammable concentrations are possible but only in the event of process closures rupture, ventilation failure, etc.

70. Where combustible dusts are present or probable. Division 1 is where hazardous concentrations are probable, where their existence would be simultaneous with electrical equipment failure, or where electrically conducting dusts are involved. Division 2 is where hazardous concentrations are not likely but where deposits of dust might interfere with heat dissipation from electrical equipment or be ignited by electrical equipment.

71. Where combustible fibers or flyings are present. Division 1 is where easily ignitible fibers or materials producing combustible flyings are handled, manufactured, or used. Division 2 is where such fibers or flyings are stored or handled, except in the process of manufacture.

72. The use of nonflammable gases to flush flammable gases or vapors from an enclosed space.

73. The mixing of a chemically inert, nonflammable gas with the flammable substance, displacing the oxygen until the percentage of oxygen in the mixture is too low to allow combustion.

74. The NEC says equipment must be *hermetically* sealed. However, nowhere is *hermetically* defined; so it is left to the discretion of the code enforcer. Strictly speaking, a hermetic seal is one that is perfectly air tight, so that no gas or spirit can enter or escape.

75. The embodiment of a component or assembly in a solid or semisolid medium, such as tar, wax, or epoxy. It is considered safe if the material effectively seals the ignition source from the atmosphere

INSTALLATIONS FOR HAZARDOUS LOCATIONS

Many national, state, and local codes and regulations have been compiled for custom-made equipment that is manufactured for a specific job. State and local authorities, as well as codes, should always be consulted. This assures that the electrical systems conform to all installation requirements. The National Electrical Code divides the locations of hazardous conditions into classes and divisions. If these classes and divisions are mentioned in your wiring specifications, it is best to consult your latest copy of the National Electrical Code. It will give you the exact requirements.

Hazardous Conditions

Class I locations are those in which flammable gases or vapors are, or may be, present in the air in quantities sufficient to produce explosive or ignitable mixtures.

Class II locations are those in which combustible dust is, or may be, present in the air in quantities sufficient to produce an explosive or ignitable atmosphere.

The phrase "quantities sufficient" is an attempt to define the amount of vapor or dust that will cause a dangerous atmosphere. This is difficult, since many factors are involved, some of which are variable. For instance, barometric pressure, humidity, air movement, and the amount and type of ventilation affect flammable conditions. Also, the ratio of room volume to the amount of vapor or dust, temperature, processes, and machinery can all contribute to hazardous situations.

It is vital that those who deal with dangerous materials such as gases and flammable liquids be aware of the hazards involved. Safety measures must be considered by persons who plan and install electrical equipment in hazardous locations. For exact ignition temperatures and explosive limits of commonly used hazardous substances, see the latest edition of the *National Electrical Code Handbook*.

Code Definitions

Articles of the National Electrical Code (NEC) deal specifically with problems associated with hazardous locations. These locations are defined according to classes and subdivided into divisions. The three classes of locations and conditions are as follows:

- Class I locations: those in which flammable gases or vapors are, or may be, present in the air in quantities sufficient to produce explosive or ignitable mixtures.
  - Class I, Division 1: those where such hazardous concentrations of flammable gases or vapors exist continuously, intermittently, or periodically under normal operation conditions.
  - Class I, Division 2: those where such hazardous concentrations of flammable gases or vapors are handled in closed containers or closed systems.

- Class II locations: those where the presence of combustible dust presents a fire or explosive hazard.
  - Class II, Division 1: those where dust is suspended in the air continuously, intermittently, or periodically under normal operation conditions, in quantities sufficient to produce explosive or ignitable mixtures.
  - Class II, Division 2: those where such dust is not suspended in the air, but where deposits of it accumulating on the electrical equipment will interfere with the safe dissipation of heat, causing a fire hazard.

- Class III locations: those where easily ignitable fibers or flyings are present but not likely to be suspended in the air in quantities sufficient to produce ignitable mixtures.

— Class III, Division 1: those where ignitable fibers, or materials producing combustible airborne particles, are handled, manufactured, or used.

— Class III, Division 2: those where easily ignitable fibers are stored or handled (except in the process of manufacture).

Testing and approving conditions have advanced to a finer degree of classification with four separate designations: A, B, C, and D for Class I; and three categories for Class I: E, F, and G.

Equipment is tested by the Underwriters' Laboratories and the Canadian Standards Associations.

ELECTRICAL CODE PROBLEMS

1. In most cities, the local public utility company has no jurisdiction over

   (A) location and type of service to be supplied to a building.
   (B) wiring installations for light and power in buildings.
   (C) location and type of service switch and metering equipment to be installed in buildings.
   (D) maximum permissible starting current of motors when started directly across the line.

2. Most city electrical codes state that electrical metallic tubing shall not be used for interior wiring systems of more than 600 volts nor for conductors larger than

   (A) No. 6
   (B) No. 4
   (C) No. 2
   (D) No. 0

3. According to the Code, in order that armored cable will not be injured, the radius of the curve of the inner edge of any bend must be not less than

   (A) 3 times the diameter of the cable.
   (B) 5 times the diameter of the cable.
   (C) 7 times the diameter of the cable.
   (D) 10 times the diameter of the cable.

4. The Code states that feeders over 40′ in length supplying two branch circuits shall be not smaller than

   (A) 2 No. 14 AWG
   (B) 2 No. 12 AWG
   (C) 2 No. 10 AWG
   (D) 2 No. 8 AWG

5. In accordance with the Code, circuit breakers for motor branch circuits protection shall have continuous current ratings not less than

   (A) 110 percent of the full load current of the motor.
   (B) 115 percent of the full load current of the motor.
   (C) 120 percent of the full load current of the motor.
   (D) 125 percent of the full load current of the motor.

6. In accordance with the Code, all wiring is to be installed so that when completed the system will be free from shorts or grounds. A circuit installation of No. 12 wire with all safety devices in place, but lampholders, receptacles, fixtures, and or appliances not connected, shall have a resistance between conductors and between all conductors and ground not less than

   (A) 10,000 ohms.
   (B) 100,000 ohms.
   (C) 250,000 ohms.
   (D) 1,000,000 ohms.

7. The Code states that wires, cables, and cords of all kinds except weather-proof wire shall have a

   (A) distinctive marking so that the maker may be readily identified.
   (B) tag showing the minimum working voltage for which the wire was tested or approved.
   (C) tag showing the maximum current passed through the conductor under test.
   (D) tag showing the ultimate tensile strength.

8. The Code states that conductors supplying an individual motor shall have a minimum carrying capacity of

   (A) 110 percent of the motor full load current.
   (B) 120 percent of the motor full load current.
   (C) 125 percent of the motor full load current.
   (D) 135 percent of the motor full load current.

9. For not more than three conductors in raceway, based on a room temperature of 86°F, the allowable current-carrying capacity, in amperes, of a No. 12 AWG, type R conductor is

   (A) 15
   (B) 20
   (C) 30
   (D) 40

10. In accordance with the Code, the grounding connection for interior metal raceways and armored cable shall be made at a point

    (A) not greater than 5 feet from the source of supply.
    (B) not greater than 10 feet from the source of supply.
    (C) as far as possible from the source of supply.
    (D) as near as practicable to the source of supply.

11. In accordance with the Code, a grounding conductor for a direct current system shall have a current-carrying capacity not less than that of the largest conductor supplied by the system and in no case less than that of

    (A) No. 12 copper wire.
    (B) No. 10 copper wire.
    (C) No. 8 copper wire.
    (D) No. 6 copper wire.

12. In accordance with the Code, the number of No. 14 AWG, type R conductors running through or terminating in a $1\frac{1}{2}'' \times 3\frac{1}{4}''$ octagonal outlet or junction box should not be greater than

    (A) 5
    (B) 6
    (C) 7
    (D) 8

13. In accordance with the Code, motors

    (A) may be operated in series multiple.
    (B) may be operated in multiple series.
    (C) shall not be operated in series multiple.
    (D) shall not be operated in multiple.

14. Two $\frac{1}{4}$-hp motors, under the protection of a single set of overcurrent devices and with or without other current-consuming devices in the current, are considered as being sufficiently protected if the rating or setting of the overcurrent devices does not exceed

    (A) 15 amperes at 250 volts.
    (B) 15 amperes at 125 volts.
    (C) 30 amperes at 125 volts.
    (D) 30 amperes at 250 volts.

15. According to the Code, Class I locations are those in which gases and vapors

    (A) ignite on exposure to the air.
    (B) explode on exposure to the air.
    (C) are flammable gases or vapors.
    (D) are safe to work around.

16. According to the Code, Class II locations are those in which combustible dust

    (A) presents a fire or explosion hazard.
    (B) presents no fire hazard.
    (C) presents no explosion hazard.
    (D) presents a clear and imminent danger.

ANSWER KEY

1. B	5. B	9. B	13. C
2. D	6. D	10. D	14. B
3. B	7. A	11. C	15. C
4. C	8. C	12. A	16. A

DICTIONARY OF ELECTRICAL TERMS

The following list of terms is intended for use both as a dictionary and as a testing device. For your convenience, we have divided the list into a series of nineteen brief tests. As you go on to other sections in this book, you will find these terms being used over and over again. Familiarize yourself with them now and help ensure a high test score later.

> **DIRECTIONS:** In each test, the numbered TERMS are in Column I. Select the correct DEFINITION in Column II and place the corresponding number next to the term in Column I. To fix the meanings firmly in your mind, repeat the test until you are familiar with every term.

TEST ONE

TERMS

COLUMN I

1. Alternator
2. Atom
3. Adapter
4. Admittance
5. Air Gap
6. Alloy
7. Alternating Current
8. AM
9. Ambient Temperature
10. Ammeter

DEFINITIONS

COLUMN II

1. Smallest particle of an element with all its properties.
2. The measure of ease with which an alternating current flows in a circuit.
3. Amplitude Modulation.
4. The temperature of air or other medium surrounding an electrical device.
5. Measures the current flow in amperes in a circuit.
6. An electric current that reverses its direction of flow at regular intervals.
7. A path for electrical energy through air between two electrodes or core sections of a transformer.
8. AC generator.
9. A device used to change, temporarily or permanently, the terminal connections of a circuit or part.
10. A mixture of two or more metals.

ANSWER KEY

1. 8		5. 7		8. 3	
2. 1		6. 10		9. 4	
3. 9		7. 6		10. 5	
4. 2					

TEST TWO

TERMS	DEFINITIONS
COLUMN I	COLUMN II

COLUMN I

11. Ampere
12. Ampere-Hour
13. Ampere-Turn
14. Amplitude
15. Apparent Power
16. Arc
17. Armature
18. Armored Cable
19. Artificial Ground
20. Autotransformer

COLUMN II

1. The maximum departure of an alternating current or voltage from zero value, measured in either direction from zero.
2. The movable portion of a magnetic circuit.
3. A luminous discharge of electricity between separated conductors.
4. The unit of electrical current flow. If a one-ohm resistance is connected to a one-volt source, one ampere will flow.
5. A transformer in which part of the primary winding serves also as the secondary or in which part of the secondary winding is also in the primary circuit.
6. Two or more individually insulated conductors wrapped in an insulating cover and enclosed within an interlocking spirally-wound galvanized steel cover.
7. A grounding electrode, metal plate, or pipe buried in the earth.
8. The product of volts and amperes in an alternating current circuit whose voltage and current are not in phase, measured by volt-amperes.
9. A unit of magnetizing force equal to the number of amperes of current multiplied by the number of turns in the winding in which it flows.
10. A current of one ampere flowing for one hour.

ANSWER KEY

11. 4	15. 8	18. 6
12. 10	16. 3	19. 7
13. 9	17. 2	20. 5
14. 1		

TEST THREE

TERMS	DEFINITIONS

COLUMN I

21. Ballast
22. Battery
23. B & S Gage
24. Bipolar
25. Booster
26. Bound Charge
27. Breakdown Voltage
28. Bridge Circuit
29. Busway
30. C

COLUMN II

1. A choke or inductor used in a gaseous discharge (fluorescent) lamp circuit.
2. An electric charge that remains in an insulated conductor due to a nearby charge of opposite polarity.
3. Capacitor and celsius temperature scale.
4. Two parallel paths connected between a common source of potential, with each path divided into two at intermediate junction points and with an indicating element (galvanometer) bridged from one of the junctions to the other.
5. The standard gage used in the United States to specify wire sizes. (Brown & Sharpe)
6. The voltage at which the insulation between two conductors will break down.
7. A protective enclosure for buses (conductors formed by large cross-section bars or rods).
8. Two or more cells form a battery or power source.
9. A transformer or generator inserted in a circuit to increase the voltage to overcome line drop.
10. Having two magnetic poles, north and south; 2-pole.

ANSWER KEY

21. 1	25. 9	28. 4
22. 8	26. 2	29. 7
23. 5	27. 6	30. 3
24. 10		

TEST FOUR

TERMS

COLUMN I

DEFINITIONS

COLUMN II

31. Capacitor

32. Coil

33. Candelabra Lampholder

34. Candlepower

35. Capacitance

36. Capacitive Circuit

37. Capacitive Reactance

38. Capacitor Motor

39. Capacity

40. Cartridge Fuse

1. A device that can store an electrical charge.
2. The effect of capacitance in opposing the flow of alternating or pulsating current.
3. A lampholder having a nominal screw diameter of $\frac{1}{2}$ inch.
4. A unit of light equal to the intensity from a standard candle.
5. The electrical size of a condenser determining the amount of electrical energy that can be stored by a given voltage.
6. A fuse enclosed with an insulating and protective covering and provided with connections at its ends.
7. A split-phase motor in which a capacitor displaces part of the current in phase from the remainder in order that the motor may be self-starting on single-phase supply current.
8. One containing more capacitive reactance than inductive reactance or a circuit with a capacitor.
9. Electrostatic capacity.
10. Another name for an inductor or choke. A coil of wire.

ANSWER KEY

31. 1	35. 9	38. 7
32. 10	36. 8	39. 5
33. 3	37. 2	40. 6
34. 4		

TEST FIVE

TERMS	DEFINITIONS
COLUMN I	COLUMN II

COLUMN I

41. Cellular Metal Floor Raceway
42. Celsius
43. Centimeter
44. Circuit
45. Circuit-Breaker
46. Circuit Voltage
47. Circular Mil
48. Circular-Mil Foot
49. Commutation
50. Commutator

COLUMN II

1. A ring of insulated copper segments connected to the windings of an armature that bear brushes connecting the armature winding to the outside circuits to change the induced alternating current of the armature to direct current in the output.
2. A unit of cross-sectional area; equals the area of a circle with a diameter of one mil or 1/1,000 inch.
3. The greatest effective difference of potential between any two conductors in a given circuit.
4. Unit of metric system of measurement equaling approx. 0.39 inch; 1/100th of a meter.
5. A raceway formed in the hollow spaces of cellular metal floors, together with its fittings.
6. The Metric scale of measuring temperature. 0 represents temperature of melting ice, 100 the temperature of boiling water at sea level.
7. A complete path over which an electric current can flow.
8. A device to automatically open a circuit in case of overcurrent.
9. A unit of conductor size equal to a portion of the conductor having a cross-sectional area of one circular mil and length of one foot.
10. Conversion of alternating current to direct current.

ANSWER KEY

41. 5	45. 8	48. 9
42. 6	46. 3	49. 10
43. 4	47. 2	50. 1
44. 7		

TEST SIX

TERMS

COLUMN I

51. Compound Winding
52. Compound Wound Generator
53. Compound Wound Motor
54. Conductance
55. Conductivity
56. Conduit
57. Connector
58. Contact
59. Control Panel
60. Coulomb

DEFINITIONS

COLUMN II

1. Any substance in which a difference of voltage between two points causes current to flow between those points; wires, cables, etc.
2. A metallic enclosure for conductors.
3. A device to join conductors by soldering or mechanical means.
4. In a common magnetic circuit, the winding connecting in series with the load.
5. A direct-current motor having a series and shunt winding for its field.
6. A unit of electrical charge; the quantity of electricity passing in one second through a circuit in which the rate of flow is one ampere.
7. A terminal to which a connection can be made.
8. An exposed or enclosed upright panel carrying switches and other protective, controlling, and measuring devices for electric machinery or equipment.
9. The measure of ease with which a substance conducts electricity, measured in mhos.
10. A direct-current generator having a series and shunt winding for its field.

ANSWER KEY

51. 4	55. 1	58. 7
52. 10	56. 2	59. 8
53. 5	57. 3	60. 6
54. 9		

TEST SEVEN

TERMS	DEFINITIONS

COLUMN I

61. Current
62. Current Transformer
63. Hertz (Hz)
64. DC
65. Dead End
66. Demand Factor
67. Direct Current
68. Distributed Capacity
69. Double Pole
70. Double-Pole Switch

COLUMN II

1. Switch or device connected to both sides of a circuit or controlling both sides of a circuit.
2. The ratio of the maximum demand of a system to the total connected load; maximum watts used at any time divided by the total wattage of all equipment connected to the system.
3. Direct current.
4. The movement of electrons through a conductor measured in amperes, milliamperes, and microamperes.
5. A complete reversal of alternating current, passing through a complete set of changes or motions in opposite directions, from a rise to maximum, return to zero, rise to maximum in the other direction, and another return to zero.
6. The ends of circuit wires that are connected to supports but do not carry an electric load.
7. The capacity distributed between conducting elements; distinguished from capacity concentrated in a capacitor.
8. One that simultaneously opens or closes two separate circuits or both sides of the same circuit.
9. An electric current that always flows in the same direction in its circuit.
10. An instrument transformer with primary winding in series with a current-carrying conductor and secondary winding connected to a meter or device that is actuated by conductor current and current changes.

ANSWER KEY

61. 4	65. 6	68. 7
62. 10	66. 2	69. 1
63. 5	67. 9	70. 8
64. 3		

TEST EIGHT

<table>
<tr><td>TERMS</td><td>DEFINITIONS</td></tr>
<tr><td>COLUMN I</td><td>COLUMN II</td></tr>
</table>

COLUMN I

71. Double Throw Switch
72. Drop
73. Dielectric
74. Duty Cycle
75. E
76. Edison Base
77. Effective Current
78. Efficiency
79. Electrochemistry
80. Electronics

COLUMN II

1. The voltage drop developed across a resistor due to current-flow through it.
2. An insulating material used in a capacitor or other electrical device.
3. The percentage of total time during which an electrical device carries current.
4. The value of alternating current that will cause the same heating effect as a given value of direct current.
5. The ratio of energy output to energy input, expressed as a percentage.
6. The production or separation of chemical elements and compounds by the action of electric currents.
7. The science and art dealing with the flow of electricity or electrons through vacuums and gases confined within the envelopes of tubes or tanks.
8. The standard screw base used for light bulbs.
9. Voltage.
10. One that connects one circuit terminal to either of two other circuit terminals.

ANSWER KEY

71. 10	75. 9	78. 5
72. 1	76. 8	79. 6
73. 2	77. 4	80. 7
74. 3		

TEST NINE

TERMS	DEFINITIONS
COLUMN I	COLUMN II

COLUMN I

81. Fahrenheit
82. Farad
83. Feedback
84. Feeder
85. Foot-Candle
86. Four-Way Switch
87. Fuse
88. Gang Switch
89. Ground
90. Grounding Conductor

COLUMN II

1. The basic measuring unit of capacity.
2. Any conductor of a system between the service equipment (or the generator switchboard of an isolated plant) and the overcurrent devices that protect branch circuits.
3. A unit of illumination; the degree of illumination produced by a lumen-luminous flux of one lumen per square foot of surface area.
4. A wire used to connect equipment or a wiring system with ground or to a grounding electrode buried in the earth.
5. A conductor providing electrical connection between the equipment and circuit and the earth; the metal portions of a support when used as a conductor.
6. A strip of wire or metal that, when it carries an excess of current over its rated capacity, will burn out. Also called a cutout.
7. The United States' temperature measuring system. 32 degrees is the temperature of freezing water; 212 degrees is the temperature of boiling water at sea level.
8. Transfer of electric energy from one point in a system to a preceding point.
9. One used in a circuit that permits a single lamp to be controlled from any of three or more positions: it has four terminals that alternately are joined together in different pairs.
10. Two or more rotary switches on one shaft and operated by the same control.

ANSWER KEY

81. 7	85. 3	88. 10
82. 1	86. 9	89. 5
83. 8	87. 6	90. 4
84. 2		

TEST TEN

TERMS

COLUMN I

91. I
92. Impedance
93. Impulse
94. Induction Motor
95. Inductive Circuit
96. Inductive Coupling
97. Inductor
98. Insulation
99. Intermediate Lampholder
100. Internal Resistance

DEFINITIONS

COLUMN II

1. A momentary increase in the current or voltage in a circuit.

2. A circuit containing more inductive reactance than capacitive reactance, such as one with many devices having iron core coils and winding, induction motors, etc.

3. A form in which energy is transferred from a coil in one circuit to a coil in another by induction.

4. A coil, with or without an iron core, that opposes changes in current because of its self-inductance.

5. The resistance of conductors inside electrical equipment, measured between terminal connections.

6. Current.

7. An AC motor in which energy from the stationary windings is transferred to conductors on the rotor by electromagnetic induction and in which the rotor receives no current through any conductive contacts.

8. The total opposition that a circuit offers the flow of alternating current at a given frequency; combination of resistance and reactance, measured in ohms.

9. A material that has an electrical resistance high enough to allow for its use for separating one electrical circuit from another.

10. One with a screw diameter of $\frac{21}{32}$ inch.

ANSWER KEY

91.	6	95.	2	98.	9
92.	8	96.	3	99.	10
93.	1	97.	4	100.	5
94.	7				

TEST ELEVEN

TERMS	DEFINITIONS
COLUMN I	COLUMN II

COLUMN I

101. Joule
102. Jumper
103. Kilohertz (kHz)
104. Kilowatt
105. Kilowatt-Hour
106. Kirchhoff's Current Law
107. Kirchhoff's Voltage Law
108. Knife Switch
109. L
110. Lagging Current

COLUMN II

1. Sum of all voltage sources acting in a complete circuit must be equal to the sum of all the voltage drops in the circuit.
2. Switch in which one or more metal blades (usually copper), pivoted at one end, serve as the moving parts.
3. An inductance or coil.
4. A wire used as temporary connection.
5. 1,000 watts.
6. The sum of all currents flowing to a point in a circuit must be equal to the sum of all currents flowing away from that point.
7. A measure of electrical energy; a power of one watt for one second; the work done by sending one ampere through a resistance of one ohm for one second.
8. 1,000 Hertz.
9. A unit of electric energy equal to the power rate of one kilowatt continuing for one hour.
10. AC current (in an inductive circuit) whose zero values and maximum values in a given direction occur later than the zeros and corresponding maximums of the AC voltage in the same circuit.

ANSWER KEY

101. 7	105. 9	108. 2
102. 4	106. 6	109. 3
103. 8	107. 1	110. 10
104. 5		

TEST TWELVE

TERMS

COLUMN I

111. Lampholder
112. Leading Current
113. Line Starter
114. Line Voltage
115. Load
116. Lug
117. M
118. Maximum Value
119. Medium Lampholder
120. Megohm

DEFINITIONS

COLUMN II

1. The greatest value reached by AC current or voltage during any point in the cycle.
2. Mega (1,000,000). Used with regard to resistor sizes; i.e., 12 MΩ or 12 million ohms or 12 Megs.
3. A small strip of metal placed on a terminal screw or riveted to make a site for a soldered wire connection.
4. AC current (in a capacitive circuit) whose zero values and maximum values in a given direction occur before the zeros and corresponding maximums of the AC voltage in the same circuit.
5. The voltage at a wall outlet or terminal of a power line system.
6. One with a screw diameter of one inch.
7. A screw-shell device for receiving the screw base of a lamp bulb or other part; a lamp socket.
8. A motor starter that applies full line voltage to motor immediately on operation of the starter.
9. The total of equipment of consuming devices connected to a battery, generator, or supply circuit, measured in: watts, watt-hours, ohms, amperes, volts.
10. A resistance of 1,000,000 ohms.

ANSWER KEY

111. 7	115. 9	118. 1
112. 4	116. 3	119. 6
113. 8	117. 2	120. 10
114. 5		

TEST THIRTEEN

TERMS

COLUMN I

121. Mogul Lampholder
122. Multipolar
123. Mutual Inductance
124. N.E.C.
125. Negative
126. Negative Charge
127. Neutral
128. Network
129. Nichrome

130. Nonconductor

DEFINITIONS

COLUMN II

1. An insulating material, one that offers extreme opposition of the flow of electricity.
2. An alloy of nickel, iron, and chromium with high resistance and capable of withstanding high temperature, used in heating elements.
3. An electric circuit in which the parts are connected in some special manner and cannot be classed as in series, in parallel, or series-parallel.
4. National Electric Code.
5. One with a screw diameter of $1\frac{1}{2}$ inches.
6. The property of a circuit that permits the action of mutual induction; the production of varying or alternating emf in one circuit by movement across its conductors of field lines rising from another nearby circuit with varying current.
7. Neither positive nor negative; having zero potential; having electric potential intermediate between the potentials of other associated parts of the circuit, positive with reference to some parts, negative with reference to others.
8. A machine having more than two magnetic poles; two-pole type is known as bipolar or two pole.
9. A potential less than that of another potential or of the earth.
10. The condition in which a body has more than the normal quantities of negative electrons; more negative electricity than an uncharged or neutral body.

ANSWER KEY

121. 5	125. 9	128. 3
122. 8	126. 10	129. 2
123. 6	127. 7	130. 1
124. 4		

TEST FOURTEEN

TERMS	DEFINITIONS

COLUMN I

131. Noninductive
132. Nonmagnetic
133. Nonmetallic Sheathed Cable
134. Nonmetallic Surface Extension
135. Nonmetallic Waterproof Wiring
136. No-Voltage Release
137. Ohm
138. Ohm's Law
139. Open Wiring
140. Parallel Connection

COLUMN II

1. The relationship between voltage, current, and resistance in a DC circuit or the relationship between voltage, current, and impedance in AC circuits.
2. A switch held by an electromagnet in a closed position and released when voltage across the magnet winding drops to a predetermined minimum.
3. A multiple-conductor, rubber-sheathed cable used for exposed wiring in wet locations where exposed to mild corrosive fumes or vapors.
4. A connection of two or more circuits, or parts of circuits, between the same terminals of a source of current so that the same voltage difference is applied to all parts and the current through each is proportionate to the overall voltage and the resistance of the individual parts.
5. Wire or cable covered by insulating compounds and fabric braids in layers providing some mechanical strength.
6. Insulated wires supported on knobs, cleats, or other insulators but without any other enclosure or covering.
7. The unit of electrical resistance. Resistance is one ohm when a DC voltage of one volt will send a current of one ampere through.
8. Two individually insulated conductors attached to a fabric or other device arranged for convenient fastening to walls or other exposed surface.
9. Materials such as paper, glass, wood, etc., which are not affected by magnetic fields.
10. So placed that the effects of self-induction are caused to cancel and to leave a negligible remaining self-induction.

ANSWER KEY

131. 10	135. 3	138. 1
132. 9	136. 2	139. 6
133. 5	137. 7	140. 4
134. 8		

TEST FIFTEEN

TERMS	DEFINITIONS

COLUMN I

141. Peak
142. Period
143. Phillips Screw
144. Pigtail
145. Polarity in a Circuit
146. Pole
147. Polyphase
148. Polyphase Motor
149. Positive
150. Positive Charge

COLUMN II

1. One end of a magnet; one electrode of a battery.
2. The electrical condition of a body that has less than the normal quantity of negative electrons.
3. The term used to describe a terminal with fewer electrons than normal so that it attracts electrons. Electrons flow into the positive terminals of a voltage source.
4. A motor that operates from a supply system of more than one phase.
5. The maximum instantaneous value of a varying voltage or current.
6. The time required for a complete cycle of alternating current or voltage; for 60 cycles per second (60 Hz), it would be 1/60 second.
7. A flexible connection between a stationary terminal and a part that has a short range of motion.
8. A screw having an indented cross in its head in place of the slot.
9. The quality of having two opposite charges, one positive, one negative.
10. Having two or more alternating currents and potentials acting at the same time.

ANSWER KEY

141.	5	145.	9	148.	4
142.	6	146.	1	149.	3
143.	8	147.	10	150.	2
144.	7				

TEST SIXTEEN

<table>
<tr><td align="center">TERMS</td><td align="center">DEFINITIONS</td></tr>
<tr><td align="center">COLUMN I</td><td align="center">COLUMN II</td></tr>
</table>

COLUMN I

151. Potential
152. Potential Gradient
153. Potential Transformer
154. Power Factor
155. Power Factor Corrections
156. Power Level
157. Pulsating Current
158. Pulse
159. Q Factor
160. R

COLUMN II

1. Resistance.
2. The addition of capacitance to alternating current circuit containing a great deal of inductance to lessen the amount of current that does no useful work; or, inductance might be added to a circuit containing excessive capacitance.
3. An instrument transformer with its primary connected between opposite sides of a line or between points having a potential difference and with its secondary connected to a meter or other device that is actuated by the potential difference of the line.
4. The rate of change of potential with respect to the distance between two points.
5. A characteristic of a point in an electrical circuit based on its electric charge in comparison with the charge at some other reference point; would be more positive or more negative than the reference point.
6. The ratio of the voltage and current, or volt-amperes, that do useful work in an alternating current circuit or equipment to the total voltage and current, volt-amperes, flowing in the circuit.
7. The amount of electrical power passing through a given point in a circuit; may be expressed in watts, decibels, or volume units.
8. A rating used to indicate characteristics of coils and resonant circuits; reactance divided by ohmic resistance. $Q = \dfrac{XL}{R}$
9. A current that changes in value but not in direction; direct current combined with a smaller value of alternating current.
10. A momentary sharp change in voltage or current.

ANSWER KEY

151. 5	155. 2	158. 10
152. 4	156. 7	159. 8
153. 3	157. 9	160. 1
154. 6		

TEST SEVENTEEN

TERMS

COLUMN I

161. Reactance
162. Rectifier
163. Regulation
164. Relay
165. Repulsion-Induction Motor
166. Repulsion Motor
167. Repulsion-Start Induction Motor
168. RMA Color Code
169. Rotor
170. Rotary Switch

DEFINITIONS

COLUMN II

1. The change in voltage that takes place between a condition of no load and of full load, or rated load, in a transformer, generator, or other source.
2. An AC motor in which the rotor is turned by repulsion between magnetic fields induced by supply current in stator windings and other fields induced in rotor winding. Supply current only to stator windings.
3. One that is operated by turning a control knob.
4. A device that changes AC to DC. Allows current to flow in only one direction.
5. An AC motor that starts as a repulsion motor and after attaining speed runs as an induction motor; change over by automatic switch.
6. A standard method of designating resistor values by colored markings. (Radio Manufacturers Association.)
7. The member that rotates in a machine, generator, or motor.
8. An AC motor with two windings on the rotor: one, a squirrel-cage type; the other, a repulsion-start induction type.
9. Opposition offered to the flow of alternating current by the inductance or capacitance of a part; measured in ohms; designated by letter X.
10. An electromagnetic device that permits control of current in one circuit by a much smaller current in another circuit.

ANSWER KEY

161. 9	165. 8	168. 6
162. 4	166. 2	169. 7
163. 1	167. 5	170. 3
164. 10		

TEST EIGHTEEN

TERMS

COLUMN I

171. Series Circuit
172. Series-Parallel Circuit
173. Shock
174. Short Circuit
175. Shunt
176. Slip Ring
177. Solar Cell
178. Solenoid
179. Splice
180. Static Electricity

DEFINITIONS

COLUMN II

1. A form of energy present when there are two charges of opposite polarity in close proximity. Generated by friction.
2. A device that turns light energy into electrical energy.
3. A resistor placed in parallel with a meter movement to handle or bypass most of the current around the movement.
4. A circuit that has extremely low resistance.
5. A circuit with one resistor or consuming device located in a string or one after another.
6. A process whereby an outside source of electricity is such that it overrides the body's normal electrical system and causes the muscles to react involuntarily.
7. A combination of series and parallel circuits where a minimum of three resistors or devices are connected with at least one in series and with at least two in parallel.
8. A coil of wire wrapped around a hollow form, usually with some type of core material sucked into the hollow. The movement of the core is usually to move a switch or to open valves.
9. A ring of copper mounted on the shaft of a motor or generator through which a brush makes permanent (or constant) contact with the end of the rotor windings. Always used in pairs.
10. A form of electrical connection in which wires are joined directly to each other.

ANSWER KEY

171. 5	175. 3	178. 8
172. 7	176. 9	179. 10
173. 6	177. 2	180. 1
174. 4		

TEST NINETEEN

TERMS	DEFINITIONS
COLUMN I	COLUMN II

COLUMN I

181. Terminal
182. Thermocouple
183. Thermostat
184. Three-way Switch
185. Toggle Switches
186. Transformer
187. Universal Motor
188. Watt
189. X
190. Zener

COLUMN II

1. A unit of measure for electrical power.
2. A symbol used to indicate reactance.
3. A device used to step up or step down voltage.
4. A motor that will run on either AC or DC.
5. A switch operated by temperature variations.
6. Two of these switches are used to control a device from two locations.
7. A point to which electrical connections are made.
8. A type of semiconductor diode that intentionally breaks down at a predetermined voltage. Usually used for voltage regulation.
9. A device made of two different kinds of metals joined together at one end. When the junction is heated an emf is generated.
10. Devices used to turn various circuits on and off or to switch from one device to another. They are made in a number of configurations.

ANSWER KEY

181.	7	185.	10	188.	1
182.	9	186.	3	189.	2
183.	5	187.	4	190.	8
184.	6				

TEST TWENTY

TERMS	DEFINITIONS
COLUMN I	COLUMN II

191. Receptacle
192. Vector
193. Volt Meter
194. Wafer Switch
195. Watthour Meter
196. Wire Stripper
197. Semiconductor
198. Rheostat
199. Root-Means-Square
200. Z

1. Variable resistor; usually has only two points in a circuit. Used to control voltage by increasing or decreasing resistance.
2. Socket or outlet that accepts a plug to make electrical contact.
3. Material that is able to conduct electricity under certain conditions and not conduct it under others.
4. Symbol for impedance.
5. Tool for removing insulation from wire.
6. Device for checking levels of electromotive force.
7. Device used to measure electrical power.
8. Representation that indicates both direction and magnitude; used to graph function of AC.
9. Type of reading obtained by using a standard voltmeter or ammeter.
10. Rotary switch with contacts mounted on wafers.

ANSWER KEY

191.	2	195.	7	198.	1
192.	8	196.	5	199.	9
193.	6	197.	3	200.	4
194.	10				

SAFETY AND JUDGMENT IN ELECTRICAL WORK

> **DIRECTIONS:** For each question, read all choices carefully. Then select the answer that you consider correct or most nearly correct. Write the letter preceding your best choice next to the question.

1. An electrician should consider all electrical equipment "alive" unless he or she definitely knows otherwise. The main reason for this practice is to avoid

   (A) doing unnecessary work.
   (B) energizing the wrong circuit.
   (C) personal injury.
   (D) de-energizing a live circuit.

2. When working on live 600-volt equipment where rubber gloves might be damaged, an electrician should

   (A) work without gloves.
   (B) carry a spare pair of rubber gloves.
   (C) reinforce the fingers of the rubber gloves with rubber tape.
   (D) wear leather gloves over the rubber gloves.

3. When connecting a lamp bank or portable tool to a live 600-volt DC circuit, the best procedure is to make the negative or ground connection first and then the positive connection. The reason for this procedure is that

   (A) electricity flows from positive to negative.
   (B) there is less danger of accidental shock.
   (C) the reverse procedure may blow the fuse.
   (D) less arcing will occur when the connection is made.

4. If a live conductor is contacted accidentally, the severity of the electrical shock is determined primarily by

   (A) the size of the conductor.
   (B) the current in the conductor.
   (C) whether the current is AC or DC.
   (D) the contact resistance.

5. A corroded electrical connection in a circuit generally has a tendency to develop a high spot temperature. This is because the corrosion

   (A) increases the flow of current through the connection.
   (B) decreases the voltage drop across the connection.
   (C) increases the voltage drop across the connection.
   (D) decreases the effective resistance of the connection.

6. With respect to the safety value of insulation on electrical maintenance tools, it can be said properly that

   (A) it ensures the safety of the user.
   (B) the insulation provides very little real protection.
   (C) it is of value mainly to the new helper.
   (D) the insulation should not be used as the only protective measure.

7. Before using rubber gloves on high tension work, they should be

   (A) given to the helper and he or she should try them out.
   (B) treated with neats-foot oil.
   (C) washed inside and out.
   (D) tested to withstand the required voltage.

8. Metal cabinets used for lighting circuits are grounded to

   (A) eliminate electrolysis.
   (B) assure that the fuse in a defective circuit will blow.
   (C) reduce shock hazard.
   (D) simplify wiring.

9. When working near lead acid storage batteries extreme care should be taken to guard against sparks, essentially to avoid

   (A) overheating the electrolyte.
   (B) an electric shock.
   (C) a short circuit.
   (D) an explosion.

10. To prevent accidental starting of a motor that is to be worked on,

    (A) remove the fuses.
    (B) connect a lamp across the motor leads.
    (C) ground the frame.
    (D) ground the motor leads.

11. Most electric power tools, such as electric drills, come with a third conductor in the power lead that is used to connect the case of the tool to a grounded part of the electric outlet. The reason for this extra conductor is to

    (A) protect the user of the tool should the winding break down to the case.
    (B) prevent accumulation of a static charge on the case.
    (C) provide for continued operation of the tool should the regular grounded line-wire open.
    (D) eliminate sparking between the tool and the material being worked upon.

12. A good practical test that can be used in the field for detecting punctures in rubber gloves just before putting them on is to

    (A) seal the gloves by rolling down the cuffs, and then compress them against a flat surface.
    (B) fill the gloves with water, hang them up, and watch for leaks.
    (C) tie the cuffs to compressed-air line outlets and slowly inflate.
    (D) dip the gloves in soap suds and then blow into them, watching for bubbles.

13. It is always essential that a supervisor in charge of a crew of workers preparing to work on a low tension circuit caution them to

    (A) wait until the circuit has been killed.
    (B) work only when the load is zero.

    (C) consider the circuit alive at all times.
    (D) never work on any circuit alone.

14. It is best as a safety measure not to use water to extinguish fires involving electrical equipment. The main reason is that water

    (A) may damage wire insulation.
    (B) will not extinguish an electrical fire.
    (C) may transmit shock to the user.
    (D) will turn to steam and hide the fire.

15. When cleaning the insulation of electrical equipment in confined quarters it is *least* desirable to do the cleaning by

    (A) wiping with a dry cloth.
    (B) blowing with compressed air.
    (C) wiping with a cloth moistened with carbon tetrachloride.
    (D) wiping with a cloth moistened with water.

16. A steel measuring tape is undesirable for use around electrical equipment. The *least* important reason is the

    (A) magnetic effect.
    (B) short circuit hazard.
    (C) shock hazard.
    (D) danger of entanglement in rotating machines.

ANSWER KEY

1. C	5. C	9. D	13. C
2. D	6. D	10. A	14. C
3. B	7. D	11. A	15. C
4. D	8. C	12. A	16. A

ELECTRICAL JUDGMENT

> **DIRECTIONS:** For each question, read all choices carefully. Then select the answer that you consider correct or most nearly correct. Write the letter preceding your best choice next to the question

1. Of the following statements, the one that is correct is:

   (A) A "running light test" performed on rotating electrical machinery is for the purpose of checking for electrical faults.

   (B) If a circuit carries both AC and DC, the type of ammeter best suited to measure the effective value of the combined currents is the permanent magnet type.

   (C) Drawings are generally considered as a part of the specifications for any job.

   (D) The unit of light intensity may be defined as footcandles per square foot of illuminated area.

2. Which of the following statements is correct?

   (A) Of the common DC motors, the one that is least adaptable for traction work is the series motor.

   (B) Two 3-way switches cannot be used to control a lamp from two separate locations.

   (C) Emergency lighting systems in buildings should preferably be connected to two separate sources of power.

   (D) A Fire Underwriter's label on electrical materials may be accepted as proof that it is "approved material" for use on city projects.

3. An electrical code requires that all the conductors connecting an AC bus to a load be placed in a single metal conduit, tube, or equivalent and does not approve using one conduit for each wire. The principal reason for this requirement is that

   (A) a single conduit installation is cheaper.

   (B) it makes testing of the wires easier.

   (C) it is easier to pull the wires through a single conduit.

   (D) currents would circulate through the individual conduits.

4. The blueprint of a switchboard that is being installed under your supervision shows certain connections that you believe to be wrong. Your proper procedure is to

   (A) have the connections made according to the print but be prepared to make the changes if ordered.

   (B) report the apparent errors to your supervisor but continue with the remainder of the job.

   (C) hold the job until you have checked with the person whose initials are on the blueprint.

   (D) have the connections made properly and then return the blueprint marked to show the changes.

5. Assume there have been several reports of lamps in a particular 5-light series burning out shortly after renewal. However, the circuit fuse does not blow, and inspections and tests fail to show a reason for this condition. It would probably be best to

   (A) renew the series wiring of the circuit.

   (B) retest the circuit each time the lamps burn out.

   (C) request someone else to keep a close check on the lamps.

   (D) take no further action since you have no definite indication.

6. A newly appointed helper has made a blunder that has resulted in injury to another worker. As a foreman, you should certainly

   (A) recommend the dismissal of the new helper.

   (B) ignore the incident if it is the first offense.

   (C) study the accident for remedial action.

   (D) reprimand your partner for not properly instructing the helper.

7. As supervisor in charge of operations, you have twice reported that an important piece of equipment is very defective, but the repair crew has made no move to correct the defect. Under such conditions, you should

   (A) make another inspection to be sure you are right.

   (B) attempt to make repairs yourself when the unit is out of service.

   (C) keep the unit out of service and explain the reason in your operating logs.

   (D) do nothing but keep the unit in service as best possible.

8. A complex maintenance operation has been broken down into smaller and simpler jobs, and a job is to be assigned to each subordinate. Each job may be done in a number of different ways. The practical supervisory procedure would be to instruct each subordinate

   (A) to do his or her job in a specified way.
   (B) in several ways of doing his or her job.
   (C) to devise his or her own way of doing the job.
   (D) how to do all jobs.

9. An electrician should always make sure that his or her tools are kept in good condition because

   (A) a good job can never be done without perfect tools.
   (B) defective tools may cause accidents or damage.
   (C) tools that are in good condition require no care.
   (D) there is less possibility of the tools being lost.

10. When reporting minor trouble orally to your supervisor, the most important information from you would be

    (A) the exact time you discovered the trouble.
    (B) the type of trouble and its exact location.
    (C) the names of all the workers with you when you discovered the trouble.
    (D) exactly what you were doing when you noticed the trouble.

11. As an electrician, you have been assigned to a certain job and have been told that it is essential that it be finished by a certain time. If, after working diligently for some time, you realize that you cannot finish the job in time, you should

    (A) notify your supervisor immediately.
    (B) continue working and get as much done as possible.
    (C) skip what you consider minor parts of the job.
    (D) take it easy since the job cannot be done in time.

Question 12 refers to the statement below:

"The ampere-turns acting on a magnetic circuit are given by the product of the turns linked by the amperes flowing through these turns. Magnetomotive force tends to drive the flux through the circuit and corresponds to emf in the electric circuit. It is directly proportional to the ampere-turns and only differs from the numerical value of the ampere-turns by the constant factor 1.257, and the product of this factor and the ampere-turns equals the magnetomotive force. This unit of mmf is the gilbert."

12. One pole of a DC motor is wound with 500 turns of wire, through which a current of 2 amperes flows. Under these conditions, the mmf, in gilberts, acting on this magnetic circuit is most nearly

    (A) 1,000
    (B) 1,257
    (C) 500
    (D) 628

ANSWER KEY

1. C	4. B	7. C	10. B
2. C	5. A	8. A	11. A
3. D	6. C	9. B	12. B

SCRAMBLED DICTIONARY OF EQUIPMENT AND USAGE

The following tests cover equipment with which you should be familiar. You are expected to know how to use this equipment and how to solve everyday problems requiring its use. The tests measure your current knowledge and allow you to discover your weaker areas. Repeat each test until you have confidence in your ability to handle the material covered when it appears on the "real" test.

TEST ONE

> **DIRECTIONS:** Each DEFINITION in Column I refers to one of the TERMS in Column II. Select the letter that corresponds to the defined TERM and write that letter next to the appropriate DEFINITION in Column I.

DEFINITION	TERMS
COLUMN I	COLUMN II

1. Current consuming equipment, fixed or portable.	A. Mains
2. That portion of a wiring system extending beyond the final overcurrent device protecting the circuit.	B. Switchboard
3. Any conductors of a wiring system between the main switchboard or point of distribution and the branch circuit overcurrent device.	C. Fuse
4. Not readily accessible to persons unless special means for access are used.	D. Outlet
	E. Service raceway
5. A point on the wiring system at which current is taken to supply fixtures, lamps, heaters, motors, and current-consuming equipment.	F. Feeder
6. The rigid steel conduit that encloses service entrance conductors.	G. Isolated
7. That portion of overhead service conductors between the last line pole and the first point of attachment to the building.	H. Appliances
	J. Branch Circuit
8. Conductors of a wiring system between the lines of the public utility company or other source of supply and the main switchboard or point of distribution.	K. Fitting
	L. Conductor
	M. Enclosed
9. A wire or cable or other form of metal suitable for carrying electrical energy.	N. Surrounded
10. Surrounded by a case that will prevent accidental contact with live parts.	O. Service drop

ANSWER KEY

1. H	3. F	5. D	7. O	9. L
2. J	4. G	6. E	8. A	10. M

TEST TWO

> **DIRECTIONS:** In this test, the numbered MATERIALS in Column I have corresponding USES, which are lettered in Column II. Next to each MATERIAL in Column I write the letter of its most appropriate USE.

MATERIALS

COLUMN I

11. Silver
12. Mica
13. Porcelain
14. Phosphor bronze
15. Lead peroxide

USES

COLUMN II

A. Strain insulators
B. Arch shields
C. Heater wire
D. Commutators
E. Batteries
H. Relay contact points
J. Relay springs

ANSWER KEY

11. H   12. D   13. A   14. J   15. E

TEST THREE

> **DIRECTIONS:** In this test, the numbered MATERIALS in Column I are to be matched up with the ELECTRICAL EQUIPMENT PARTS listed and lettered in Column II. Next to each of the MATERIALS in Column I write the letter of the corresponding Column II PART.

MATERIALS

COLUMN I

16. Steel Laminations
17. Lead
18. Mica
19. Porcelain
20. Rubber
21. Copper
22. Carbon

ELECTRICAL EQUIPMENT PARTS

COLUMN II

A. Acid storage battery plates
B. Transformer cores
C. DC motor brushes
D. Insulating tape
E. Cartridge fuse cases
H. Commutator insulation
J. Strain insulators
K. Knife-switch blades

ANSWER KEY

16. B   18. H   20. D   21. K   22. C
17. A   19. J

TEST FOUR

> **DIRECTIONS:** In this test, each numbered PART in Column I is commonly associated with one of the PIECES OF ELECTRICAL EQUIPMENT listed and lettered in Column II. You are to match up the PARTS in Column I with the PIECES in Column II. Next to each of the PARTS in Column I write the letter of the PIECE with which it is most commonly associated.

PARTS   PIECES OF ELECTRICAL EQUIPMENT

COLUMN I   COLUMN II

23. Current setting plug   A. Oil circuit breaker
24. Lead connectors   B. AC power cable
25. Closing solenoid   C. Induction overload relay
26. Thermostat   D. Storage battery
27. Pothead   E. Electric water heater

ANSWER KEY

23. C	24. D	25. A	26. E	27. B

TEST FIVE

> **DIRECTIONS:** In this test, Column I consists of numbered EQUIPMENT PARTS, each of which is made from one of the MATERIALS listed and lettered in Column II. You are to match up the PARTS in Column I with their corresponding MATERIALS in Column II. Write next to the numbered PART in Column I the letter of the MATERIAL from which it is commonly made.

EQUIPMENT PARTS   MATERIALS

COLUMN I   COLUMN II

28. DC circuit breaker arcing-tips   A. Copper
29. Cartridge fuse casing   B. Silver
30. Pig-tail jumpers for contacts   C. Porcelain
31. Commutator bars   D. Carbon
32. Bearing oil-rings   E. Plastic
33. Cores for wound heater-coils   H. Wood
34. Center contact in screw lamp-sockets   J. Lead
35. Acid storage battery terminals   K. Brass
36. Push-button pilot light cover   L. Phosphor bronze
37. Operating sticks for disconnecting switches   M. Fiber

ANSWER KEY

28. D	30. B	32. K	34. L	36. E
29. M	31. A	33. C	35. J	37. H

TEST SIX

DIRECTIONS: Column I lists various JOB DESCRIPTIONS. Column II lists a variety of TOOLS, one of which is used for each of the jobs in Column I. You're to match up the TOOLS in Column II with the JOBS in Column I. Write next to each JOB the letter preceding the proper TOOL to use for that job.

JOB DESCRIPTIONS   TOOLS

COLUMN I   COLUMN II

	JOB	TOOL	
38.	Testing an armature for a shorted coil	A.	Neon Light
39.	Measurement of electrical pressure	B.	Growler
40.	Measurement of electrical energy	C.	Voltmeter
41.	Measurement of electrical power	D.	Ohmmeter
42.	Direct measurement of electrical insulation resistance	E.	Wattmeter
43.	Direct measurement of electrical resistance	F.	Ammeter
	(1 ohm to 10,000 ohms)	G.	Megger
44.	Direct measurement of electrical current	H.	Watthour Meter
45.	Testing to find if supply is DC or AC	J.	Manometer
46.	Testing the electrolyte of a battery	K.	Cable Clamp Pliers
47.	Cutting an iron bar	L.	Pair of Test Lamps
48.	Bending conduit	M.	Hack Saw
49.	A standard for checking the size of wire	N.	Hydrometer
		O.	Hickey
		P.	American Wire Gage
		Q.	Micrometer
		R.	Hygrometer
		S.	Rip Saw

ANSWER KEY

38. B	41. E	44. F	46. N	48. C
39. C	42. G	45. A	47. M	49. P
40. H	43. D			

TEST SEVEN

DIRECTIONS: In this test, Column I lists a number of DEVICES that are properly associated in operations with the CONDITIONS listed in Column II. You are asked to match up the CONDITIONS in Column II with the DEVICES in Column I. Write next to each of the DEVICES in Column I the letter preceding the CONDITION in Column II with which that device is properly associated.

DEVICES   CONDITIONS

COLUMN I   COLUMN II

50. Transformer   A. Alternating current only
51. Rectifier   B. Direct current only
52. Rotary Converter   C. Both alternating *and* direct current
53. Storage Battery   D. Either alternating current *or* direct
54. Induction Motor   current
55. Tungsten Lamp
56. Soldering Iron
57. Generator Exciter

ANSWER KEY

50. A   52. C   54. A   56. D   57. B

51. C   53. B   55. D

TEST EIGHT

DIRECTIONS: Column I lists various JOB DESCRIPTIONS. Column II lists a variety of TOOLS, one of which is used for each of the JOBS in Column I. You're to match up the TOOLS in Column II with the JOBS in Column I. Write next to each JOB the letter preceding the proper TOOL to use for that job.

JOB DESCRIPTIONS   TOOLS

COLUMN I   COLUMN II

58. Check brush pressure   A. Micrometer
59. Check contact area between the contact and   B. Megger
contact studs of a DC breaker   C. Wheatstone Bridge
60. Check contact between fingers and blade of an O.C.B.   D. (0–6 lbs.) Spring
61. Measure insulation resistance of a cable   Balance
62. Measure resistance of ammeter shunts   E. Feeler Gage

ANSWER KEY

58. D   59. A   60. E   61. B   62. C

TEST NINE

DIRECTIONS: In this test, Column I lists several ITEMS that are frequently represented by the SYMBOLS listed in Column II. You are asked to match up the SYMBOLS with the ITEMS they stand for. Write next to each ITEM in Column I the letter preceding the SYMBOL in Column II that stands for that item.

ITEMS

SYMBOLS

COLUMN I

COLUMN II

63. Lighting Panel
64. Special-purpose Outlet

A.

G.

65. Floor Outlet

B.

H.

66. Three-way Switch

67. Normally Closed Contact

C. S₃

I.

68. Resistor

69. Watt Hour Meter

D.

J.

70. Two-pole Electrically Operated Contactor with Blowout Coil

71. Capacitor

E.

72. Bell

F.

ANSWER KEY

63. B	65. E	67. F	69. J	71. H
64. D	66. C	68. G	70. I	72. A

TEST TEN

DIRECTIONS: In this quiz, Column I lists TERMS that are used to rate the devices listed in Column II. You are to match up each TERM with the DEVICE it rates. Write next to each of the RATING TERMS in Column I the letter preceding the one DEVICE in Column II to which it is properly applied.

RATING TERMS

DEVICES

COLUMN I

COLUMN II

73. 11,000 to 110 volts
74. 440 volts; 5 hp
75. 120 volts; 1,000 watts
76. 1,000 ohms; 10 watts
77. 100 amperes; 50 millivolts
78. 120 ampere-hours
79. 5 amperes; 2 seconds

A. Motor
B. Relay
C. Storage Battery
D. Transformer
E. Heater
F. Meter Shunt
G. Resistor

ANSWER KEY

73. D	75. E	77. F	78. C	79. B
74. A	76. G			

TOOLS, EQUIPMENT, AND INSTALLATION METHODS

> **DIRECTIONS:** For each question, read all the choices carefully. Then select the answer that you consider correct or most nearly correct. Write the letter preceding your best choice next to the question.

TOOLS AND EQUIPMENT

1. Mica is commonly used in electrical construction for

    (A) commutator bar separators.
    (B) switchboard panels.
    (C) strain insulators.
    (D) heater cord insulation.

2. The purpose of having a rheostat in the field circuit of a DC shunt motor is to

    (A) control the speed of the motor.
    (B) minimize the starting current.
    (C) limit the field current to a safe value.
    (D) reduce sparking at the brushes.

3. A frequency meter is constructed as a potential device, that is, to be connected across the line. A logical reason for this is that

    (A) only the line voltage has frequency.
    (B) a transformer may then be used with it.
    (C) the reading will be independent of the varying current.
    (D) it is safer than a series device.

4. The cross-sectional area of the bus bar shown in Figure 4 is

    (A) 1 square inch.
    (B) 3 square inches.
    (C) 9 square inches.
    (D) 12 square inches.

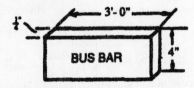

Figure 4

5. The electrical connector shown in Figure 5 would most likely be used in a power plant to connect

    (A) two branch cables to a main cable.
    (B) a single cable to the terminals of two devices.
    (C) a single cable to a flat bus bar.
    (D) a round bus bar to a flat one.

Figure 5

6. The fitting shown in Figure 6 is used in electrical construction to

    (A) clamp two adjacent junction boxes together.
    (B) act as a ground clamp for the conduit system.
    (C) attach flexible metallic conduit to a junction box.
    (D) protect exposed wires where they pass through a wall.

Figure 6

7. The diameter of a bare solid No. 14 AWG copper wire is approximately

    (A) 0.064 mils.
    (B) 0.64 mils.
    (C) 6.4 mils.
    (D) 64 mils.

8. A direct-current supply may be obtained from an alternating-current source by means of

    (A) a frequency changer set.
    (B) an inductance-capacitance filter.
    (C) a semiconductor diode rectifier circuit.
    (D) None of the above

9. To measure the value of armature circuit resistance corresponding to rated current for a 100-HP, direct-current, 240-volt compound motor you would use

(A) a 0-50 millivoltmeter and a 0-500 milliammeter.
(B) A 0-50 millivoltmeter and a 0-500 milliwattmeter.
(C) a 0-15 voltmeter and a 0-500 ammeter.
(D) a megger.

10. The current-carrying capacity of a No. 2 aluminum wire as compared to that of a No. 2 copper wire is

(A) 80 percent.
(B) 84 percent.
(C) 74 percent.
(D) 88 percent.

11. The minimum size of grounding conductor for a direct or alternating-current system is

(A) No. 14   (C) No. 8
(B) No. 10   (D) No. 6

12. The following equipment is required for a "2-line return-call" electric bell circuit:

(A) 2 bells, 2 metallic lines, 2 ordinary push-buttons, and one transformer
(B) 2 bells, 2 metallic lines, 2 return-call push-buttons, and 2 transformers
(C) 2 bells, 2 metallic lines, 2 return-call push-buttons, and one transformer
(D) 2 bells, 2 metallic lines, one ordinary push-button, one return-call push-button, and one transformer

13. The convenience outlet in Figure 13 that is known as a *polarized* outlet is number

(A) 1   (C) 3
(B) 2   (D) 4

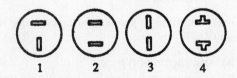

Figure 13

14. A polarized plug generally has

(A) two parallel prongs of the same size.
(B) prongs at an angle with one another.
(C) magnetized prongs.
(D) prongs marked plus and minus.

15. The outlet in Figure 15 that will accept the plug is

(A) 1   (C) 3
(B) 2   (D) 4

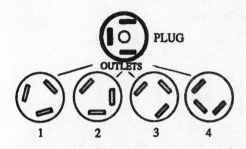

Figure 15

16. The standard colors of the outer coverings of wires used in series lighting circuits are

(A) Positive—black; Negative—white; Series—red
(B) Positive—black; Negative—red; Series—white
(C) Positive—white; Negative—black; Series—red
(D) Positive—red; Negative—white; Series—black

17. In comparing Nos. 00, 8, 12, and 6 AWG wires, the smallest of the group is

(A) No. 00   (C) No. 12
(B) No. 8   (D) No. 6

18. An electrician who counts 64 turns of wire on a reel that is 2 feet in diameter knows that the length of wire on the reel is nearest to

(A) 100 feet.   (C) 400 feet.
(B) 200 feet.   (D) 600 feet.

19. The letters RIWP when applied to electrical wire indicate the wire

(A) has a solid conductor.
(B) has rubber insulation.
(C) is insulated with paper.
(D) has a lead sheath.

20. The core of an electromagnet is usually

(A) aluminum.
(B) lead.
(C) brass.
(D) iron.

21. A good magnetic material is

(A) copper.
(B) iron.
(C) tin.
(D) brass.

22. A material NOT used in the makeup of lighting wires or cables is

(A) rubber.
(B) paper.
(C) lead.
(D) cotton.

23. Silver is a better conductor of electricity than copper; however, copper is generally used for electrical conductors. The main reason for using copper instead of silver is its

(A) cost.
(B) weight.
(C) strength.
(D) melting point.

24. The device shown in Figure 24 is clearly intended for use in electrical construction to

(A) support conduit on a wall.
(B) join cable to a terminal block.
(C) ground a wire to a water pipe.
(D) attach a chain-hung lighting fixture to an outlet box.

Figure 24

25. The four illustrations in Figure 25 show pairs of equal-strength permanent magnets on pivots, each magnet being held in the position shown by a mechanical locking device. When they are mechanically unlocked, the magnets that are LEAST likely to change their positions are pair number

(A) 1   (C) 3
(B) 2   (D) 4

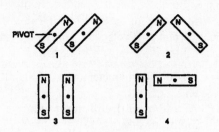

Figure 25

26. It is NOT correct to state that

(A) current flowing through a resistor causes heat.
(B) rectifiers change DC to AC.
(C) the conduit of an electrical system should be grounded.
(D) ammeters are used in series in the circuit.

27. The device used to change AC to DC is a

(A) frequency changer.
(B) regulator.
(C) transformer.
(D) rectifier.

28. An electrical device that transmits rotation from a driving to a driven member without mechanical contact—with stepless adjustable control and with almost instantaneous response—is the

(A) eddy current coupling.
(B) universal coupling.
(C) planetary coupling.
(D) coupling transformer.

29. Electrical contacts are opened or closed when the electrical current energizes the coils of a device called a

(A) reactor.
(B) transtat.
(C) relay.
(D) thermostat.

30. Boxes and fittings intended for outdoor use should be of

(A) weatherproof type.
(B) stamped steel of not less than No. 16 standard gauge.
(C) stamped steel plated with cadmium.
(D) ample strength and rigidity.

31. A hickey is

(A) not used in the electrical trade.
(B) only a part of a fixture.
(C) a tool used to bend small sizes of rigid conduit.
(D) used only in the plumbing trade.

32. The electrician's tapered reamer is used for

(A) reaming the ends of rigid conduit after it is cut.
(B) reaming the threads on couplings.
(C) making holes in panel boxes.
(D) reaming the holes in bushings.

33. The device often connected across relay contacts to minimize arcing when the contacts open is a

(A) spring.
(B) resistor.
(C) reactor.
(D) capacitor.

34. Lock nuts are sometimes used in making electrical connections on studs. In these cases, the purpose of the lock nuts is to

(A) make a tighter connection.
(B) be able to connect several wires to one stud.
(C) make it difficult to tamper with the connection.
(D) prevent the connection from loosening under vibration.

35. When a gauge number such as No. 4 is used in connection with a twist drill, it refers to the

(A) length.
(B) hardness.
(C) number of cutting edges.
(D) diameter.

36. When the term 10-32 is used in connection with machine screws commonly used in lighting work, the number 32 refers to the

(A) screw length.
(B) screw thickness.
(C) diameter of hole.
(D) threads per inch.

ANSWER KEY

1. A	7. D	13. A	19. B	25. C	31. C
2. A	8. C	14. B	20. D	26. B	32. A
3. C	9. C	15. C	21. B	27. D	33. D
4. A	10. B	16. A	22. B	28. A	34. D
5. C	11. C	17. C	23. A	29. C	35. D
6. C	12. B	18. C	24. A	30. A	36. D

USING TOOLS

Fastening

1. To fasten an outlet box to a finished hollow tile wall, it is best to use

   (A) wooden plugs.
   (B) toggle bolts.
   (C) through bolts and fishplates.
   (D) expansion bolts.

2. The fastening devices commonly used in conjunction with split-lead expansion inserts to hold small outlet boxes on concrete walls are

   (A) wood screws.
   (B) lag screws.
   (C) toggle bolts.
   (D) through bolts.

3. An outlet box should be fastened to a concrete wall by the use of

   (A) expansion bolts.
   (B) toggle bolts.
   (C) wood plugs and nails.
   (D) porcelain inserts and screws.

4. When installing a new meter on a panel, to obtain accurate mounting,

   (A) drill from the back of the panel.
   (B) drill oversize holes.
   (C) use a template.
   (D) use the meter to mark hole centers.

5. To fasten an outlet box to a terra cotta arch, you should use

   (A) wooden plugs and nails.
   (B) expansion bolts.
   (C) toggle bolts.
   (D) tenpenny nails.

6. To fasten an outlet box between the studs in a wall constructed of metal lath and plaster, you should use

   (A) strong lath twine.
   (B) iron wire.
   (C) cement or plaster.
   (D) an approved box hanger.

7. To fasten an outlet box on a steel bulkhead, you should use

   (A) solder.
   (B) wood screws.
   (C) machine screws.
   (D) expansion bolts.

8. To fasten an outlet box to a concrete ceiling, you should use

   (A) wooden plugs.
   (B) toggle bolts.
   (C) Mollys.
   (D) expansion bolts.

9. A small meter panel is to be fastened to a hollow tile wall. This is best done by using

   (A) expansion bolts.
   (B) swing bolts.
   (C) self-threading screws.
   (D) toggle bolts.

10. Toggle bolts are appropriate for fastening an outlet box to a

    (A) concrete ceiling.
    (B) brick wall.
    (C) hollow-tile wall.
    (D) wooden partition.

Soldering

11. When soldering two copper surfaces together, they are kept clean while heating by

    (A) applying the solder quickly.
    (B) frequently rubbing with emery cloth.
    (C) not permitting the open flame to touch them.
    (D) the use of a flux.

12. A soldering iron should NOT be heated to excess because this will usually

    (A) anneal the copper tip.
    (B) ruin the tin on the surface of the tip.
    (C) loosen the copper tip on the iron rod.
    (D) burn the wooden handle.

13. Acid is not a good flux for use in soldering small electrical connections mainly because it is

    (A) nonconducting.
    (B) expensive.
    (C) messy to use.
    (D) corrosive.

14. The flux commonly used for soldering electrical wire is

    (A) tin chloride.
    (B) zinc chloride.
    (C) rosin.
    (D) silver amalgam.

15. In melting solder, the formation of excessive dross is an indication that

    (A) the solder temperature is too low.
    (B) the tin content of the solder is too high.
    (C) the tin content of the solder is too low.
    (D) too much heat is being applied.

Wiring

16. The most important reason for using friction tape over a splice is to

    (A) prevent damage to the rubber tape.
    (B) increase the insulation resistance.
    (C) make the splice as small as possible.
    (D) prevent the wire ends from separating should the wire be pulled.

17. When moving a reel containing cable, it is important to roll it in the direction indicated by the arrow marked on the reel. The reason for this is to

    (A) prevent unwinding and damaging the cable.
    (B) protect the lagging from injury.
    (C) make sure that the cable end is always on top.
    (D) avoid reverse bends when installing the cable.

18. To cut Wiremold, you would

    (A) use an approved cutter like an M.M. cutter.
    (B) use a hack saw and remove the burr with a file.
    (C) use a chisel.
    (D) use a large pair of tin snips.

19. To cut oval duct, you would

    (A) use a hack saw and remove the burr with a file.
    (B) use an approved cutter like an M.M. cutter.
    (C) use a cold chisel.
    (D) use a pair of tin snips.

20. To cut rigid conduit, you should

    (A) use a cold chisel and ream the ends.
    (B) use a 3-wheel pipe cutter.
    (C) use a hack saw and ream the ends.
    (D) order it cut to size.

21. The length of a "Running Thread" should NOT be less than

    (A) a desired length.
    (B) the length of a coupling plus a lock nut.
    (C) twice the length of the coupling.
    (D) $\frac{1}{2}$ the length of the coupling.

22. When you bend a 90-degree bend in a piece of rigid conduit, the radius of the inner edge shall be not less than

    (A) $1\frac{1}{2}$ inches.

    (B) $2\frac{1}{2}$ inches.

    (C) $3\frac{1}{2}$ inches.

    (D) $4\frac{1}{2}$ inches.

23. The length of a Panel Thread should NOT be less than

    (A) the thickness of the panel box plus the thickness of the locknut and bushing.
    (B) twice the length of the coupling.
    (C) the thickness of the box plus the thickness of the locknut and bushing plus $\frac{1}{2}$ the length of the coupling.
    (D) the length of a standard pipe thread.

24. A one-inch pipe that is suitable for use as an electric conduit must be capable of withstanding, without damage, a 90-degree bend about a radius of approximately

    (A) 7.5 inches.
    (B) 10 inches.
    (C) 15 inches.
    (D) 20 inches.

25. The one of the following that would prove LEAST useful in uncoupling several pieces of conduit in a shop is a

    (A) chain wrench.
    (B) strap wrench.
    (C) stillson wrench.
    (D) box wrench.

26. The total length of threads on a standard $\frac{3}{4}''$ conduit should be about

    (A) $\frac{1}{2}$ inch.

    (B) $\frac{3}{4}$ inch.

    (C) 1 inch.

    (D) $1\frac{1}{2}$ inches.

27. When using compressed air to clean electrical equipment, it is recommended that the air pressure should not exceed 50 pounds. The reason for this is that higher pressures

    (A) introduce a personal hazard to the user.
    (B) will damage electrical connections at the terminals.
    (C) might blow dust onto other equipment in the vicinity.
    (D) may loosen insulating tapes.

28. If it is necessary to increase slightly the tension of an ordinary coiled spring in a relay, the proper procedure is to

    (A) cut off one or two turns.
    (B) compress it slightly.
    (C) stretch it slightly.
    (D) unhook one end, twist, and replace.

29. Lubrication is never used on

    (A) a knife switch.
    (B) a die when threading conduit.
    (C) wires being pulled into a conduit.
    (D) a commutator.

30. To reverse the direction of rotation of a repulsion motor, you should

    (A) move the brushes so that they cross the pole axis.
    (B) interchange the connection of either the main or auxiliary winding.
    (C) interchange the connections to the armature winding.
    (D) interchange the connections to the field winding.

ANSWER KEY

1.	B	7.	C	13.	D	19.	A	25.	D
2.	A	8.	D	14.	C	20.	C	26.	B
3.	A	9.	D	15.	D	21.	B	27.	D
4.	C	10.	C	16.	A	22.	C	28.	A
5.	C	11.	D	17.	A	23.	C	29.	D
6.	D	12.	B	18.	B	24.	B	30.	A

ELECTRICAL MEASUREMENT

DIRECTIONS: For each question, read all the choices carefully. Then select the answer that you consider correct or most nearly correct. Write the letter preceding your best choice next to the question.

MEASURING DEVICES

1. A DC wattmeter is essentially a combination of

    (A) a voltmeter and an ammeter.
    (B) two ammeters.
    (C) two voltmeters.
    (D) a current and a potential transformer.

2. Of the following meters, the one that does NOT have the zero at the center of the scale is the

    (A) control battery ammeter.
    (B) main tie-line ammeter.
    (C) main tie-line reactive volt-ammeter.
    (D) main tie-line wattmeter.

3. A shunt in conjunction with a shunt-type ammeter is used in measuring DC current where

    (A) it is desired to isolate the instrument from the main circuit.
    (B) the current fluctuates greatly in value.

(C) it is not practical to carry the full load current through the instrument.

(D) the accompanying DC voltage is high.

4. Very high AC voltages are usually measured with a

(A) voltmeter and current transformer.
(B) millivoltmeter and shunt.
(C) voltmeter and multiplier.
(D) potential transformer and voltmeter.

5. In the course of normal operation, the instrument that will be LEAST effective in indicating that a generator may overheat because it is overloaded is

(A) an ammeter.
(B) a voltmeter.
(C) a wattmeter.
(D) a stator thermacouple.

6. Large currents in DC circuits are practically always measured with a(n)

(A) ammeter and shunt.
(B) millivoltmeter and multiplier.
(C) ammeter and current transformer.
(D) millivoltmeter.

7. A millivoltmeter having a full-scale deflection of 50 millivolts is used with a 100-ampere, 50-millivolt shunt in a DC circuit. This combination is normally used to measure

(A) voltage.
(B) current.
(C) power.
(D) resistance.

8. In telemetering equipment, the purpose of the glow tube is to provide

(A) adequate illumination to read the meter.
(B) protection against high line voltage.
(C) rectification of the line current.
(D) a means of discharging the equipment.

9. A cycle counter is used in testing

(A) relays.
(B) ammeters.
(C) wattmeters.
(D) voltmeters.

10. The insulation resistance of a transformer winding is readily measured with

(A) a wattmeter.
(B) an ammeter.
(C) a megger.
(D) a Kelvin bridge.

11. To measure the voltage across a load you would connect a(n)

(A) voltmeter across the load.
(B) ammeter across the load.
(C) voltmeter in series with the load.
(D) ammeter in series with the load.

12. Your supervisor has told you to measure the insulation resistance of some feeders. To do this, you will use

(A) a megger.
(B) a bell test.
(C) a magneto test.
(D) a service person from the utility company.

13. You are to check the power factor of a certain electrical load. You cannot get a power factor meter. You would use

(A) an ammeter, a wattmeter, and a voltmeter.
(B) a voltmeter and an ammeter.
(C) a wattmeter.
(D) a kilowatt hour meter.

14. The power factor of a single-phase alternating current motor may be found by using which of the following sets of AC instruments?

(A) One voltmeter and one phase-rotation meter
(B) One voltmeter and one ammeter
(C) One voltmeter, one ammeter, and one wattmeter
(D) One voltmeter, one ammeter, and one watthour meter

15. The correct value of the resistance of a field coil can be measured by using

(A) a Schering bridge.
(B) an ammeter and a voltmeter.
(C) a Kelvin double bridge.
(D) a Maxwell bridge.

16. The hot-wire voltmeter

(A) is a high precision instrument.
(B) is used only for DC circuits.
(C) reads equally well on DC and/or AC circuits.
(D) is used only for AC circuits.

17. An AC ammeter is calibrated to read RMS values. This also means that this meter is calibrated to read the

(A) average value.
(B) peak value.
(C) effective value.
(D) square value.

18. To increase the range of DC ammeters you would use a(n)

    (A) current transformer.
    (B) inductance.
    (C) capacitor.
    (D) shunt.

19. The electric meter NOT in itself capable of measuring both DC and AC voltages is the

    (A) D'Arsonval voltmeter.
    (B) electrodynamometer voltmeter.
    (C) iron vane voltmeter.
    (D) inclined-coil voltmeter.

20. To increase the range of an AC ammeter, which of the following is most commonly used?

    (A) Current transformer
    (B) Inductance
    (C) Capacitor
    (D) Straight shunt (not U-shaped)

21. The type of meter that is suitable for direct current only is the

    (A) iron-vane type.
    (B) permanent magnet type.
    (C) electrodynamometer type.
    (D) hot-wire type.

22. The open-circuit test on a transformer is a test for measuring

    (A) its copper losses.
    (B) its iron losses.
    (C) its insulation resistance.
    (D) the equivalent resistance of the transformer.

23. A shunt is used in parallel with a DC ammeter measuring large currents to

    (A) dampen the meter pointer.
    (B) reduce the current that goes through the meter.
    (C) protect the meter against shorts.
    (D) increase the sensitivity of the meter.

24. An electrician may use a megger to

    (A) measure the amount of illumination.
    (B) determine the speed of an electric motor.
    (C) measure the resistance of a lighting cable.
    (D) test a lighting circuit for a ground.

25. To increase the range of a volmeter,
    (A) add a shunt.
    (B) add resistance in series with the meter movement.
    (C) add resistance in parallel with the meter movement.
    (D) put a diode in the circuit.

ANSWER KEY

1. A	6. A	11. A	16. C	21. B
2. B	7. B	12. A	17. C	22. B
3. C	8. B	13. A	18. D	23. B
4. D	9. A	14. C	19. A	24. D
5. B	10. C	15. B	20. A	25. B

USE OF MEASURING DEVICES

1. When applying a high-potential test voltage to the primary winding of a rebuilt transformer,

    (A) one end of the primary winding must be grounded.
    (B) the secondary winding must be short-circuited.
    (C) all other parts of the transformer must be insulated from ground.
    (D) the secondary winding, transformer case, and core must be grounded.

2. To test and calibrate a polyphase watthour meter using a single phase AC supply, the best method is to connect the

    (A) voltage coils in series, current coils in parallel.
    (B) current coils in series, voltage coils in parallel.
    (C) current coils in parallel, voltage coils in series.
    (D) voltage coils in series, current coils in series.

3. A certain circuit requires a maximum of 10 amperes when operating properly. If a calibrated ammeter in the circuit reads 12 amperes, it is possible that

(A) a partial short exists somewhere in the circuit.
(B) one of the branch circuits is open.
(C) the ground connection is open.
(D) a high-resistance connection exists somewhere in the circuit.

4. The purpose of subjecting a newly completed lighting equipment installation to a high-potential test would be to

(A) find the maximum voltage that the equipment will withstand.
(B) measure the insulation resistance of the wiring.
(C) check the dielectric strength of the insulation.
(D) make sure that the equipment will withstand operating voltage.

5. If a test lamp lights and continues to glow when placed in series with a capacitor and a suitable source of DC, it is a good indication that the capacitor is

(A) fully charged.
(B) short-circuited.
(C) fully discharged.
(D) open-circuited.

6. The insulation resistance of a cable is to be determined by the use of a voltmeter with a multiplier and a 600-volt DC source. The line voltage is first measured, and then the insulation is connected in series with the meter and a second reading across the line is taken. If the second reading is very low compared to the first, it indicates that the

(A) meter is defective.
(B) cable insulation is bad.
(C) cable insulation is good.
(D) DC source has a partial short.

7. Before disconnecting an ammeter from an energized current transformer circuit, the current transformer

(A) primary should be shorted.
(B) secondary should be shorted.
(C) primary should be opened.
(D) secondary should be opened.

8. A power-factor meter is connected to a single-phase, 2-wire circuit by means of

(A) 2 wires.
(B) 3 wires.
(C) 4 wires.
(D) 5 wires.

Questions 9–11 refer to Figure 9 below.

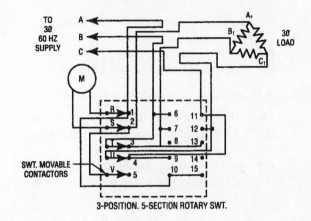

Figure 9

9. With switch movable contactors R, S, T, U, and V in positions 1, 2, 3, 4, and 5 as shown, Meter M is connected between points

(A) A-A′, and load is improperly connected to supply.
(B) A-A′, and load is properly connected to supply.
(C) C-C′, and load is improperly connected to supply.
(D) C-C′, and load is properly connected to supply.

10. With switch movable contactors R, S, T, U, and V in positions 6, 7, 8, 9, and 10, the function of meter M is to measure the

(A) current in line B-B′.
(B) voltage in line B-B′.
(C) power drawn by the load.
(D) power factor of the load.

11. With switch movable contactors R, S, T, U, and V in positions 11, 12, 13, 14, and 15, meter M is connected between points

(A) A-A′, and load is improperly connected to supply.
(B) A-A′, and load is properly connected to supply.
(C) C-C′, and load is improperly connected to supply.
(D) C-C′, and load is properly connected to supply.

12. In order to properly connect a single-phase wattmeter to a circuit, you should use

    (A) two current and two potential leads.
    (B) two current leads only.
    (C) two potential leads only.
    (D) two current leads and two power leads.

13. A DC milliammeter may be used to measure voltages

    (A) when a proper shunt is used with the meter.
    (B) if a high external resistor is connected in series with the meter.
    (C) by simply connecting the meter across the line.
    (D) if a high external resistor is connected across the terminals of the meter.

14. To properly remove an ammeter from a high voltage bus already supplying load,

    (A) the load should preferably be reduced.
    (B) one should make sure that the switchboard is grounded.
    (C) the voltage at the bus should preferably be reduced when possible.
    (D) the case of the instrument should be grounded and the secondary winding of the current transformer short-circuited.

15. To check the full-load efficiency of a transformer, its losses (core and copper) must be known. These losses

    (A) cannot be obtained except by actually loading the transformer.
    (B) may be obtained without loading the transformer by performing a short-circuit and an open-circuit test on it.
    (C) may be found by measuring the input to the transformer with the secondary open.
    (D) may be obtained by measuring the winding resistance and calculating the I^2R losses.

16. When reading a watthour meter, the hands should always be read as indicating the figure that they have last passed. If a hand is very close to a figure, whether or not it has actually passed this figure must be determined from the

    (A) reading taken one hour earlier.
    (B) reading taken one hour later.

    (C) position of the hand on the next higher dial.
    (D) position of the hand on the next lower dial.

17. Testing for a blown cartridge fuse by connecting a test lamp from one clip to the other across the suspected fuse will in all cases indicate a

    (A) good fuse if the lamp lights up.
    (B) blown fuse if the lamp remains dark.
    (C) blown fuse if the lamp lights up.
    (D) good fuse if the lamp remains dark.

18. The method usually used to determine the area of the contacts actually making contact on a DC circuit breaker is to

    (A) note the impression made on a piece of paper upon which the contacts have been closed.
    (B) insert a 0.005 feeler gage between the closed contacts.
    (C) pass current through the closed contacts and measure the millivolt drop.
    (D) multiply the width by the length of each contact.

19. If a ground occurs on one side of a 120-volt battery control circuit, the voltage on the ground detector lamps will be

    (A) 60 volts on each lamp.
    (B) 60 volts on one lamp and 0 volts on the other.
    (C) 120 volts on one lamp and 0 volts on the other.
    (D) 0 volts on each lamp.

20. A generator watthour meter is read at 10:00 a.m. and again at 10:30 a.m. when the unit is taken off the line. Find the average load by subtracting the first reading from the second reading and multiplying by

    (A) the meter constant.
    (B) the meter constant and dividing by two.
    (C) two and by the meter constant.
    (D) one thousand.

21. A 600-volt lamp cluster could NOT be used on a 600-volt circuit to test

    (A) the continuity of the circuit.
    (B) if the circuit is energized.
    (C) the exact voltage of the circuit.
    (D) for a ground on the circuit.

ANSWER KEY

1. D	6. C	10. A	14. D	18. A
2. B	7. B	11. D	15. B	19. C
3. A	8. B or C	12. A	16. D	20. C
4. D	9. B	13. B	17. C or D	21. C
5. B				

PROBLEMS IN MEASUREMENT

1. The input to a motor-generator set is 1,500 watts, and the motor and generator losses total 250 watts. The efficiency of the set is nearest to

   (A) 88.2 percent.
   (B) 83.2 percent.
   (C) 71.4 percent.
   (D) 16.7 percent.

2. A kilowatthour meter with a constant of 100 and connected to measure the power output of a 35,000 kVA unit reads 4324 at the beginning of a day and 1564 at the end of the day. The total output for the day is

   (A) 840,000 kWh.
   (B) 724,000 kWh.
   (C) 294,400 kWh.
   (D) 276,000 kWh.

3. If one of the two wattmeters used to measure the total power to a 3-phase balanced delta-connected load indicates zero, the power factor of the load is

   (A) 100 percent.
   (B) 80 percent.
   (C) 50 percent.
   (D) 0 percent.

4. A voltage of about 40 volts is needed temporarily to make a particular test taking several hours. Someone suggests to you that a 10-ohm resistor and a 20-ohm resistor be connected in series across the 120-volt source that is available, claiming that 40 volts will then be obtained across the 10-ohm resistor. If these resistors are on hand and each is rated at 200 watts, you should turn down the suggestion because

   (A) the 20-ohm resistor will be overloaded.
   (B) the 10-ohm resistor will be overloaded.
   (C) too much power will be wasted.
   (D) the combination will give too high a voltage.

5. On a certain voltmeter, the same scale is used for three ranges; these are 0–750, 0–300, and 0–120 volts. If the scale is marked only for the 0–120 volt range, a scale reading of 112 when the 750 volt range is being used corresponds to an actual voltage of

   (A) 622
   (B) 688
   (C) 700
   (D) 742

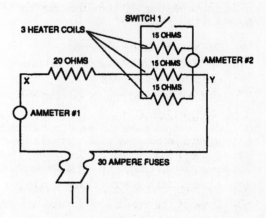

Figure 6

Questions 6–11 refer to Figure 6 above. Assume that the two ammeters are of negligible resistance and that switch 1 is open unless otherwise stated.

6. The equivalent resistance of the 3 heater coils connected as shown is

   (A) 5 ohms.   (C) 15 ohms.
   (B) 10 ohms.   (D) 45 ohms.

7. If ammeter 2 reads 6 amperes, ammeter 1 will read

   (A) 2 amperes.
   (B) 6 amperes.
   (C) 9 amperes.
   (D) 18 amperes.

8. When each of the 3 heater coils carries 2 amperes, the power consumed by the 3 heater coils will total

   (A) 20 watts.
   (B) 180 watts.
   (C) 540 watts.
   (D) 1350 watts.

9. When switch 1 is closed, the equivalent resistance of the whole circuit (points X to Y) is

   (A) 20 ohms.
   (B) 25 ohms.
   (C) 27.5 ohms.
   (D) 30 ohms.

10. No matter what current is flowing through the circuit, the voltage drop across the 20-ohm resistor as compared to that across the heater coils will

   (A) always be equal.
   (B) always be lower.
   (C) always be higher.
   (D) be lower only if switch 1 is closed.

11. If the line voltage is 120 volts, then the fuses will blow if

    (A) the 20-ohm resistor is shorted.
    (B) the 20-ohm resistor is shorted and two heater coils are open circuited.
    (C) switch 1 is closed and the 20-ohm resistor is shorted.
    (D) the 20-ohm resistor develops an open circuit and switch 1 is closed.

12. The power, in watts, taken by a load connected to a three-phase circuit is generally expressed by

    (A) EI P.F. 2
    (B) EI P.F.
    (C) 3 EI P.F.
    (D) $\dfrac{EI}{3}$ P.F.

Questions 13–15 refer to Figure 13 below.

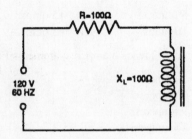

Figure 13

13. The value of the impedance, in ohms, of the above circuit is most nearly

    (A) 200   (C) 150
    (B) 50   (D) 140

14. The current, in amperes, flowing in the above circuit is most nearly

    (A) .6   (C) 1.2
    (B) 2.4   (D) .85

15. The power, in watts, consumed in the above circuit is most nearly

    (A) 72   (C) 576
    (B) 144   (D) 36

16. A capacitor whose capacity is one microfarad is connected in parallel with a capacitor whose capacity is 2 microfarads. This combination is equal to a single capacitor having a capacity, in microfarads, of approximately

    (A) $\frac{2}{3}$ (C) 3
    (B) 1   (D) $\frac{3}{2}$

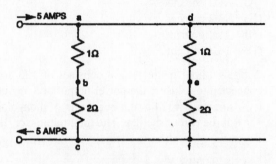

Figure 17

17. With reference to Figure 17, the current flowing through resistance ab is

    (A) 5 amperes.
    (B) 4 amperes.
    (C) $2\frac{1}{2}$ amperes.
    (D) $1\frac{1}{2}$ amperes.

18. With reference to Figure 17, the voltage difference between points b and e is

    (A) 1 volt.
    (B) 10 volts.
    (C) 5 volts.
    (D) 0 volts.

19. If the full rating of a transformer is 90 kW at 90 percent power factor, then the kVA rating is

    (A) 81
    (B) 90
    (C) 100
    (D) 141

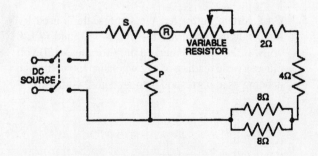

Figure 20

Items 20–27 refer to Figure 20 above.

20. If resistance "S" (of low value) and "P" (of high value) are both associated with the same meter, the meter is

(A) a wattmeter.
(B) a voltmeter.
(C) an ammeter.
(D) a varmeter.

21. When the DC voltage "E" is 100 and the current through the variable resistor is 1 ampere, the variable resistor is fixed at

(A) 78 ohms.
(B) 86 ohms.
(C) 90 ohms.
(D) 100 ohms.

22. With the same load resistances and the same fixed value of the variable resistor as used in Figure 20, the DC voltage "E" is replaced by an AC voltage of 100. The current through the variable resistor is

(A) 0.707 ampere.
(B) 1.00 ampere.
(C) 1.41 amperes.
(D) 1.73 amperes.

23. When the voltage drop across the 8-ohm resistances in 50 volts, that across the 2-ohm resistance is

(A) 10 volts.
(B) 12.5 volts.
(C) 25 volts.
(D) 100 volts.

24. The *ratio* of the voltage drop across the 2-ohm resistance to that across the 4-ohm resistance

(A) increases with an increase in line voltage.
(B) will increase if the two 8-ohm resistances are shorted.
(C) decreases as the line current decreases.
(D) is independent of line current.

25. If the current through the 2-ohm resistance is 2 amperes, the total power consumed by the 2-, 4-, and both 8-ohm resistances is

(A) 40 watts.
(B) 56 watts.
(C) 88 watts.
(D) 200 watts.

26. A relay "R," of negligible resistance, in series with the line as shown and set to operate at 4 amperes line current is taken out of service for repairs. The

only available spare is also of negligible resistance and has a maximum current setting of 3 amperes. This spare will function properly if it is installed

(A) in series with one of the 8-ohm resistances.
(B) in series and between the 2-and 4-ohm resistances.
(C) in parallel across the 4-ohm resistance.
(D) to directly replace the original relay.

27. With a fixed voltage "E," increasing the amount of the variable resistance put in the circuit will increase the voltage

(A) drop across the 2-ohm resistance.
(B) "V" across the line.
(C) drop across the 8-ohm resistance.
(D) drop across the variable resistor.

28. The power consumed by a 2-ampere series circuit consisting of a 100-ohm resistor in series with a capacitor of 100 ohms capacitive reactance is

(A) 100 watts.
(B) 200 watts.
(C) 300 watts.
(D) 565 watts.

29. The power consumed by a 4-ampere series circuit consisting of a 100-ohm resistor and a coil with 100 ohms inductive reactance is

(A) 400 watts.
(B) 282.28 watts.
(C) 141.14 watts.
(D) 565 watts.

30. If the current through a series circuit is 8 amperes and there are two 500-ohm resistances acting as loads, the total current drawn from the power source would be

(A) 8 amperes.
(B) 4 amperes.
(C) 2 amperes.
(D) 16 amperes.

31. If the total current in a parallel circuit is 4 amperes and it is feeding into a parallel arrangement of resistors where 4 resistors of the same size are connected, then the current through each resistor would be

(A) the same.
(B) equal but not proportional.
(C) unequal.
(D) 4 amperes.

32. The power consumed by an inductive load on an AC line is found by

   (A) multiplying its DC resistance by the current.
   (B) multiplying the current by its inductive reactance.
   (C) checking its phase angle first.
   (D) multiplying the DC resistance by the inductance.

33. In Figure 20, the equivalent resistance of the two 8-ohm resistors is

   (A) 2 ohms.
   (B) 4 ohms.
   (C) 16 ohms.
   (D) 8 ohms.

34. If an ammeter has 10 amperes flowing through it in a circuit with a resistance of 100 ohms, the voltage drop measured across the resistor will be

   (A) 10 volts.
   (B) 1000 volts.
   (C) 100 volts.
   (D) 5 volts.

35. The wattage rating of the resistor for the circuit in Question 34 would have to be a *minimum* of

   (A) 10 watts.
   (B) 100 watts.
   (C) 1000 watts.
   (D) 10,000 watts.

ANSWER KEY

1. B	7. D	13. D	19. C	25. A	31. A
2. D	8. B	14. D	20. A	26. A	32. B
3. C	9. A	15. A	21. C	27. D	33. B
4. A	10. C	16. C	22. B	28. D	34. B
5. C	11. C	17. C	23. C	29. D	35. D
6. A	12. C	18. D	24. D	30. A	

VOLTAGE PROBLEMS

DIRECTIONS: For each question, read all choices carefully. Then select the answer that you consider correct or most nearly correct. Write the letter preceding your best choice next to the question.

1. A potential relay is connected across a 600-volt DC source. The resistance of the relay coil is 2,400 ohms. If a resistance of 400 ohms is connected in series with the relay coil and a resistance of 1,200 ohms is connected in parallel with the relay coil, the voltage across the coil will be

   (A) 200 volts.
   (B) 400 volts.
   (C) 500 volts.
   (D) 550 volts.

2. If a fourth lamp in a lighted 5-lamp series on a 600-volt circuit is removed from its socket, the voltage across the terminals of the empty socket is

   (A) 0
   (B) 120
   (C) 480
   (D) 600

3. Two transformers with ratios of 1:2 are to be connected in parallel. To test for proper connections, the circuit of Figure 3 is used. The transformers are connected in parallel if the voltmeter shown reads

(A) 120 volts.
(B) 240 volts.
(C) 0 volts.
(D) 480 volts.

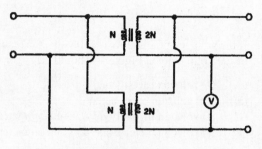

Figure 3

4. Three single-phase transformers having ratios of 10:1 are connected with their primaries in wye and their secondaries in delta. If the low-voltage windings are used as the primaries and the line voltage on the primary side is 208 volts, then the line voltage on the secondary side is

(A) 3,600 volts.
(B) 2,080 volts.
(C) 1,200 volts.
(D) 692 volts.

5. In accordance with the voltages shown in Figure 5, the power supply must be

(A) 3-wire DC.
(B) 3-phase AC.
(C) 2-phase AC.
(D) single-phase AC.

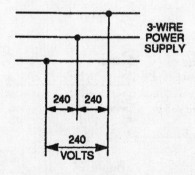

Figure 5

6. If the voltmeter in Figure 6 reads 34 volts, the circuit voltage is about

(A) 68
(B) 85
(C) 102
(D) 119

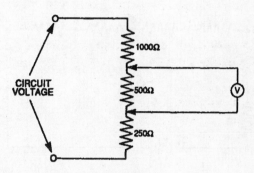

Figure 6

7. The range of both voltmeters shown in Figure 7 is 0-300 volts. In this case, the AC meter will indicate the correct voltage and the DC meter will indicate

(A) zero.
(B) a few volts too high.
(C) a few volts too low.
(D) the correct voltage.

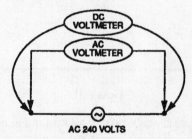

Figure 7

8. The reading of the voltmeter in Figure 8 should be

(A) 50
(B) 10
(C) 5
(D) 0

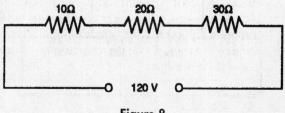

Figure 8

9. The reading of the voltmeter in Figure 9 will be highest when the test prods are held on points

   (A)   1 and 4
   (B)   2 and 5
   (C)   3 and 6
   (D)   4 and 7

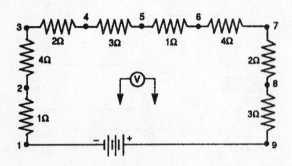

Figure 9

10. The reading of the voltmeter in Figure 10 should be nearest to

   (A)   30
   (B)   90
   (C)   120
   (D)   240

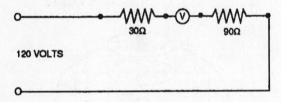

Figure 10

11. Each of the four resistors shown in Figure 11 has a resistance of 50 ohms. If R_2 becomes open-circuited, the reading of the voltmeter will

   (A)   increase slightly.
   (B)   decrease slightly.
   (C)   fall to zero.
   (D)   become 240 volts.

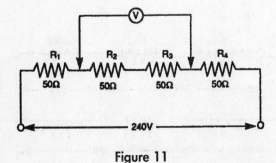

Figure 11

12. In electrical wiring diagrams, electrical measuring devices are often abbreviated in symbolic form. Of the following, the symbol commonly used to represent a direct current watt-hour meter is

   (A)
   (B)   —Ⓥ—
   (C)   —Ⓜ—
   (D)   —Ⓦ—

13. If the voltage of the supply is 120 volts, the readings of the voltmeters in Figure 13 should be

   (A)   60 volts on each meter.
   (B)   120 volts on each meter.
   (C)   80 volts on meter 1 and 40 volts on meter 2.
   (D)   80 volts on meter 2 and 40 volts on meter 1.

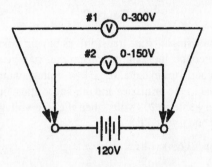

Figure 13

14. If the voltmeter in Figure 14 reads 34 volts, the circuit voltage is about

   (A)   68
   (B)   85
   (C)   102
   (D)   119

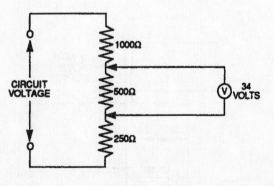

Figure 14

15. Meter 1 in Figure 15 is a(n)

    (A) ammeter.
    (B) frequency meter.
    (C) wattmeter.
    (D) voltmeter.

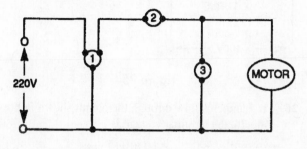

Figure 15

16. The reading of the voltmeter in Figure 16 should be

    (A) 600   (C) 120
    (B) 300   (D) 0

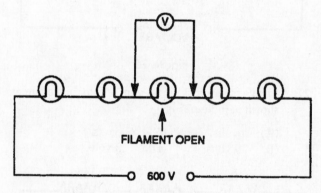

Figure 16

17. If the voltage of each of the dry-cells shown in Figure 17 is 1.5 volts, the voltage between X and Y is

    (A) 3   (C) 9
    (B) 6   (D) 12

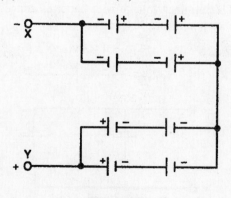

Figure 17

18. The reading of the voltmeter in Figure 18 will be

    (A) 0 volts.
    (B) 80 volts.
    (C) 120 volts.
    (D) 240 volts.

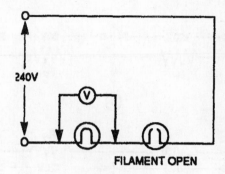

Figure 18

19. The two voltmeters shown in Figure 19 are identical. If the battery voltage is 120 volts, the readings of the voltmeters should be

    (A) 120 volts on each meter.
    (B) 60 volts on each meter.
    (C) 120 volts on meter 1 and 240 volts on 2.
    (D) 120 volts on meter 1 and 0 volts on 2.

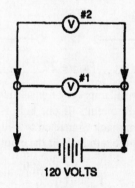

Figure 19

20. The voltage "X" in Figure 20 is

    (A) 25   (C) 15
    (B) 20   (D) 5

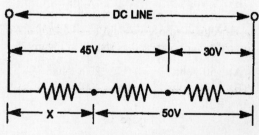

Figure 20

21. With the voltage drop across the four resistors in Figure 21 as shown, the voltmeter will read

    (A) 50 volts.   (C) 100 volts.
    (B) 70 volts.   (D) 170 volts.

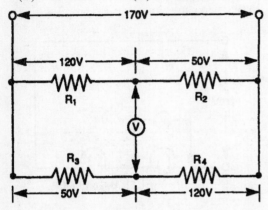

Figure 21

22. In Figure 22, the voltage drop is 24 volts across resistor

    (A) 1   (C) 3
    (B) 2   (D) 4

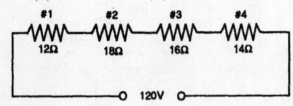

Figure 22

23. Five 110-volt lamps are often used in series for testing 600-volt circuits. If one bulb is removed from such a lamp bank connected to 600-volts, the voltage across the terminals of the empty socket is

    (A) 110   (C) 600
    (B) 490   (D) 0

24. A battery consisting of four 2-volt cells in series will have a voltage of

    (A) $\frac{1}{2}$ volt.   (C) 4 volts.
    (B) 2 volts.   (D) 8 volts.

25. The voltage across terminal 1 and terminal 2 of the transformer connected as shown in Figure 25 is

    (A) 50 volts.   (C) 200 volts.
    (B) 100 volts.   (D) 400 volts.

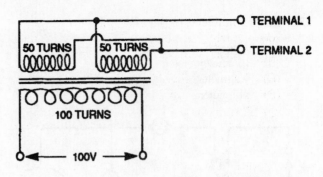

Figure 25

26. If 2 amperes flow through the circuit shown in Figure 26, the terminal voltage is

    (A) 2 volts.   (C) 12 volts.
    (B) 6 volts.   (D) 24 volts.

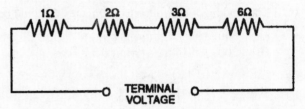

Figure 26

27. The voltage across the 30-ohm resistor in the circuit shown in Figure 27 is

    (A) 4 volts.   (C) 60 volts.
    (B) 20 volts.   (D) 120 volts.

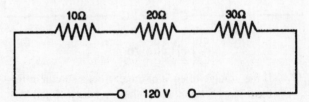

Figure 27

28. The terminal voltage with batteries connected as shown in Figure 28 is

    (A) 0 volts.   (C) 3 volts.
                            (D) 6 volts.
    (B) $1\frac{1}{2}$ volts.

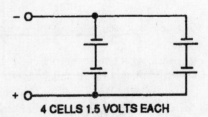

Figure 28

29. If a ground occurs on one side of a 120-volt battery control circuit, the voltage on the ground detector lamps will be

   (A) 120 volts on one lamp and 0 volts on the other.
   (B) 60 volts on each lamp.
   (C) 0 volts on each lamp.
   (D) 60 volts on one lamp and 0 volts on the other.

30. A 2,400-volt 3-phase system with a grounded neutral has a phase-to-ground voltage of approximately

   (A) 800 volts.　　(C) 1,700 volts.
   (B) 1,390 volts.　(D) 7,200 volts.

31. When a high-potential test voltage is applied to electrical equipment, the purpose is to

   (A) break down the insulation.
   (B) measure the insulation resistance.
   (C) make sure the insulation will withstand operating voltage.
   (D) measure dielectric strength of the insulation.

32. Current transformer secondary circuits are not usually fused because

   (A) the secondary current cannot exceed 5 amperes.
   (B) the wiring is heavy enough to carry large currents safely.
   (C) protection is provided by fuses in the primary circuit.
   (D) excessive voltage may be developed in the secondary circuit if it is opened by a blown fuse.

33. The insulation resistance of a DC cable was checked by means of a high-resistance DC voltmeter. When the cable was cold, the reading obtained was 10 volts. If the test were to be repeated after the cable had been in service carrying load for several hours, you would expect the voltage reading to be

   (A) unchanged.
   (B) 0 volts.
   (C) lower than 10 volts.
   (D) higher than 10 volts.

34. An automatic voltage regulator as applied to a generator is

   (A) a transformer whose secondary coils can be rotated, producing a change in secondary voltage.
   (B) a booster generator, by means of which a variation of voltage can be obtained.
   (C) a device commonly used to vary the voltage of a generator by changing its impedance.

   (D) a device commonly used to hold the voltage of a generator or bus constant under varying load conditions.

35. If the voltage of the supply is 120 volts, the readings of the voltmeters in Figure 35 should be

   (A) 60 volts on each meter.
   (B) 120 volts on each meter.
   (C) 80 volts on meter 1 and 40 volts on meter 2.
   (D) 80 volts on meter 2 and 40 volts on meter 1.

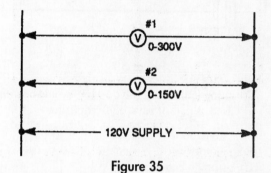

Figure 35

36. The most practical method of determining if a 600-volt circuit is "dead" is to

   (A) examine the fuse to see if it is blown.
   (B) touch it with the back of the hand.
   (C) check with the nearest substation.
   (D) test it with a known good bank of lamps.

37. Certain vacuum tubes have four elements inside the glass envelope: a heater, a cathode, a grid, and a plate. In most vacuum tube circuits, the highest "plus" DC voltage is applied to the

   (A) plate.
   (B) grid.
   (C) cathode.
   (D) heater.

38. Assume you have decided to test a sealed box having two terminals by using the hook-up shown, in Figure 38. When you hold the test prods on the terminals, the voltmeter needle swings upscale and then quickly returns to zero. As an initial conclusion, you would be correct in assuming that the box contained a

   (A) capacitor.
   (B) choke.
   (C) rectifier.
   (D) resistor.

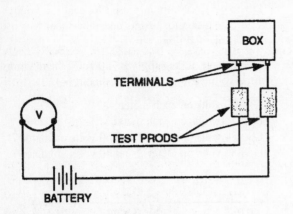

Figure 38

39. The rating terms "240 volts, 10 HP" would be properly used as part of the specifications for

    (A) transformers.
    (B) motors.
    (C) storage batteries.
    (D) heaters.

40. It is correct to state that a DC voltmeter can be used directly to measure

    (A) power.
    (B) frequency.
    (C) polarity.
    (D) power factor.

41. For a given line voltage, four heater coils will consume the most power when connected

    (A) all in series.
    (B) all in parallel.
    (C) with two parallel pairs in series.
    (D) one pair in parallel with the other two in series.

42. The factor that will have the LEAST effect on the voltage at the most distant point from the source of supply for a two-wire circuit is

    (A) whether the supply is 25 hertz or 60 hertz AC.
    (B) the length of the circuit.
    (C) the amount of load on the circuit.
    (D) the gauge of the circuit wires.

43. If a 5-ohm, a 10-ohm, and a 15-ohm resistor are connected in series across a 120-volt circuit, the voltage across the 15-ohm resistor will be

    (A) 120 volts.
    (B) 60 volts.
    (C) 40 volts.
    (D) 20 volts.

44. The middle lamp burns out and is removed from a bank of five lamps connected in series across a 600-volt DC line. The voltage across the empty socket is

    (A) 600, and that across a good lamp 120.
    (B) 120, and that across a good lamp 0.
    (C) 600, and that across a good lamp 0.
    (D) 120, and that across a good lamp 120.

45. When applying a high-potential test voltage to the primary winding of a rebuilt transformer,

    (A) one end of the primary winding must be grounded.
    (B) the secondary winding must be short-circuited.
    (C) all other parts of the transformer must be insulated from ground.
    (D) the secondary winding, transformer case, and core must be grounded.

46. For measuring DC voltage, the most accurate type of meter is the

    (A) hot wire.   (C) induction.
    (B) soft iron vane.   (D) D'Arsonval.

47. In the common 3-phase, 4-wire supply system, the voltage (in volts) from line to neutral is most nearly

    (A) 110   (C) 208
    (B) 120   (D) 220

48. With reference to question 47, the neutral line

    (A) does not carry current at any time.
    (B) carries current at all times.
    (C) has a potential difference with respect to ground of approximately 0 volts.
    (D) has a potential difference with respect to ground of 208 volts.

49. To transmit power economically over considerable distances, it is necessary that the voltage be high. High voltages are readily obtainable with

    (A) DC currents.
    (B) AC currents.
    (C) rectified currents.
    (D) carrier currents.

50. With reference to question 49, the one favorable economic factor in the transmission of power by using high voltages is the

    (A) reduction of conductor cross-section.
    (B) decreased amount of insulation required by the line.
    (C) increased I^2R loss.
    (D) decreased size of generating stations.

51. In a 2-phase, 3-wire system, the voltage between the common wire and either of the other two wires is 200 volts. The voltage between these other two wires is then approximately

   (A) 200 volts.   (C) 141 volts.
   (B) 283 volts.   (D) 100 volts.

52. In order to magnetize a steel bar, a magneto-motive force of 1000 ampere turns is necessary. The voltage that must be applied to a coil of 100 turns and 10 ohms resistance is

   (A) 1   (C) 100
   (B) 10   (D) 1000

53. A single-phase synchronous converter is connected on its DC side to a 141.4-volt DC source of supply. The AC single-phase voltage delivered by this machine is approximately

   (A) 300   (C) 150
   (B) 200   (D) 100

54. The voltage induced in a loop of wire rotating in a magnetic field is

   (A) DC.   (C) rectified AC.
   (B) pulsating DC. (D) AC.

55. In a balanced 3-phase, wye-connected load, the

   (A) line to neutral voltage equals the line voltage.
   (B) line to neutral voltage equals the line voltage multiplied by the square root of 3.
   (C) line voltage equals the line to neutral voltage divided by the square root of 3.
   (D) line voltage equals the line to neutral voltage multiplied by the square root of 3.

56. A potential relay is connected across a 600-volt DC source. The resistance of the relay coil is 2,000 ohms. If a resistance of 500 ohms is connected in series with the relay coil and a resistance of 2,000 ohms is connected in parallel with the relay coil, the voltage across the coil will be

   (A) 100 volts.   (C) 400 volts.
   (B) 200 volts.   (D) 500 volts.

57. Each of the two lighting transformers in a certain transformer closet is supplied from a different phase of the same 3-phase primary feeder. The secondary voltage of each transformer is 600 volts. If a secondary terminal of one transformer is connected to a secondary terminal of the other transformer, the voltage between the two unconnected terminals will be either

   (A) 0 or 1,200 volts.
   (B) 600 or 1,040 volts.

   (C) 0 or 1,040 volts.
   (D) 600 or 1,200 volts.

58. A potential relay is connected across a 600-volt DC source. The resistance of the relay coil is 3,000 ohms. If a resistance of 500 ohms is connected in parallel with the relay coil, the voltage across the coil will be

   (A) 150 volts.   (C) 400 volts.
   (B) 200 volts.   (D) 600 volts.

59. A potential of 24 volts is impressed across a potentiometer having a total resistance of 1,000 ohms. If a fixed resistance of 500 ohms is connected across one half of the potentiometer, the voltage across the fixed resistance is

   (A) 6   (C) 12
   (B) 8   (D) 16

60. If a 10-ohm, a 20-ohm, and a 30-ohm resistor are connected in series across a 120-volt circuit, the voltage across the 20-ohm resistor will be

   (A) 120 volts.   (C) 40 volts.
   (B) 60 volts.   (D) 20 volts.

61. Two amperes of current are drawn by a circuit consisting of four resistors connected in parallel. What voltage is dropped across each of the resistors? (The resistors are 100 ohms, 100 ohms, 50 ohms, and 25 ohms, respectively.)

   (A) Varies with the resistance
   (B) The same across each
   (C) The 100-ohm resistors are the same, but the others are unequal.
   (D) The 50-ohm resistor has one half the 100-ohm resistor voltage.

62. What is the voltage across the 100-ohm resistors in question 61?

   (A) Same as all the others
   (B) 50 volts
   (C) 100 volts
   (D) 400 volts

63. Four resistors of 100 ohms each are connected across a power supply. The total current drawn from the power supply is 4 amperes. What is the voltage across each resistor?

   (A) 100 volts   (C) 25 volts
   (B) 400 volts   (D) 141.14 volts

64. The voltage across the terminals of a blown fuse is

   (A) the voltage of the power source.
   (B) 120 volts.
   (C) zero.
   (D) 240 volts.

65. In order to measure the voltage dropped across a resistor, the meter should be connected in

(A) series.
(B) parallel.
(C) series-parallel.
(D) one lead to ground and one to the source.

66. A voltmeter inserted in series with a load will

(A) measure the applied voltage.
(B) become part of the circuit.
(C) measure the circuit current.
(D) measure the total resistance.

67. When the range switch in a voltmeter is moved from 0–100 volts to 0–1000 volts, the internal resistance of the voltmeter

(A) is increased.
(B) is decreased.
(C) stays the same.
(D) is placed across the meter movement.

68. Which of these three-phase connections produces an advantage in voltage?

(A) Delta
(B) Wye
(C) Delta-wye
(D) Wye-delta

ANSWER KEY

1. B	10. C	19. A	28. C	37. A	45. D	53. D	61. B
2. D	11. D	20. A	29. A	38. A	46. D	54. D	62. A
3. C	12. D	21. B	30. B	39. B	47. B	55. D	63. B
4. C	13. B	22. A	31. C	40. C	48. C	56. C	64. A
5. B	14. D	23. C	32. D	41. B	49. B	57. B	65. B
6. D	15. C	24. D	33. D	42. A	50. A	58. D	66. B
7. A	16. A	25. A	34. D	43. B	51. B	59. B	67. A
8. D	17. B	26. D	35. B	44. C	52. C	60. C	68. C
9. B	18. A	27. C	36. D				

WATTAGE PROBLEMS

> **DIRECTIONS:** For each question, read all choices carefully. Then select the answer that you consider correct or most nearly correct. Write the letter preceding your best choice next to the question.

1. When connecting wattmeters to AC motor circuits consuming large amounts of current, it is necessary to use

(A) current transformers.
(B) potential transformers.
(C) power shunts.
(D) isolation transformers.

2. The wattmeters P_1 and P_2 are connected as shown in Figure 2 to measure the power drawn by a balanced 3-phase load with a power factor of about 85 percent. In what direction will the meters deflect?

(A) P_1 deflects upscale, and P_2 deflects downscale (reverses).
(B) P_2 deflects upscale, and P_1 deflects downscale (reverses).

(C) Both P_1 and P_2 deflect upscale.
(D) Both P_1 and P_2 deflect downscale (reverses).

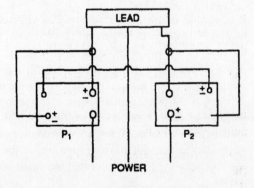

Figure 2

3. The total current in a circuit that contains two 5-ohm resistances in parallel is 10 amperes. The power consumed by this circuit is

    (A)   25 watts.
    (B)   250 watts.
    (C)   500 watts.
    (D)   1,000 watts.

4. During a test, a standard 110-volt, 5-ampere wattmeter is connected to a single-phase circuit by means of a 3:1 current transformer and a 20:1 potential transformer. With a primary current of 5 amperes at 2,200 volts and unity power factor, the wattmeter reading, to the nearest watt, will be

    (A)   60 watts.
    (B)   183 watts.
    (C)   330 watts.
    (D)   550 watts.

5. Four 120-watt, 120-volt heaters are connected in series on a 600-volt circuit. The total heat given off by the four heaters will be

    (A)   480 watts.
    (B)   600 watts.
    (C)   680 watts.
    (D)   750 watts.

6. A megawatt is

    (A)   ten watts.
    (B)   one hundred watts.
    (C)   one thousand watts.
    (D)   one million watts.

7. An integrating watthour meter has four dials. If, from left to right, the respective pointers are between 7 and 8, between 4 and 5, between 0 and 1, and between 3 and 4, the reading is

    (A)   7403
    (B)   7413
    (C)   3047
    (D)   8514

8. In a given circuit when the power factor is unity, the reactive power is

    (A)   a maximum.
    (B)   zero.
    (C)   equal to I^2R.
    (D)   a negative quantity.

9. If a 3-phase motor connected to a 208-volt source takes 100 amperes at 90 percent power factor, then the input power to this motor is most nearly

    (A)   18,720 watts.
    (B)   20,800 watts.
    (C)   32,400 watts.
    (D)   56,160 watts.

10. In an AC circuit, a low value of reactive volt amperes compared with the watts indicates

    (A)   maximum current for the load.
    (B)   low efficiency.
    (C)   high power factor.
    (D)   unity power factor.

11. In an AC circuit, the ratio of the power in kilowatts to the total kilovoltamperes is the

    (A)   load factor.
    (B)   power factor.
    (C)   diversity factor.
    (D)   conversion factor.

12. The power used by the heater shown in Figure 12 is

    (A)   120 watts.
    (B)   720 watts.
    (C)   2,400 watts.
    (D)   4,320 watts.

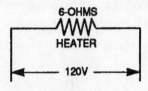

Figure 12

13. If the motor shown in Figure 13 runs for one half an hour, the energy consumed is

    (A)   120 watt-hours.
    (B)   1,500 watt-hours.
    (C)   3,000 watt-hours.
    (D)   90,000 watt-hours.

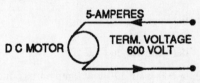

Figure 13

14. If a 100-watt tungsten lamp is compared with a 25-watt tungsten lamp of the same voltage rating, the resistance of the 100-watt lamp is

    (A)   higher.
    (B)   lower.
    (C)   the same.
    (D)   higher with AC, lower with DC.

15. Two 500-watt lamps connected in series across a 110-volt line draw 2 amperes. The total power consumed is

    (A)   1,000 watts.
    (B)   250 watts.
    (C)   220 watts.
    (D)   55 watts.

16. The number of watts of heat given off by a resistor is expressed by the formula I^2R. If 10 volts is applied to a 5-ohm resistor, the heat given off will be

    (A)   500 watts.
    (B)   250 watts.
    (C)   50 watts.
    (D)   20 watts.

17. It is now possible to obtain a 200-watt light bulb that is as small in all dimensions as the standard 150-watt light bulb. The principal advantage to users resulting from this reduction in size is that

    (A) maintenance electricians can carry many more light bulbs.
    (B) two sizes of light bulbs can be kept in the same storage space.
    (C) the higher wattage bulb can now fit into certain lighting fixtures.
    (D) less breakage is apt to occur in handling.

18. When the energy cost for a motor is $4.62 at 3 cents per kilowatt-hour, the energy consumed is

    (A) 13.86 kWh.   (C) 762 kWh.
    (B) 154 kWh.   (D) 1386 kWh.

19. The term "60-watt" is most commonly used in identifying a

    (A) fuse.   (C) cable.
    (B) lamp.   (D) switch.

20. The power factor of an AC circuit containing both a resistor and a capacitor is

    (A) 0
    (B) between 0 and 1.0
    (C) 1.0
    (D) between 1.0 and 2.0

21. When a 100-watt, 120-volt lamp burns continuously for 8 hours at rated voltage, the energy used is

    (A) 800 watt-hours.
    (B) 960 watt-hours.
    (C) 12,000 watt-hours.
    (D) 96,000 watt-hours.

22. Meter 1 in Figure 22 is a(n)

    (A) ammeter.
    (B) frequency meter.

(C) wattmeter.
(D) voltmeter.

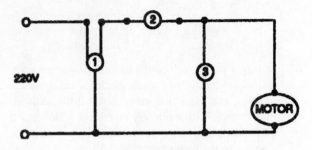

Figure 22

23. The formula used to convert volt-amperes to watts is

    (A) TP = AP × PF
    (B) TP = Ohms × Volts × Cosine of the angle theta
    (C) AP = TP × PF
    (D) AP = Volt-Amperes × 1.73

24. AP is the abbreviation for

    (A) Applied Power.
    (B) Associated Power.
    (C) Apparent Power.
    (D) Approximate Power.

25. True power is measured in the basic unit of

    (A) Watts.
    (B) Volt-Amperes.
    (C) Megavolt-amperes.
    (D) Kilowatts.

26. Power factor is also expressed as

    (A) Cosine theta.
    (B) True Power.
    (C) Apparent Power.
    (D) Applied Power.

ANSWER KEY

1. A	5. D	9. C	12. C	15. C	18. B	21. A	24. C
2. D	6. D	10. C	13. B	16. D	19. B	22. C	25. A
3. B	7. A	11. B	14. B	17. C	20. B	23. A	26. A
4. B	8. B						

CURRENT PROBLEMS

> **DIRECTIONS:** For each question, read all choices carefully. Then select the answer that you consider correct or most nearly correct. Write the letter preceding your best choice next to the question.

1. In an AC circuit delivering a constant power at a varying power factor, the current is

   (A) lowest when the power factor is leading.
   (B) lowest when the power factor is lagging.
   (C) constant for all power factors.
   (D) lowest at 100 percent power factor.

2. With a reversal of power, an AC ammeter in good condition will read

   (A) zero.
   (B) the reactive current.
   (C) the correct current.
   (D) backward.

3. The heating effect of 10 amperes AC as compared with 10 amperes DC are

   (A) the same.
   (B) 1.41 times as great.
   (C) 1.73 times as great.
   (D) .707 times as great.

4. A choke coil with an iron core is connected to an alternating current source. The current flow is inversely proportional to the

   (A) reactance.   (C) resistance.
   (B) impedance.   (D) inductance.

5. A milliampere is

   (A) one million amperes.
   (B) 1/1,000,000 ampere.
   (C) 1/1,000 ampere.
   (D) one thousand amperes.

6. A relay coil with a resistance in series is connected in parallel with a contactor coil to a battery. If the current is 5 amperes in the relay coil, 5 amperes in the resistor, and 3 amperes in the contactor coil, the battery current is

   (A) 13 amperes.   (C) 5 amperes.
   (B) 2 amperes.   (D) 8 amperes.

7. The reading of the ammeter in Figure 7 should be

   (A) 4.0   (C) 1.0
   (B) 2.0   (D) 0.5

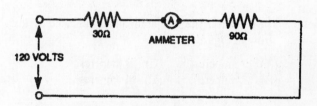

Figure 7

8. The instrument shown in Figure 8 is properly connected to measure

   (A) AC amperes.   (C) AC volts.
   (B) DC amperes.   (D) DC volts.

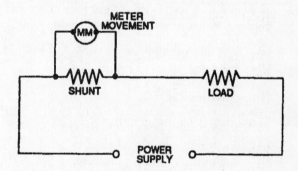

Figure 8

9. A coil of wire wound on an iron core draws exactly 5 amperes when connected across the terminals of a 10-volt storage battery. If this coil is now connected across the 10-volt secondary terminals of an ordinary power transformer, the current drawn will be

   (A) less than 5 amperes.
   (B) more than 5 amperes.
   (C) exactly 5 amperes.
   (D) more or less than 5 amperes, depending on the frequency.

10. The current flowing through the 6-ohm resistor in the circuit shown in Figure 10 is

    (A) 1 ampere.
    (B) 3 amperes.
    (C) 6 amperes.
    (D) 11 amperes.

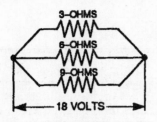

Figure 10

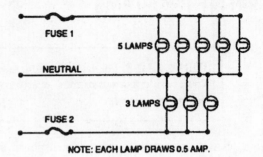

NOTE: EACH LAMP DRAWS 0.5 AMP.

Figure 14

11. The current in the wire at the point indicated by the arrow in Figure 11 is

(A) 1 ampere. (C) 3 amperes.
(B) 2 amperes. (D) 4 amperes.

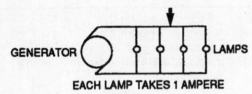

Figure 11

12. A copper wire with twice the diameter of another copper wire has a current-carrying capacity

(A) four times as great.
(B) twice as great.
(C) half as great.
(D) three times as great.

13. The current in the 4-ohm resistor in Figure 13 is

(A) 5 amperes. (C) 3 amperes.
(B) 4 amperes. (D) 1 ampere.

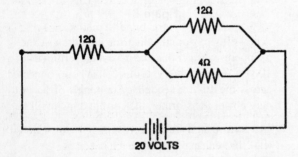

Figure 13

14. If fuse 1 blows in the 3-wire DC system shown in Figure 14, the current in the neutral wire will

(A) increase by 1.0 ampere.
(B) increase by 0.5 ampere.
(C) decrease by 1.0 ampere.
(D) decrease by 0.5 ampere.

15. If the permissible current is 1,000 amperes for each square inch of cross section, the bus bar shown in Figure 15 can carry

(A) 2,250 amperes.
(B) 2,000 amperes.
(C) 1,750 amperes.
(D) 1,500 amperes.

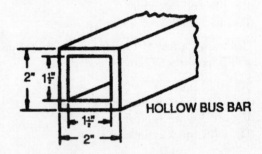

Figure 15

16. If the voltmeter in Figure 16 reads 80 volts, the current in the 11-ohm resistor is

(A) 10 amperes.
(B) 6.3 amperes.
(C) 12 amperes.
(D) 8.3 amperes.

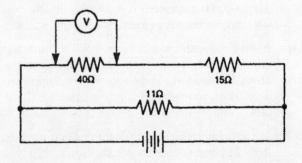

Figure 16

17. If ammeter 2 in Figure 17 reads 60 amperes, the reading of ammeter 1 should be about

    (A) 4 amperes. (C) 60 amperes.
    (B) 15 amperes. (D) 900 amperes.

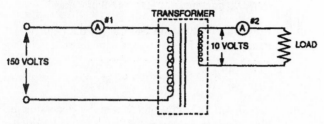

Figure 17

18. Regardless of the battery voltage, it is clear by inspection that the highest current in Figure 18 is in the

    (A) 1-ohm resistor.
    (B) 2-ohm resistor.
    (C) 3-ohm resistor.
    (D) 4-ohm resistor.

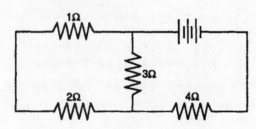

Figure 18

19. The term "15-ampere" is commonly used in identifying

    (A) an insulator. (C) a conduit.
    (B) a fuse. (D) an outlet box.

20. Two dissimilar ammeters are connected in parallel and the combination connected in series with a circuit. If one of the meters reads 4 amperes when the other meter reads 8 amperes, the current in the circuit

    (A) is 12 amperes.
    (B) is 6 amperes.
    (C) is 4 amperes.
    (D) cannot be determined from these readings.

21. If one heater in Figure 21 takes 10 amperes and the other heater takes 5 amperes, the current in wire 2 will be

    (A) 15 amperes.

    (B) $7\frac{1}{2}$ amperes.

    (C) 5 amperes.
    (D) zero.

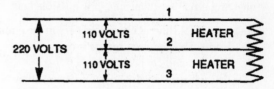

Figure 21

22. The maximum allowable current-carrying capacity of two-conductor No. 14 Romex cable is

    (A) 10 amperes. (C) 15 amperes.
    (B) 12 amperes. (D) 18 amperes.

23. If the currents in resistors Nos. 1, 2, and 3 in Figure 23 are 4.8, 7.5, and 6.2 amperes, respectively, then the current (in amperes) in resistor No. 4 is

    (A) 1.3 (C) 3.5
    (B) 2.7 (D) 6.1

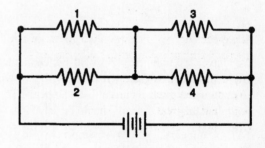

Figure 23

24. If the allowable current in a copper bus bar is 1,000 amperes per square inch of cross-section, the width of a standard $\frac{1}{4}''$ bus bar designed to carry 1,500 amperes would be

    (A) 2″ (C) 6″
    (B) 4″ (D) 8″

25. Four heaters, each having a resistance of 30 ohms, are connected in series across a 600-volt train circuit. The current taken by each heater is

    (A) 5 amperes. (C) 20 amperes.
    (B) 17 amperes. (D) 80 amperes.

26. Reactance in a circuit decreases the current in the circuit

    (A) only when alternating current is flowing.
    (B) only when direct current is flowing.
    (C) only in case the circuit contains resistance.
    (D) only in case the circuit contains no resistance.

27. A certain circuit requires a maximum of 10 amperes when operating properly. If a calibrated ammeter in the circuit reads 12 amperes, it is possible that

(A) a partial short exists somewhere in the circuit.
(B) one of the branch circuits is open.
(C) the ground connection is open.
(D) a high-resistance connection exists somewhere in the circuit.

28. If the allowable current density for copper bus bars is 1,000 amperes per square inch, the current-carrying capacity of a circular copper bar having a diameter of two inches is approximately

(A) 1,050 amperes.
(B) 2,320 amperes.
(C) 3,140 amperes.
(D) 4,260 amperes.

29. The current in amperes of a 220-volt, 5-HP DC motor having an efficiency of 90 percent is approximately

(A) 18.8   (C) 14.3
(B) 17   (D) 20.5

30. You have a 100-ampere, 13-kV oil switch that has a trip coil rated up to 5 amperes. You wish the switch to open when the line current is 80 amperes. To accomplish this, the trip coil should be set at

(A) 4 amperes.   (C) 3 amperes.
(B) 5 amperes.   (D) 1 ampere.

31. Three 20-ohm resistances are connected in wye across a 208-volt, 3-phase circuit. The line current in amperes is approximately

(A) 18   (C) 5.2
(B) 10.4   (D) 6.0

32. The current in amperes of a 1-HP, 120-volt, single-phase induction motor having an efficiency of 90 percent and operating at 0.8 power factor is approximately

(A) 6.9   (C) 8.6
(B) 7.8   (D) 6.2

33. A standard stranded cable contains 19 strands. When measured with a micrometer, the diameter of each strand is found to be 105.5 mils. If, under certain conditions, the allowable current density is 600 cm per ampere, the allowable current-carrying capacity of this conductor is

(A) 236 amperes.   (C) 352.5 amperes.
(B) 176.3 amperes.   (D) 705 amperes.

34. The current input per phase under rated-load conditions for a 200-HP, 3-phase, 2300-volt, 0.8 PF induction motor that is 90 percent efficient is

(A) 52 amperes.   (C) 41.6 amperes.
(B) 90 amperes.   (D) 46.8 amperes.

35. Referring to question 34, the power input under rated-load conditions is approximately

(A) 149 kW.   (C) 166 kW.
(B) 96 kW.   (D) 332 kW.

36. A 600-volt DC circuit feeds a motor-generator set. If the generator delivers 4.8 kW at 120 volts and the overall efficiency of the set at this load is 80 percent, the motor line current is

(A) 6.4 amperes.   (C) 12 amperes.
(B) 10 amperes.   (D) 30 amperes.

37. An induction-type overload relay has the current plug in the 10-ampere tap and is set to operate in 0.4 second at 30 amperes. This setting means that the relay will

(A) have a minimum operating time of 0.4 second.
(B) always require 30 amperes to operate.
(C) operate in 0.2 second at 15 amperes.
(D) not operate on less than 10 amperes.

38. If a current transformer has a ratio of 100:5 and an ammeter connected to its secondary reads 1.5 amperes, the actual line current is

(A) 7.5 amperes.   (C) 30 amperes.
(B) 0.075 ampere.   (D) 600 amperes.

39. Figure 39 represents the circuit of a DC ammeter. If the value of R_1 is increased while the value of R_2 remains unchanged, the

(A) deflection of the instrument is no longer proportional to the current.
(B) range of the ammeter is decreased.
(C) range of the ammeter remains the same.
(D) range of the ammeter is increased.

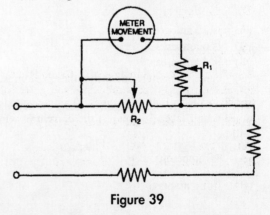

Figure 39

40. In reference to Figure 39, if the value of R_2 is decreased while the value of R_1 remains unchanged, the

    (A) range of the ammeter is increased.
    (B) range of the ammeter is decreased.
    (C) range of the ammeter remains the same.
    (D) deflection of the instrument is no longer proportional to the current.

41. Three 30-ohm resistances are connected in delta across a 208-volt, 3-phase circuit. The line current, in amperes, is approximately

    (A) 6.93 (C) 120
    (B) 13.86 (D) 12.00

42. If two 60-watt, 120-volt lamps are connected in series across a 120-volt supply, the current taken will be

    (A) less than $\frac{1}{4}$ ampere.

    (B) exactly $\frac{1}{4}$ ampere.

    (C) between $\frac{1}{4}$ and $\frac{1}{2}$ ampere.

    (D) exactly $\frac{1}{2}$ ampere.

43. A 3-wire DC supply system has an unbalanced load of 20 amperes in one of the outside wires and 30 amperes in the other outside wire. The current in the middle or neutral wire is

    (A) 10
    (B) 25
    (C) 30
    (D) 50

44. A 100-watt, 120-volt lamp, at normal voltage, will draw about

    (A) $\frac{2}{3}$ ampere.

    (B) $\frac{5}{6}$ ampere.

    (C) 1 ampere.
    (D) 1.2 amperes.

45. A series resistor combination of 3, 6, and 9 ohms is connected to a power source furnishing 36 volts. What is the current flowing through an ammeter inserted between the 6- and 9-ohm resistor?

    (A) 2 amperes (C) 4 amperes
    (B) 12 amperes (D) 6 amperes

46. A set of eight identical Christmas tree lamps in series draws 0.15 amperes when connected across a 115 volt line. What is the total current in the circuit?

    (A) 0.0013 amperes
    (B) 766.66 amperes
    (C) 0.15 amperes
    (D) 14.375 amperes

47. If in a series string of ten 12-volt lamps one lamp burns out and you short the burned-out filament, the total current in the circuit will

    (A) decrease. (C) stay the same.
    (B) increase. (D) double.

48. An ammeter is connected in series in a circuit because

    (A) it is not a power consumer.
    (B) it has no effect on the circuit.
    (C) it has high internal resistance.
    (D) it has low internal resistance.

49. A 500-ohm resistor is placed across a 100-volt source; an ammeter in the circuit would read

    (A) 500 amperes. (C) 2 amperes.
    (B) 100 amperes. (D) 0.2 amperes.

50. A 500-ohm and a 1000-ohm resistor are inserted in a circuit with 500 volts available. The ammeter in series with the two parallel resistors would read

    (A) 500 amperes. (C) 1000 amperes.
    (B) 1.5 amperes. (D) 1500 amperes.

51. The heating effect of 10 amperes DC as compared with 10 amperes AC is

    (A) the same.
    (B) 1.41 times as great.
    (C) 1.73 times as great.
    (D) 0.707 times as great.

52. Two equal series resistors, R_1 and R_2, have a voltage measured across each of 50 volts, the current through R_1 is

    (A) 50 amperes. (C) the same as R_2.
    (B) 5 amperes. (D) zero.

ANSWER KEY

1.	D	10.	B	19.	B	28.	C	37.	D
2.	C	11.	B	20.	A	29.	A	38.	C
3.	A	12.	A	21.	C	30.	A	39.	D
4.	B	13.	D	22.	C	31.	D	40.	A
5.	C	14.	B	23.	D	32.	C	41.	D
6.	D	15.	C	24.	C	33.	C	42.	C
7.	C	16.	A	25.	A	34.	A	43.	A
8.	B	17.	A	26.	A	35.	C	44.	B
9.	A	18.	D	27.	A	36.	B		

45.	A
46.	C
47.	B
48.	D
49.	D
50.	B
51.	A
52.	C

RESISTANCE PROBLEMS

DIRECTIONS: For each question, read all choices carefully. Then select the answer that you consider correct or most nearly correct. Write the letter preceding your best choice next to the question.

---

1. A field discharge resistance is connected across a generator field when the field breaker is opened. The purpose of this is to

   (A) prevent excessive voltage rise in the field when the circuit is opened.

   (B) reduce the current the breaker must interrupt.

   (C) prevent excessive current flow in the field when the circuit is opened.

   (D) allow the generator voltage to drop very slowly.

2. One foot of a certain size of nichrome wire has a resistance of 1.63 ohms. To make a heating element for a toaster that will use 5 amperes at 110 volts, the number of feet of wire needed is approximately

   (A) 17.9   (C) 5.5

   (B) 8.2   (D) 13.5

3. The speed of a 3-phase, slip-ring induction motor is increased with

   (A) a decrease in the secondary circuit resistance.

   (B) an increase in the secondary circuit resistance.

   (C) a decrease in the voltage impressed on the stator.

   (D) an increase in the stator current.

4. In a 5-HP, 220-volt shunt motor rated at 19.2 amperes and 1,500 RPM, the armature resistance is

   (A) smaller than that of the shunt field.

   (B) larger than that of the shunt field.

   (C) the same as that of the shunt field.

   (D) always one half that of the shunt field.

5. The resistance, in ohms, of a 25-ampere, 50-millivolt shunt is approximately

   (A) 2   (C) 0.02

   (B) 0.2   (D) 0.002

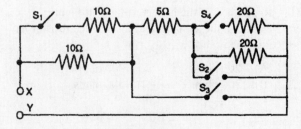

Figure 6

Questions 6–10 refer to the diagram in Figure 6. All switches are normally open.

6. With switches No. 1 and No. 2 closed, the combined resistance of the circuit in ohms is

   (A) 30   (C) 10

   (B) 25   (D) $2\frac{1}{2}$

7. The switches to be closed in order to obtain a combined resistance of 5 ohms are

   (A) Nos. 1 and 3.   (C) Nos. 1 and 2.

   (B) Nos. 2 and 3.   (D) Nos. 1 and 4.

8. If 3 amperes flow through the 5-ohm resistor with all switches open, the voltage between the terminals X and Y is

   (A) 15   (C) 90

   (B) 60   (D) 105

9. If the line current is 10 amperes with all switches closed, the power consumed by the circuit is

   (A) 500 watts.   (C) 1,000 watts.

   (B) 750 watts.   (D) 2,000 watts.

10. With only switch No. 4 closed and a line voltage of 225 volts, the drop across one of the 10-ohm resistors is

   (A) 225   (C) 64.3

   (B) 90   (D) 56.3

11. The insulation resistance of a motor is commonly measured by the use of a(n)

   (A) ammeter.

   (B) wattmeter.

   (C) voltmeter.

   (D) Wheatstone bridge.

12. A resistance of 20 ohms after being measured with an accurate bridge is found to be 20.05 ohms. It can be said that the percent accuracy of this resistance is

   (A) 0.25 percent.

   (B) 0.5 percent.

   (C) 1 percent.

   (D) 1.5 percent.

13. A 50-millivolt meter shunt having a resistance of 0.005 ohms is to be used with a 5-milliampere meter whose resistance is 10 ohms. When the current in this shunt is 8 amperes, the current through the meter is

    (A) 4 amperes.
    (B) 4 milliamperes.
    (C) 2 amperes.
    (D) 2 milliamperes.

14. Accurate resistances, the values of which are not materially affected by changes in room temperature, are usually made of an alloy commonly called

    (A) manganin.
    (B) paganin.
    (C) Excellin.
    (D) Siemens Martin.

15. In Figure 15, the resistor that carries the most current is the one whose resistance, in ohms, is

    (A) 4   (C) 2
    (B) 3   (D) 1

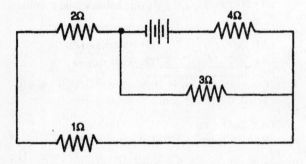

Figure 15

16. The resistance of 1,000 feet of 10 AWG wire is approximately 1 ohm. If the resistance of a coil of 10 AWG wire is 1.19 ohms, the length of wire in the coil is nearest to

    (A) 1,109 feet.   (C) 1,190 feet.
    (B) 1,119 feet.   (D) 1,199 feet.

17. If three resistors of 175 ohms, 75 ohms, and 17 ohms, respectively, are connected in parallel, the combined resistance will be

    (A) greater than 175 ohms.
    (B) between 175 ohms and 75 ohms.
    (C) between 75 ohms and 17 ohms.
    (D) less than 17 ohms.

18. The resistance of a copper wire to the flow of electricity

    (A) increases as the diameter of the wire increases.
    (B) decreases as the diameter of the wire decreases.
    (C) decreases as the length of the wire increases.
    (D) increases as the length of the wire increases.

19. The rating term "1,000 ohms, 10 watts" would generally be applied to a

    (A) heater.   (C) resistor.
    (B) relay.   (D) transformer.

20. The sketch in Figure 20 shows the four resistance dials and the multiplying dial of a resistance bridge. The four resistance dials can be set to any value of resistance up to 10,000 ohms, and the multiplier can be set at any of the nine points shown. In their present positions, the five pointers indicate a reading of

    (A) 13.60   (C) 130,600
    (B) 136,000   (D) 13.06

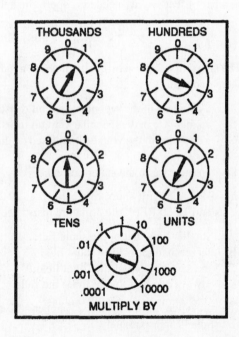

Figure 20

21. Regardless of the battery voltage in Figure 21, it is clear that the smallest current is in the resistor having a resistance of

    (A) 200 ohms.   (C) 400 ohms.
    (B) 300 ohms.   (D) 500 ohms.

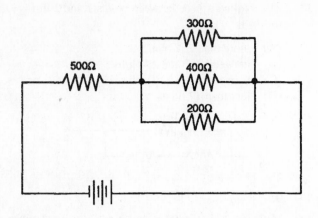

Figure 21

22. In Figure 22, the total resistance in the circuit shown between terminal 1 and terminal 2 is

(A) $1\frac{1}{2}$ ohms. (C) 9 ohms.

(B) 6 ohms. (D) 15 ohms.

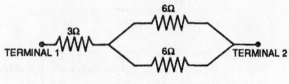

Figure 22

23. A high resistance connected in parallel with a potential relay across a 120-volt battery will

(A) increase the voltage across the relay.
(B) make the relay inoperative.
(C) have no effect on the relay.
(D) increase the current through the relay.

24. A heater consists of four 15-foot lengths of wire connected in series. If the resistance of the wire is 0.14 ohms per foot, the total resistance of the heater is

(A) 0.52 ohms. (C) 6.0 ohms.
(B) 2.1 ohms. (D) 8.4 ohms.

25. If a low resistance is connected in parallel with a higher resistance, the combined resistance is

(A) always less than the low resistance.
(B) always more than the high resistance.
(C) always between the values of the high and the low resistance.
(D) higher or lower than the low resistance, depending on the value of the higher resistance.

26. Comparing the resistance of ammeters, frequency meters, and meggers, the instruments with the lowest resistances are

(A) frequency meters.
(B) meggers.
(C) ammeters.
(D) voltmeters.

27. The resistance of a 1,000-foot length of a certain size copper wire is required to be 10.0 ohms +2 percent. This wire would NOT be acceptable if the resistance was

(A) 10.12 ohms. (C) 10.22 ohms.
(B) 10.02 ohms. (D) 9.82 ohms.

28. If the slider connecting both resistors in Figure 28 is 9 inches from the left-hand end of the resistors, the resistance between terminals 1 and 2 is

(A) 1,125 ohms. (C) 750 ohms.
(B) 875 ohms. (D) 625 ohms.

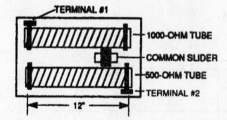

Figure 28

29. When a DC voltage of 1.50 volts is applied to a certain coil, the current in the coil is 6 amperes. The resistance of this coil is

(A) $\frac{1}{4}$ ohm. (C) $7\frac{1}{2}$ ohms.

(B) 4 ohms. (D) 9 ohms.

30. The resistance box shown in Figure 30 can be set to any value of resistance up to 10,000 ohms. The reading shown is

(A) 3875 (C) 5783
(B) 5738 (D) 8375

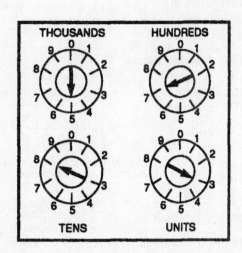

Figure 30

31. The total resistance in ohms between points X and Y in Figure 31 is

(A) 0.30   (C) 15
(B) 3.33   (D) 30

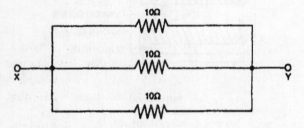

Figure 31

32. The resistance of a 1,000-foot coil of a certain size copper wire is 10 ohms. If 300 feet is cut off, the resistance of the remainder of the coil is

(A) 7 ohms.   (C) 0.7 ohm.
(B) 3 ohms.   (D) 0.3 ohm.

33. A wire that is three AWG sizes larger than another wire has half the resistance, twice the weight, and twice the area. If a No. 10 wire has a resistance of 1 ohm per 1,000 feet, has an area of 10,000 circular mils, and weighs 32 pounds per 1,000 feet, the resistance of 1,000 feet of No. 19 wire is

(A) 8 ohms.   (C) $1\frac{1}{2}$ ohms.

(B) 6 ohms.   (D) $\frac{1}{8}$ ohm.

34. The total resistance between points 1 and 2 in Figure 34 is

(A) more than 257 ohms.
(B) between 257 and 19 ohms.
(C) between 19 and 17 ohms.
(D) less than 17 ohms.

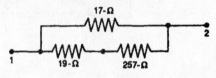

Figure 34

35. If the 6-volt lamp in Figure 35 burns at normal voltage and current, resistance R must be most nearly

(A) 120 ohms.   (C) 12 ohms.
(B) 60 ohms.   (D) 6 ohms.

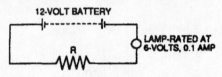

Figure 35

36. When the movable arm of the uniformly wound resistor in Figure 36 is in the position shown, the resistance in ohms between terminals 2 and 3 is

(A) 2,000   (C) 1,500
(B) 1,800   (D) 1,200

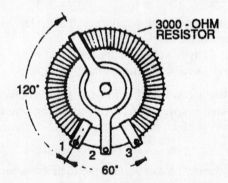

Figure 36

37. If the 10-ohm resistor marked "X" burns out, the reading of the voltmeter in Figure 37 will become

(A) 0   (C) 80
(B) 20   (D) 100

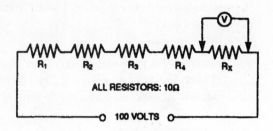

Figure 37

38. Nichrome wire having a resistance of 150 ohms per 1,000 feet is to be used for a heater requiring a total resistance of 6 ohms. The length of wire required is

(A) 4 feet.   (C) 25 feet.
(B) 9 feet.   (D) 40 feet.

39. If a 220-volt heater is used on 110 volts, the amount of heat produced will be

(A) one fourth as much.
(B) one half as much.
(C) twice as much.
(D) four times as much.

40. A completely short-circuited heater resistance will be

(A) hotter than normal.
(B) cooler than normal.
(C) inoperative.
(D) white hot.

41. A resistance of 5 ohms connected in series with a resistance of 10 ohms will result in combined resistance of

(A) 2 ohms.

(B) $3\frac{1}{3}$ ohms.

(C) 15 ohms.

(D) $7\frac{1}{2}$ ohms.

42. Two wires, A and B, have the same cross-sectional area. The resistance of A is 500 ohms and that of B is 100 ohms. The number of times A is longer than B is

(A) 5   (C) 3
(B) 4   (D) 2

43. The resistance of a circuit containing 1 ohm, 2 ohms, and 3 ohms, in parallel, is

(A) 6 ohms.   (C) 0.545 ohms.
(B) 4.5 ohms.   (D) 5.45 ohms.

44. A field discharge resistance in a generator circuit is

(A) connected in series with the field to limit field current.
(B) connected across the field terminals, after the field current has been interrupted by opening the field switch, to prevent high voltages in the field circuit.
(C) connected across the field terminals, while the field current is being interrupted, to prevent high voltages in the field circuit.
(D) connected between the field circuit and ground to prevent accumulation of static.

45. Of the following, the copper wire or cable having the highest electrical resistance in 100-foot length is

(A) No. 10 AWG
(B) No. 12 AWG
(C) 4/0 AWG
(D) 250,000 CM

46. A rule-of-thumb is that the resistance of wire doubles (or halves) for each three AWG sizes. According to this rule, the resistance of a No. 18 AWG wire compared to that of a No. 12 AWG wire is

(A) one quarter.   (C) double.
(B) one half.   (D) 4 times.

47. The resistance of a tungsten-filament lamp is about 13 times as high when the lamp is on as when it is off. Accordingly, the cold resistance of a 40-watt, 120-volt incandescent lamp, in ohms, is about

(A) 3   (C) 364
(B) 28   (D) 43,500

48. If two 4.8 ohm resistors are connected in parallel, the resulting resistance will be

(A) 9.6 ohms.   (C) 1.2 ohms.
(B) 2.4 ohms.   (D) 0.6 ohm.

49. Essentially, the pull-out torque of a wound-rotor induction motor

(A) is independent of the rotor resistance.
(B) increases rapidly as the rotor resistance is decreased.
(C) decreases rapidly as the rotor resistance is decreased.
(D) may rise or fall as the rotor resistance is increased, depending on the particular motor.

50. The resistance of a 3.6 kW heater when operated from a 120-volt circuit is

    (A) 120
    (B) 30
    (C) 4
    (D) 3

51. Of the following materials, the one that has a nearly zero temperature coefficient of resistance is

    (A) copper.
    (B) manganine.
    (C) carbon.
    (D) porcelain.

52. In order to determine the insulation resistance between the frame and armature conductors of a motor, a 25,000-ohm voltmeter is connected in series with this resistance and to a 220-volt circuit. The voltmeter reads 5 volts. The insulation resistance of the motor is

    (A) 25,000 ohms.
    (B) 125,000 ohms.
    (C) 1,100,000 ohms.
    (D) 1,075,000 ohms.

53. The resistance of each coil of a delta-connected rotor of an AC motor is one ohm. The resistance per phase (between terminals) is

    (A) $\frac{1}{3}$ ohm.
    (B) $\frac{3}{2}$ ohms.
    (C) $\frac{2}{3}$ ohm.
    (D) 3 ohms.

54. The resistance of copper wire is

    (A) directly proportional to its cross-sectional area.
    (B) directly proportional to its length.
    (C) inversely proportional to its length.
    (D) inversely proportional to its diameter.

55. If two equal resistance coils are connected in parallel, the resistance of this combination is equal to

    (A) the resistance of one coil.
    (B) $\frac{1}{2}$ the resistance of one coil.
    (C) twice the resistance of one coil.
    (D) $\frac{1}{4}$ the resistance of one coil.

56. The insulation resistance of 50 feet of No. 12 BS rubber covered wire as compared to the insulation resistance of 100 feet of this wire is

    (A) $\frac{1}{2}$ as much.
    (B) the same.
    (C) 4 times as much.
    (D) twice as much.

57. The resistance of a 150v-scale voltmeter is 10,000 ohms. The power, in watts, consumed by this voltmeter when it is connected across a 100-volt circuit is

    (A) 10
    (B) 5
    (C) 2.5
    (D) 1

58. A storage battery consists of three lead cells connected in a series. On open circuit, the emf of the battery is 6.4 volts. When it delivers a current of 80 amperes, its terminal voltage drops to 4.80 volts. Its internal resistance, in ohms, is approximately

    (A) 0.01
    (B) 0.02
    (C) 0.03
    (D) 0.04

59. In reference to question 58, the terminal voltage, in volts, when the battery delivers 50 amperes is approximately

    (A) 5.9
    (B) 5.4
    (C) 4.9
    (D) 4.4

60. Two copper conductors have the same length, but the cross-section of one is twice that of the other. If the resistance of the one having a cross-section of twice the other is 10 ohms, the resistance of the other conductor, in ohms, is

    (A) 5
    (B) 10
    (C) 20
    (D) 30

61. In reference to a 130-volt, 36-watt lamp, the ratio between the cold and hot resistance of the lamp is approximately

    (A) 1 to 3.5
    (B) 1 to 7
    (C) 1 to 12
    (D) 1 to 20

62. A storage battery of 60 cells has an open circuit voltage of 120 volts. When supplying 50 amperes, the voltage is 110 volts. The internal resistance of the battery is

    (A) .20 ohms.
    (B) 2.0 ohms.
    (C) 2.2 ohms.
    (D) 2.4 ohms.

63. When connected across a direct current source of supply, the shunt-field coils of a generator take 0.1 amperes. A 450-ohm resistor is connected in series with the coils across the same source, thereby reducing the current to 0.08 amperes. The resistance of the field is

    (A) 81 ohms.
    (B) 360 ohms.
    (C) 1,800 ohms.
    (D) 2,500 ohms.

64. The equivalent resistance of a circuit having 4 parallel branches the individual resistances of which are 1, 2, 5, and 10 ohms is nearest to

(A) 18 ohms.   (C) 0.55 ohms.
(B) 5.5 ohms.   (D) 0.18 ohms.

65. The insulation resistance of a 1,000-foot piece of cable is 100 megohms between conductor and lead sheath. If three 2,000-foot lengths of this cable were spliced in series to make a feeder, the insulation resistance of this feeder would be nearest to

(A) 17 megohms.   (C) 150 megohms.
(B) 67 megohms.   (D) 600 megohms.

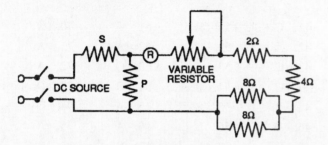

Figure 66

Questions 66–73 refer to the wiring diagram in Figure 66.

66. If resistances "S" (of low value) and "P" (of high value) are both associated with the same meter, the meter is

(A) a wattmeter.   (C) an ammeter.
(B) a voltmeter.   (D) a varmeter.

67. When the DC voltage "E" is 100 and the current through the variable resistor is 1 ampere, the variable resistor is fixed at

(A) 78 ohms.   (C) 90 ohms.
(B) 86 ohms.   (D) 100 ohms.

68. With the same load resistances and the same fixed value of the variable resistor as used in question 67, the DC voltage "E" is replaced by an AC voltage of 100. The current through the variable resistor is

(A) 0.707 ampere.   (C) 1.41 amperes.
(B) 1.00 ampere.   (D) 1.73 amperes.

69. When the voltage drop across the 8-ohm resistances is 50 volts, that across the 2-ohm resistance is

(A) 10 volts.   (C) 25 volts.
(B) 12.5 volts.   (D) 100 volts.

70. The *ratio* of the voltage drop across the 2-ohm resistance to that across the 4-ohm resistance

(A) increases with an increase in line voltage.
(B) will increase if the two 8-ohm resistances are shorted.
(C) decreases as line current decreases.
(D) is independent of line current.

71. If the current through the 2-ohm resistance is 2 amperes, the total power consumed by the 2-, 4-, and both 8-ohm resistances is

(A) 40 watts.   (C) 88 watts.
(B) 56 watts.   (D) 200 watts.

72. A relay "R," of negligible resistance, in series with the line as shown and set to operate at 4 amperes line current is taken out of service for repairs. The only available spare is also of negligible resistance and has a maximum current setting of 3 amperes. This spare will function properly if it is installed

(A) in series with one of the 8-ohm resistances.
(B) in series and between the 2- and 4-ohm resistances.
(C) in parallel across the 4-ohm resistance.
(D) to directly replace the original relay.

73. With a fixed voltage "E" increasing the amount of the variable resistance put in, the circuit will increase the voltage

(A) drop across the 2-ohm resistance.
(B) "V" across the line.
(C) drop across the 8-ohm resistance.
(D) drop across the variable resistor.

74. If three unknown resistors are connected in series across an AC source of power, it is certain that the

(A) power consumed by each resistor will be the same.
(B) total current in the circuit is the sum of the current in each of the three resistors.
(C) voltage drop across each will be the same.
(D) current through each will be the same.

75. What is the resistance of a third resistor if the first two are 8 ohms and 12 ohms and the total resistance of the circuit measures 25 ohms?

(A) 5 ohms   (C) 4 ohms
(B) 7 ohms   (D) 6 ohms

76. Three resistors of unequal value are placed in parallel. Their total resistance is

    (A) three times as great as that of the smallest resistor.

    (B) always less than that of the smallest resistor.

    (C) found by adding.

    (D) found by subtracting.

77. Five resistors of 20 ohms each are placed in series. One of the resistors has 5 amperes through it. The current through the other two resistors would be

    (A) 10 amperes.   (C) 15 amperes.

    (B) 5 amperes.   (D) 3 amperes.

78. Three resistors of 20 ohms, 20 ohms, and 10 ohms are placed in parallel. Their total resistance is

    (A) 5 ohms.   (C) 10 ohms.

    (B) 20 ohms.   (D) 50 ohms.

ANSWER KEY

1. A	11. C	21. C	31. B	41. C	51. B	61. C	70. D
2. D	12. A	22. B	32. A	42. A	52. D	62. A	71. A
3. A	13. B	23. C	33. A	43. C	53. C	63. C	72. A
4. A	14. A	24. D	34. D	44. C	54. B	64. C	73. D
5. D	15. A	25. A	35. B	45. B	55. B	65. A	74. D
6. C	16. C	26. C	36. B	46. D	56. B	66. A	75. A
7. A	17. D	27. C	37. D	47. B	57. D	67. C	76. B
8. D	18. D	28. A	38. D	48. B	58. B	68. B	77. B
9. A	19. C	29. A	39. A	49. A	59. B	69. C	78. A
10. B	20. D	30. C	40. C	50. C	60. C		

SWITCHES, WIRING, AND INSULATION

> **DIRECTIONS:** For each question, read all choices carefully. Then select the answer that you consider correct or most nearly correct. Write the letter preceding your best choice next to the question.

TYPES OF SWITCHES AND THEIR USE

1. Mercury toggle switches are sometimes used instead of regular toggle switches because they

    (A) cost less.

    (B) are lighter.

    (C) are easier to install.

    (D) do not wear out quickly.

2. TPDT would be used to identify a

    (A) wire.   (C) fuse.

    (B) conduit.   (D) switch.

3. A make-and-break contact is provided in an electric bell to

    (A) keep the coil from overheating.

    (B) make the armature vibrate.

    (C) make the bell single-stroke.

    (D) prevent arcing at the push-button.

4. A make-before-break switch is used to

(A) prevent tying two sources together.
(B) open one circuit before closing another.
(C) close one circuit before opening another.
(D) shorten the switch movement.

5. A limit switch is used on a piece of electrical apparatus to shut off the power when the

(A) travel reaches a definite limit.
(B) current exceeds a definite limit.
(C) voltage is below a definite limit.
(D) frequency exceeds a definite limit.

6. The usual function of disconnect switches in a high-voltage circuit is to

(A) open or close the circuit under load.
(B) isolate from live buses equipment not in service.
(C) maintain continuity of service should the breakers fail.
(D) open the circuit in the event of overload.

7. High-voltage switches in power plants are commonly so constructed that their contacts are submerged in oil. The purpose of the oil is to

(A) help quench arcing.
(B) lubricate the contacts.
(C) cool the switch mechanism.
(D) insulate the contacts from the switch framework.

8. The operating mechanism of a Westinghouse solenoid-operated oil switch has an air dashpot associated with the closing core to diminish the shock to the oil switch parts on closing. You would expect this dashpot to

(A) speed up the closing operation.
(B) reduce the force necessary to close the switch.
(C) make the closing operation more positive.
(D) slow down the closing operation.

9. If the mercury switch in Figure 9 is turned to the horizontal position, the mercury will flow and break the connection between the lead-in wires, thus opening the circuit. By logical reasoning, such a switch would be most useful when

(A) the circuit must be opened quickly.
(B) there is likely to be explosive gas near the switch location.
(C) there is no restriction on noise.
(D) the switch need not be operated often.

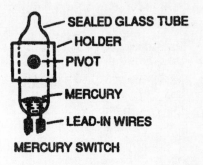

MERCURY SWITCH

Figure 9

10. Toggle switches of the type generally used on lighting circuits are

(A) quick closing and quick opening.
(B) quick closing and slow opening.
(C) slow closing and slow opening.
(D) slow closing and quick opening.

11. Which of the following is NOT used correctly in describing a toggle switch?

(A) Single-hole mounting
(B) Slow-acting
(C) 3-way
(D) Double-pole

12. The letters SPST stand for what kind of switch?

(A) Switch prong, single top
(B) Switch pole, single top
(C) Switch plus, single terminal
(D) Single-pole, single throw

13. The letters DPDT stand for what kind of switch?

(A) Double prong, double throw
(B) Double pole, double throw
(C) Double probe, double terminal
(D) Duplex pole, double terminal

14. The three-way switch has

(A) three terminals.
(B) two poles.
(C) three poles.
(D) two poles and a terminal.

15. To switch a lamp on or off from three locations, you need

(A) two three-way switches.
(B) three three-way switches.
(C) two three-way switches and one four-way switch.
(D) three four-way switches.

ANSWER KEY

1. D	4. C	7. A	10. A	13. B
2. D	5. A	8. D	11. B	14. A
3. B	6. B	9. B	12. D	15. C

PROBLEMS

Questions 1–7 in Column I are combinations of open and closed switches in Figure 1, each of which will result in one of the lamp conditions listed in Column II. For each combination in Column I, select the resulting lamp condition from Column II.

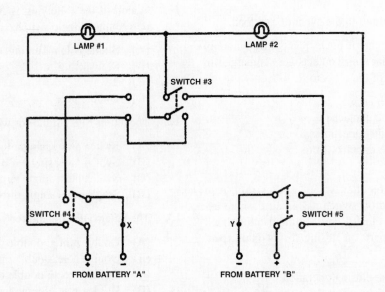

Figure 1

POSITION OF SWITCHES   LAMP CONDITIONS

COLUMN I

1. No. 3 closed to the right, No. 4 and No. 5 open
2. No. 3 closed to the right, No. 4 open, No. 5 closed
3. No. 3 closed to the right, No. 4 closed, No. 5 open
4. No. 3 closed to the left, No. 4 open, No. 5 closed
5. No. 3 closed to the left, No. 4 closed, No. 5 open
6. No. 3 closed to the right, No. 4 and No. 5 closed
7. No. 3 closed to the left, No. 4 and No. 5 closed, and jumper connected between X and Y

COLUMN II

(A) Both lamps dark
(B) Both lamps lighted
(C) Only lamp No. 1 lighted
(D) Only lamp No. 2 lighted

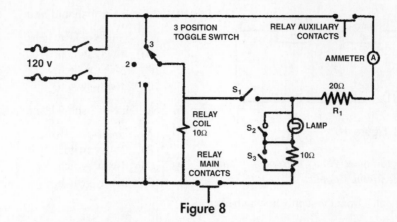

Figure 8

Questions 8–15 are based on Figure 8. Switches S1 and S3 are normally closed, and switch S2 is normally open. In each question, assume the line switch is closed and the toggle switch remains on point 3 unless otherwise stated.

8. Figure 8 is commonly known as a

(A) parts diagram.
(B) working drawing.
(C) schematic wiring diagram.
(D) detail drawing.

9. With conditions as stated above, the relay will pick up and the

(A) lamp will be dark.
(B) ammeter will show a reading.
(C) lamp will be bright.
(D) resistor R1 will be open circuited.

10. If the main relay contacts are momentarily opened by quickly inserting and removing a fiber shim between the main relay contacts, the

(A) lamp will go out and stay out.
(B) lamp will go out and then relight.
(C) relay will drop out and stay out.
(D) relay will drop out and then pick up again.

11. If the toggle switch is moved from point 3 to point 2, the

(A) ammeter will show a reading.
(B) relay will drop out.
(C) lamp will have full-line voltage.
(D) resistor R1 will be open circuited.

12. If the toggle switch is moved from point 3 to point 1, the

(A) lamp will be bright.
(B) relay will drop out.
(C) ammeter will show a high reading.
(D) line fuse will blow.

13. With the toggle switch again on point 3, if S2 is closed and S3 is opened, the current in the relay coil will be

(A) 4 amperes.   (C) 12 amperes.
(B) 5 amperes.   (D) 20 amperes.

14. With conditions as in question 13, the equivalent resistance of the circuit between points 1 and 3 will be

(A) 7.25 ohms.   (C) 20 ohms.
(B) 25 ohms.   (D) infinite.

15. With conditions as in question 13, if S1 is opened the voltage drop across R1 is

(A) $33\frac{1}{3}$ volts.

(B) 50 volts.

(C) $66\frac{2}{3}$ volts.

(D) 80 volts.

16. If an oil switch is used as a service switch in your building, which is supplied with 13,500 volts, you must use between said service switch and the service wires

(A) a removable link.
(B) nothing.
(C) a fuse.
(D) a disconnect switch.

17. You have a 100-ampere, 13-kV oil switch that has a trip coil rated up to 5 amperes. You also have a CT rated to 100 to 5 amperes. You wish the switch to open at 80 amperes line current. The setting of the trip coil to accomplish this should be

(A) 4 amperes.   (C) 3 amperes.
(B) 5 amperes.   (D) 1 ampere.

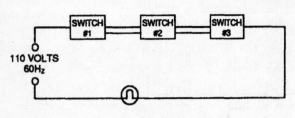

Figure 18

Questions 18–20 refer to Figure 18, a diagram of a lamp independently controlled from 3 points.

18. The conductor running from the supply to switch No. 1 should be the

    (A) blue wire.   (C) black wire.
    (B) white wire.   (D) ground wire.

19. Switch No. 1 should be a

    (A) single-pole switch.
    (B) 4-way switch.
    (C) 2-way switch.
    (D) 3-way switch.

20. Switch No. 2 should be a

    (A) single-pole switch.
    (B) 2-way switch.
    (C) 4-way switch.
    (D) 3-way switch.

Questions 21–26 in Column I are combinations of closed switches in Figure 21, each of which will result in one of the lamp conditions listed in Column II. For each combination in Column I, select the resulting lamp condition from Column II.

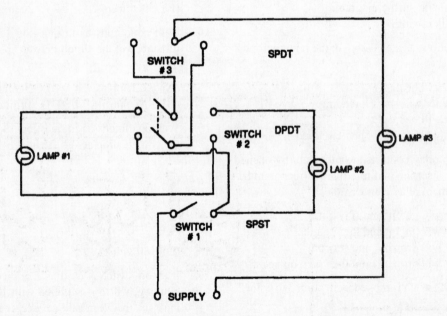

Figure 21

COMBINATIONS OF CLOSED SWITCHES			LAMP CONDITIONS
COLUMN I			COLUMN II

	switch No. 1	switch No. 2	switch No. 3	
21.	left	left	right	(A) No. 1 and No. 3 light
22.	left	left	left	(B) No. 2 and No. 3 light
23.	left	right	right	(C) only No. 3 light
24.	right	right	left	(D) no light
25.	right	left	right	
26.	right	right	right	

27. You may have to open a knife switch that may be carrying a very heavy load current. The proper way to open the switch is to

(A) open it with a jerk so as to quickly break any arc.
(B) open it slowly so that there will not be a flashover at the contacts.
(C) open it with care, to avoid damage to the auxiliary blade by the arc.
(D) tie a 5-foot rope on the switch handle and stand clear of the switch.

28. To control a lamp independently from five different points, you would use

(A) two 3-way and three 4-way switches.
(B) four 3-way switches and one 4-way switch.
(C) three 3-way and two 4-way switches.
(D) three 4-way and two SPST switches.

29. A lighting fixture is to be controlled independently from two different locations. The type of switch required in each of the two locations is

(A) single-pole, single-throw.
(B) single-pole, double-throw.

(C) double-pole, single-throw.
(D) double-pole, double-throw.

30. To control a lamp independently from three different points, you would use

(A) two 3-way switches and one SPST switch.
(B) two 3-way switches and one 4-way switch.
(C) two SPST switches and one 3-way switch.
(D) two 4-way switches and one SPST switch.

Questions 31–38 refer to Figure 31.

31. When the switch is closed in the "down" position, the required charging generator voltage would be most nearly

(A) 240 volts.   (C) 110 volts.
(B) 130 volts.   (D) 60 volts.

32. When the switch is closed in the "up" position, the voltage between line 1 and line 3 would be approximately

(A) 240 volts.   (C) 60 volts.
(B) 120 volts.   (D) 0 volts.

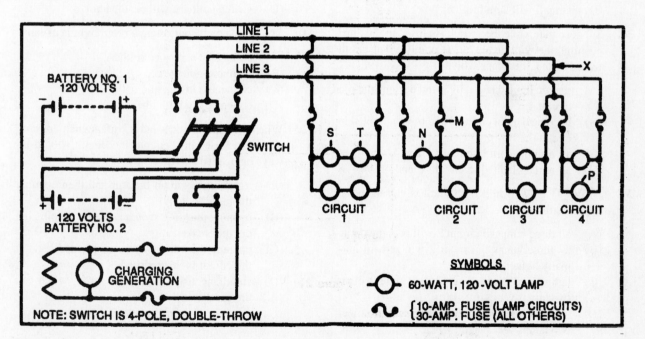

Figure 31

33. With the switch closed in the "up" position, the voltage between line 2 and line 3 would be approximately

    (A) 240 volts.   (C) 60 volts.
    (B) 120 volts.   (D) 0 volts.

34. If lamp P in circuit 4 burns out while the switch is closed in the "up" position,

    (A) the other lamp in circuit 4 and both lamps in circuit 3 should remain lighted.
    (B) all lamps in circuits 3 and 4 should become dark.
    (C) both lamps in circuit 3 should remain lighted, and both lamps in circuit 4 should become dark.
    (D) the lower lamp in circuit 3 should become dark while the upper lamps in circuits 3 and 4 should remain lighted.

35. If lamp T in circuit 1 becomes short-circuited while the switch is closed in the "up" position, the most probable result will be that

    (A) one of the circuit fuses will blow.
    (B) both of the circuit fuses will blow.
    (C) all other lamps in the circuit will burn brighter.
    (D) lamp S will burn brighter.

36. Suppose that while the switch is closed in the "up" position, the wire breaks off at point X. The result would be that the lamps would

    (A) remain lighted in circuit 3 and become dark in circuit 4.
    (B) become dark in circuit 3 and remain lighted in circuit 4.
    (C) all become dark in circuits 3 and 4.
    (D) all remain lighted in circuits 3 and 4.

37. If fuse M blows while the switch is closed in the "up" position,

    (A) all three lamps in circuit 2 will become dark.
    (B) all three lamps in circuit 2 will remain normally lighted.
    (C) lamp N will become very bright and the other two lamps very dim.
    (D) lamp N will become very dim and the other two lamps very bright.

38. Under normal conditions, with the switch closed in the "up" position, the current in line 2 is the current taken by one lamp multiplied by

    (A) 11   (C) 4
    (B) 7   (D) 1

39. If switch "S" in Figure 39 is closed, how will the ammeter readings change?

    (A) Both will increase.
    (B) No. 1 only will increase.
    (C) Both will decrease.
    (D) No. 2 only will increase.

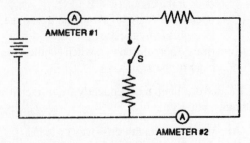

Figure 39

40. If a snap switch rated at 5 amperes is used for an electric heater that draws 10 amperes, the most likely result is that the

    (A) circuit fuse will be blown.
    (B) circuit wiring will become hot.
    (C) heater output will be halved.
    (D) switch contacts will become hot.

41. The wall switch controlling a room light is usually

    (A) connected across both lines.
    (B) a double-pole type.
    (C) connected in one line only.
    (D) connected in both lines.

42. When a circuit breaker and a knife switch are connected in series in a circuit, the circuit should always be opened by

    (A) tripping the circuit breaker and then opening the knife switch.
    (B) opening the knife switch and then tripping the circuit breaker.
    (C) opening the knife switch quickly and leaving the circuit breaker closed.
    (D) simultaneously opening the knife switch and the breaker.

43. The two coils in Figure 43 are wound in the directions indicated, and both coils have exactly the same number of turns. When the switch is closed, the north pole of the permanent magnet will be

(A) repelled by both the left-hand and right-hand cores.

(B) attracted by both the left-hand and right-hand cores.

(C) attracted by the left-hand core and repelled by the right-hand core.

(D) repelled by the left-hand core and attracted by the right-hand core.

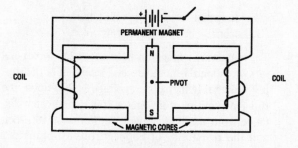

Figure 43

44. In Figure 44, the double-pole, double-throw switch that is properly connected as a reversing switch is

(A) 1   (C) 3
(B) 2   (D) 4

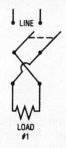
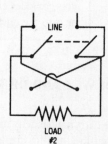
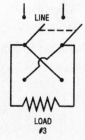
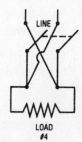

Figure 44

45. In Figure 44, the switch that will place a *short* across the power line when closed is

(A) 1   (C) 3
(B) 2   (D) 4

ANSWER KEY

1. A	10. B	19. D	28. A	37. C
2. D	11. A or B	20. C	29. B	38. D
3. A	12. B	21. D	30. B	39. B
4. A	13. C	22. D	31. B	40. D
5. C	14. A	23. D	32. A	41. C
6. D	15. D	24. B	33. B	42. A
7. B	16. D	25. C	34. A	43. A
8. C	17. A	26. D	35. D	44. B
9. C	18. C	27. A	36. D	45. D

WIRING EQUIPMENT

> **DIRECTIONS:** For each question, read all choices carefully. Then select the answer that you consider correct or most nearly correct. Write the letter preceding your best answer next to the question.

TYPES OF WIRE AND THEIR USES

1. The carrying capacity of aluminum wire when compared to a similar size of copper wire that has the same kind of insulation is

   (A) 84 percent.   (C) 74 percent.
   (B) 94 percent.   (D) 100 percent.

2. A cable composed of two insulated stranded conductors laid parallel and having a common cover is called a

   (A) twin cable.
   (B) duplex cable.
   (C) concentric cable.
   (D) sector cable.

3. In multiple-conductor armored cable construction, a color scheme is used for identifying purposes. The color coding of a 3-conductor cable should be which one of the following?

   (A) One white, one red, and one black
   (B) Two black and one white
   (C) Two white and one black
   (D) One white, one black, and one blue

4. Type RL wires and cables would most likely be used for which one of the following applications?

   (A) Power control switchboard
   (B) Interior dry locations subject to high temperatures
   (C) Interior high voltage applications
   (D) Underground power distribution

5. In panel wiring, solid wire is preferred to stranded wire because it

   (A) will carry more current.
   (B) has better insulation.
   (C) can be "shaped" better.
   (D) uses less copper.

6. Of the following, the poorest conductor of electricity is

   (A) carbon.   (C) copper.
   (B) aluminum.   (D) silver.

7. Of the following, the best conductor of electricity is

   (A) tungsten.   (C) aluminum.
   (B) iron.   (D) carbon.

8. The maximum voltage-drop between a DC motor and its switchboard is not to exceed 1 percent of the supply voltage. If the supply voltage is 200 volts, the full-load current of the motor 100 amperes, the distance from the switchboard to the motor 100 feet, and the resistivity of copper from 10 ohms per CM-foot, the size wire required in CM is

   (A) 25,000   (C) 100,000
   (B) 50,000   (D) 200,000

9. A type of electric wire protected by a spiral metal cover is known as

   (A) BX.   (C) Ampex.
   (B) Romex.   (D) Conduit.

10. A stranded conductor has 37 strands, each 90 mils in diameter. The area in circular mils of this conductor is most nearly

    (A) 3,300   (C) 236,000
    (B) 123,200   (D) 300,000

11. A length of wire 1,800′ long is made up in a coil. If this coil has an average diameter of 6″, then the number of turns in the coil is most nearly

    (A) 1,000   (C) 1,450
    (B) 1,150   (D) 7,200

12. Laminated iron is used in AC magnetic circuits to

    (A) increase heat radiation.
    (B) make assembly easier.
    (C) reduce eddy currents.
    (D) reduce permeability.

13. A copper wire one tenth of an inch in diameter has a cross-sectional area of

    (A) 1,000 cir. mils.   (C) 10,000 cir. mils.
    (B) 7,854 cir. mils.   (D) 31,416 cir. mils.

14. After No. 2 AWG, the next smaller copper wire or cable size is No.

(A) 0   (C) 3
(B) 1   (D) 4

15. After No. 10 AWG, the next smaller copper wire size in common use is No.

(A) 8   (C) 11
(B) 9   (D) 12

16. In Figure 16, the diameter of the cable compared to the diameter of a single conductor is between

(A) two and three times.
(B) three and four times.
(C) four and five times.
(D) five and six times.

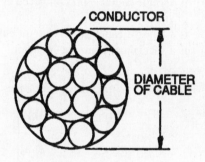

Figure 16

17. The conductors in a large lead-covered telephone cable are usually

(A) stranded and rubber insulated.
(B) solid and rubber insulated.
(C) stranded and paper insulated.
(D) solid and paper insulated.

18. The sketch in Figure 18 that correctly represents the cross-section of a standard stranded copper conductor is

(A) 1   (C) 3
(B) 2   (D) 4

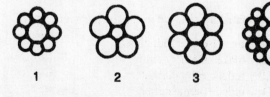

Figure 18

19. In measuring to determine the size of a stranded insulated conductor, the proper place to use the wire gage is on

(A) the insulation.
(B) the outer covering.
(C) the stranded conductor.
(D) one strand of the conductor.

20. If the following copper wire sizes were arranged in the order of increasing current-carrying capacity, the correct arrangement would be

(A) 18; 6; 0000; 500,000
(B) 500,000; 0000; 6; 18
(C) 0000; 18; 6; 500,000
(D) 0000; 6; 18; 500,000

21. Comparing No. 8 and No. 12 bare copper wire of equal lengths, the No. 8 wire will have lower

(A) weight.   (C) resistance.
(B) cost.   (D) strength.

22. If the following bare copper wire sizes were arranged in the order of increasing weight per 1,000 feet, the correct arrangement would be

(A) No. 00, No. 40, No. 8
(B) No. 40, No. 00, No. 8
(C) No. 00, No. 8, No. 40
(D) No. 40, No. 8, No. 00

23. The wire size most commonly used for branch circuits in residences is

(A) No. 14   (C) No. 12
(B) No. 16   (D) No. 18

24. Standard tables are available showing the safe carrying capacity of copper wire of various sizes to avoid damage to insulation from overheating. The allowable current given is dependent on the

(A) voltage.
(B) length of wire.
(C) type of current (AC or DC).
(D) room temperature.

25. The sketch in Figure 25 shows the ends of four bare copper wires full size with diameters as given. From left to right, the No. 14 wire is

(A) first.   (C) third.
(B) second.   (D) fourth.

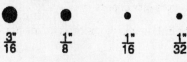

Figure 25

26. High-voltage cable that is to be installed in underground ducts is generally protected with a

    (A) steel wire armor.
    (B) lead sheath.
    (C) tarred jute covering.
    (D) copper outer jacket.

27. "Nichrome" wire is commonly used for

    (A) transformer windings.
    (B) lamp filaments.
    (C) heater coils.
    (D) battery connections.

28. After No. 4, the next larger American Wire Gage size is No.

    (A) 2   (C) 5
    (B) 3   (D) 6

29. If one copper wire has a diameter of 0.128 inch, and another copper wire has a diameter of 0.064 inch, the resistance of 1,000 feet of the first wire compared to the same length of the second wire is

    (A) one half.   (C) double.
    (B) one quarter.   (D) four times.

30. As compared with solid wire, stranded wire of the same gage size is

    (A) given a higher current rating.
    (B) easier to skin.
    (C) larger in total diameter.
    (D) better for high voltage.

31. A stranded wire is given the same size designation as a solid wire if it has the same

    (A) cross-sectional area.
    (B) weight per foot.
    (C) overall diameter.
    (D) strength.

32. A multi-conductor cable

    (A) has a number of separate circuits.
    (B) is a single circuit cable composed of a number of strands.
    (C) is a flexible cable to carry motor current.
    (D) is a special car-heating conductor.

ANSWER KEY

1. A	5. C	9. A	13. C	17. D	21. C	25. C	29. B
2. A	6. A	10. D	14. C	18. C	22. D	26. B	30. C
3. A	7. C	11. B	15. D	19. D	23. A	27. C	31. A
4. D	8. C	12. C	16. C	20. A	24. D	28. B	32. A

WIRING SYSTEMS AND DIAGRAMS

1. The factor that determines the current-carrying capacity of a 2-wire circuit is

    (A) whether the supply is AC or DC.
    (B) the gage of the circuit wire.
    (C) the length of the circuit.
    (D) the number of outlets in the circuit.

2. In a balanced 3-phase, wye-connected circuit, the line voltages are equal

    (A) to the voltage between any line and the neutral.
    (B) but the line currents are unequal.
    (C) and so are the line currents.
    (D) to the line currents.

3. Defects in wiring that permit current to jump from one wire to another before the intended path has been completed are called

    (A) grounds.   (C) opens.
    (B) shorts.   (D) breaks.

4. With reference to AC supply circuits, the waves of voltage and current ordinarily encountered in practice are

    (A) sine waves.
    (B) triangular waves.
    (C) circular waves.
    (D) rectangular waves.

5. If an inductive circuit-carrying current is short-circuited, the current in the circuit will

    (A) cease to flow immediately.
    (B) continue to flow indefinitely.
    (C) continue to flow for an appreciable time after the instant of short circuit.
    (D) increase greatly.

6. A parallel AC circuit in resonance will

    (A) have a high impedance.
    (B) act like a resistor of low value.
    (C) have current in each section equal to the line current.
    (D) have a high voltage developed across each inductive and capacitive section.

7. A certain amount of power is transmitted at a certain voltage and line loss. If the same amount of power is to be transmitted at twice the original voltage and same line loss, the effect on the weight of the transmission line is

    (A) none.
    (B) to increase it four times.
    (C) to decrease it to one fourth.
    (D) to decrease it to one half.

8. The type of alternating current distribution system commonly used to supply both light and power is

    (A) 3-phase, 3-wire.
    (B) single-phase, 2-wire.
    (C) 2-phase, 3-wire.
    (D) 3-phase, 4-wire.

9. An input circuit has both AC and DC current flowing into it. It is desired that a coupling unit be used to transfer only AC. The type of coupling circuit that would most effectively do this is

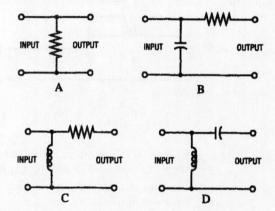

10. The letters SPST frequently found on wiring plans refer to a type of

    (A) cable.   (C) fuse.
    (B) switch.   (D) motor.

11. The letters RILC are used in identifying

    (A) transformers.
    (B) motors.
    (C) cables.
    (D) storage batteries.

12. An elementary wiring diagram is

    (A) any single line diagram.
    (B) one showing all the elements of a 3-element meter.
    (C) one showing sequences of operation of switches and relays.
    (D) one showing conduit and cable runs.

13. The term "exposed wiring" refers to wires that

(A) have no insulation when installed.
(B) run in conduit along the outside wall of a building.
(C) are not in conduit or raceway.
(D) have had part of their insulation worn away.

14. In a three-phase, 4-wire system in which the voltage between lines is 5,500 volts, the voltage to neutral is most nearly

(A) 9,500 V.   (C) 3,175 V.
(B) 5,500 V.   (D) 1,830 V.

16. In the circuit diagram in Figure 15, the voltage between the secondary leads "A" and "B" is

(A) 208 volts.   (C) 416 volts.
(B) 120 volts.   (D) 240 volts.

17. In the circuit diagram in Figure 15, the voltage between secondary leads "C" and "D" is

(A) 120 volts.   (C) 416 volts.
(B) 208 volts.   (D) 240 volts.

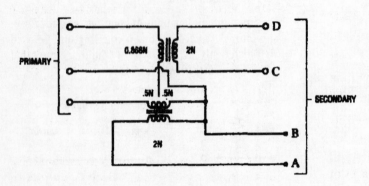

Figure 15

15. If the primary leads in Figure 15 are connected to a 3-phase, 3-wire, 208 volt system and the transformation ratios are as indicated on the diagram, the secondary leads will form a

(A) 3-phase, 4-wire system.
(B) 2-phase, 4-wire system.
(C) 4-phase, 5-wire system.
(D) 3-phase, 3-wire system.

ANSWER KEY

1. B	5. C	9. D	12. C	15. B
2. C	6. A	10. B	13. B or C	16. C
3. B	7. C	11. C	14. C	17. C
4. A	8. D			

CORRECT WIRING TECHNIQUES

1. A certain lighting circuit requires the installation of No. 10 AWG wire. If No. 10 wire is not available, it would be poor practice to use two No. 12 AWG wires in parallel instead, because

   (A) they would take up too much room in the conduit.
   (B) they would require twice as long to install.
   (C) an open circuit in one wire may overload the other.
   (D) the total conductor area would be smaller.

2. When applying rubber tape to a wire splice, it should be applied with

   (A) no tension, to avoid stretching.
   (B) just enough tension to hold it in place.
   (C) as much tension as possible short of tearing the tape.
   (D) sufficient tension to pull it to approximately half its original width.

3. The function of a spiking test on a power cable is to

   (A) determine if the sheath has deteriorated.
   (B) determine if the cable is alive.
   (C) find weak spots in the copper.
   (D) test for compound leakage.

4. The one of the following that is NOT a common splicing rule is

   (A) wires of the same size should be spliced together in line.
   (B) a joint or splice must be as mechanically strong as the wire itself.
   (C) a splice must provide a path for the electric current that will be as good as another wire.
   (D) all splices must be mechanically and electrically secured by means of solder.

5. Two-phase power may be converted to 3-phase power by

   (A) means of transformers connected in open-V.
   (B) means of Scott connected transformers.
   (C) means of an autotransformer.
   (D) none of the above methods.

6. The most valid objection for not fusing the middle wire of a 3-wire system with a grounded neutral is that

   (A) it will increase the replacement cost of the fuses.
   (B) shutdown will be increased due to the blowing of the neutral fuse.
   (C) blowing of the neutral fuse may unbalance the voltages on the two sides of the system with possible burnout of some of the lamps.
   (D) the size of the neutral wire must be made twice as large as the ungrounded line wires.

7. The size of the mandrel to be pulled through a duct before the cable is pulled shall be approximately

   (A) one inch smaller than the duct.
   (B) one-half inch smaller than the duct.
   (C) one-quarter inch smaller than the duct.
   (D) the same size as the duct.

8. When removing wooden lagging from a reel of cable or wire that is about to be installed, it is good practice to place the lagging in a neat pile away from the reel mainly to avoid

   (A) interference with the pulling of the cable.
   (B) damage to the lagging.
   (C) losing the lagging.
   (D) criticism for untidiness.

9. When wiring a 600-volt DC series circuit, the first positive connection must be to the center contact of the socket. The most likely reason for this requirement is to

   (A) lessen the voltage drop in the circuit.
   (B) make the wiring uniform.
   (C) reduce the amount of wire required to make the connections.
   (D) lessen the hazards of a shock when screwing a bulb into its socket.

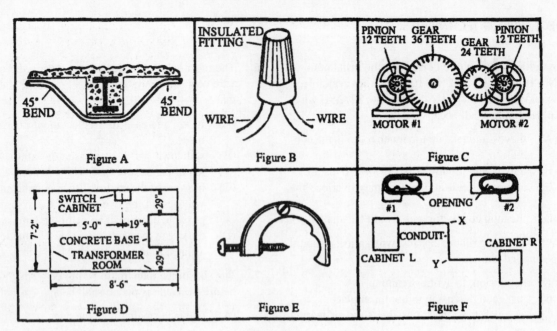

Figure 10

Questions 10–15 refer to Figure 10. Each question gives the proper Figure to use with that question.

10. When a wire is pulled into the conduit shown in Figure A, it must go around bends amounting to a total of

(A) 0°   (C) 180°
(B) 90°   (D) 360°

11. Wires are often spliced by the use of a fitting like the one shown in Figure B. The use of this fitting does away with the need for

(A) skinning.
(B) cleaning.
(C) twisting.
(D) soldering.

12. The two identical motors in Figure C are connected to the same power supply and are wired so that they normally tend to turn in the same direction. When the power is turned on,

(A) the motors will stall.
(B) both motors will turn at normal speed in the same direction.
(C) motor 1 will turn in its normal direction, driving motor 2 backward.
(D) motor 2 will turn in its normal direction, driving motor 1 backward.

13. The dimensions of the concrete base shown in Figure D are

(A) 14″ × 28″
(B) 23″ × 28″
(C) 23″ × 29″
(D) 14″ × 29″

14. The device shown in Figure E is a

(A) C-clamp.
(B) test clip.
(C) battery connector.
(D) ground clamp.

15. Figure F shows two types of conduit fitting (Nos. 1 and 2) used as pull boxes at sharp bends in conduit runs. The Figure also shows the layout of a conduit run on the wall between cabinets L and R. If wire is to be pulled into the conduit starting at cabinet L, and the wire is to be continuous without a splice from cabinet L to cabinet R, the best choice of fittings is to have a

(A) a 1 at corner X and a 2 at corner Y.
(B) 2 at both corners X and Y.
(C) 1 at both corners X and Y.
(D) a 2 at corner X and a 1 at corner Y

16. When removing the insulation from a wire before making a splice, care should be taken to avoid nicking the wire mainly because the

(A) current-carrying capacity will be reduced.
(B) resistance will be increased.
(C) wire tinning will be injured.
(D) wire is more likely to break.

17. When applying rubber tape to a lighting circuit splice, it is necessary to

    (A) have the cambric backing against the conductors.
    (B) heat the tape properly before applying.
    (C) use rubber cement on the conductors.
    (D) stretch the tape properly during application.

18. Of the following, it would be most difficult to solder a copper wire to a metal plate made of

    (A) copper.   (C) iron.
    (B) brass.   (D) tin.

19. To make a good soldered connection between two stranded wires, it is LEAST important to

    (A) twist the wires together before soldering.
    (B) use enough heat to make the solder flow freely.
    (C) clean the wires carefully.
    (D) apply solder to each strand before twisting the two wires together.

20. It is good practice to connect the ground wire for a building electrical system to a

    (A) gas pipe.
    (B) cold-water pipe.
    (C) vent pipe.
    (D) steam pipe.

21. Of the following, the least undesirable practice if a specified wire size is not available for part of a circuit is to

    (A) use two wires of $\frac{1}{2}$ capacity in parallel as a substitute.
    (B) use the next larger size wire.
    (C) use a smaller size wire if the length is short.
    (D) reduce the size of the fuse and use smaller wire.

22. To straighten a long length of wire that has been tightly coiled before pulling it into a conduit run, a good method is to

    (A) roll the wire into a coil in the opposite direction.
    (B) fasten one end to the floor and whip it against the floor from the other end.
    (C) draw it over a convenient edge.
    (D) hold the wire at one end and twist it with pliers from the other end.

23. The LEAST important action in making soldered connection between two wires is to

    (A) use the proper flux.
    (B) clean the wires well.
    (C) use plenty of solder.
    (D) use sufficient heat.

24. When tightening a terminal screw connection, the end of the wire should pass around the screw in the same direction as the screw is turned so that

    (A) the wire will act as a locknut.
    (B) the screw can be removed more easily.
    (C) any pull on the wire will tighten the screw.
    (D) the wire will not turn off.

25. The most practical way to determine in the field if a large coil of No. 14 wire has the required length for a given job is to

    (A) weigh the coil and compare with a new 1,000-foot coil.
    (B) measure the electrical resistance and compare with a 1,000-foot coil.
    (C) measure the length of one turn and multiply by the number of turns.
    (D) unwind the coil and lay the wire alongside the conduit before pulling it in.

26. To determine which wire of a 2-wire, 120-volt AC line is the grounded wire, one correct procedure is to

    (A) connect a center-zero voltmeter across the line and note the direction of movement of the pointer.
    (B) quickly touch each line wire in turn to a cold-water pipe.
    (C) connect one lead of a test lamp to the conduit, and test each side of the line with the other lead.
    (D) thrust the two line wires about an inch apart into a slice of raw potato and watch for discoloration.

27. The wires in the right-hand junction box in Figure 27 are to be spliced so that the switch will control both lighting fixtures and the fixtures will be connected in parallel. The wires to be spliced, in accordance with good wiring practice, are

    (A) 1 to 4, 2 to 6, 3 to both 5 and 7.
    (B) 1 to 6, 2 to 5, 3 to both 4 and 7.
    (C) 1 to 7, 2 to both 5 and 6, 3 to 4.
    (D) 1 to 5, 2 to both 6 and 7, 3 to 4.

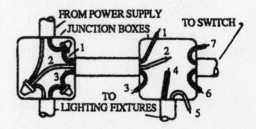

Figure 27

28. Wire splices in modern home and business building wiring systems are made both mechanically firm and of low resistance by means of

    (A) mechanical connectors.
    (B) spot welding.
    (C) brazing.
    (D) plastic tape.

ANSWER KEY

1. C	5. B	9. D	13. B	17. D	21. B	25. C
2. D	6. C	10. C	14. D	18. C	22. B	26. C
3. D	7. C	11. D	15. D	19. D	23. C	27. B
4. D	8. A	12. C	16. D	20. B	24. D	28. A

CONDUITS

> **DIRECTIONS:** For each question, read all choices carefully. Then select the answer that you consider correct or most nearly correct. Write the letter preceding your best choice next to the question.

1. With respect to pulling wires into a conduit, it is usually specified that a certain percentage of the conduit area must be left unoccupied. The purpose of this requirement is to permit

   (A) pulling in the wires without undue strain or abrasion.
   (B) pulling in additional wires later if needed.
   (C) pulling out the wires for replacement even if the insulation has swelled.
   (D) circulation of air so that the insulation will not be damaged by heat.

2. When installing electric wiring, it is essential that all conduits be

   (A) concealed.
   (B) rigidly supported.
   (C) left exposed.
   (D) given identifying markers.

3. The internal diameter of $\frac{1}{2}$-inch electrical conduit is approximately

   (A) 0.422 inch.
   (B) 0.5 inch.
   (C) 0.552 inch.
   (D) 0.622 inch.

4. The most important reason for using a condulet-type fitting in preference to making a bend in a one-inch conduit run is to

   (A) obtain a neater job.
   (B) cut down length of conduit needed.
   (C) avoid possible flattening of conduit when bending.
   (D) make wire pulling easier.

5. Electrical wires are run through conduit in order to

   (A) increase the current-carrying capacity of the wires.
   (B) protect the wires from damage.

   (C) decrease the cost of initial installation.
   (D) increase the breakdown voltage of the wires.

6. When a conduit enters a knockout in an outlet box, it should be provided with a

   (A) locknut on the inside and a bushing on the outside.
   (B) bushing on the inside and a locknut on the outside.
   (C) bushing and a locknut on the outside.
   (D) bushing and a locknut on the inside.

7. The main reason for grounding conduit installations is to

   (A) reduce leakage between wires.
   (B) prevent short circuits.
   (C) save wiring.
   (D) prevent conduit from becoming alive to ground.

8. The inside edge on the end of conduit is reamed after cutting mainly to

   (A) aid in screwing on the bushing.
   (B) prevent injury to the wire.
   (C) make pulling the wire easier.
   (D) finish the end of the thread.

9. A conduit is to be run diagonally across a 6-foot-by-8-foot room. If the ends of the conduit are to be one foot from the room corners, the conduit should be cut to

   (A) 8 feet.
   (B) 9 feet.
   (C) 10 feet.
   (D) 12 feet.

DIRECTIONS: The sketches in Column I are of WIRING DEVICES suitable for the DOTTED LOCATIONS on one of the four sketches in Column II. For each DEVICE in Column I, select the suitable LOCATION from Column II. Write its letter on the line in Column I.

WIRING DEVICES

COLUMN I

DOTTED LOCATIONS

COLUMN II

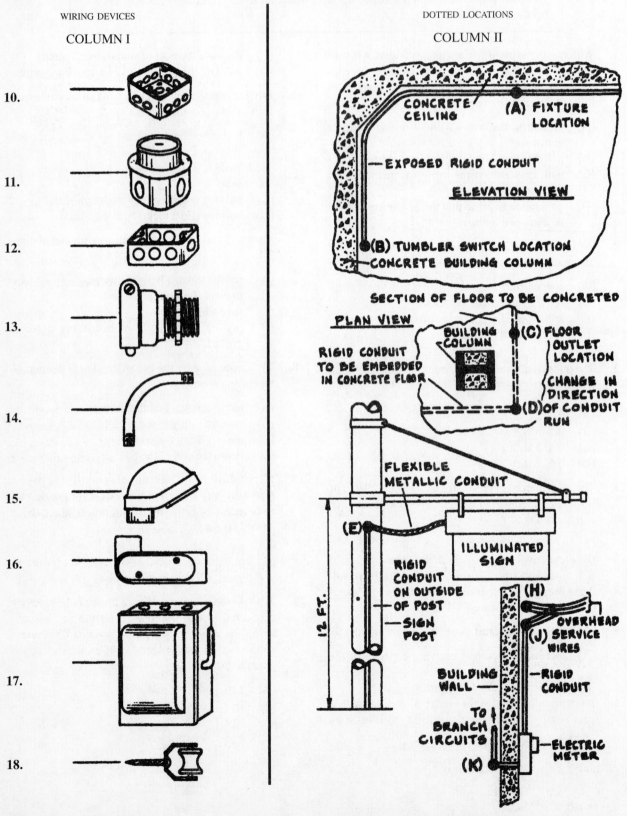

10. _____

11. _____

12. _____

13. _____

14. _____

15. _____

16. _____

17. _____

18. _____

CONCRETE CEILING (A) FIXTURE LOCATION

— EXPOSED RIGID CONDUIT

ELEVATION VIEW

(B) TUMBLER SWITCH LOCATION
CONCRETE BUILDING COLUMN

SECTION OF FLOOR TO BE CONCRETED

PLAN VIEW

BUILDING COLUMN (C) FLOOR OUTLET LOCATION

RIGID CONDUIT TO BE EMBEDDED IN CONCRETE FLOOR

CHANGE IN DIRECTION (D) OF CONDUIT RUN

FLEXIBLE METALLIC CONDUIT

(E) ILLUMINATED SIGN

RIGID CONDUIT ON OUTSIDE OF POST
SIGN POST

12 FT.

(H)
OVERHEAD (J) SERVICE WIRES

BUILDING WALL —

—RIGID CONDUIT

TO BRANCH CIRCUITS

(K)

—ELECTRIC METER

19. To support conduit on a hollow tile wall, use

   (A) through-bolts.
   (B) lag screws.
   (C) machine screws.
   (D) toggle bolts.

20. In Figure 20, if each circuit originates at the switch-board, the total amount of wire required for the conduit runs shown (neglecting connections) is

   (A) 5,300 feet.
   (B) 2,650 feet.
   (C) 2,400 feet.
   (D) 1,600 feet.

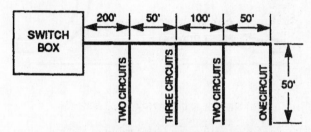

NOTE: TWO WIRES PER CIRCUIT

Figure 20

21. According to the National Electrical Code, a run of conduit between two outlet boxes should not contain more than four quarter-bends. The most likely reason for this limitation is that more bends will

   (A) result in cracking the conduit.
   (B) make the pulling of the wire too difficult.
   (C) increase the wire length unnecessarily.
   (D) not be possible in one standard length of conduit.

22. Standard iron conduit comes in 10-foot lengths. The number of such lengths required for a run of 23 yards is

   (A) 3   (C) 6
   (B) 4   (D) 7

23. Rigid conduit is generally secured to sheet metal outlet boxes by means of

   (A) threadless couplings.
   (B) box connectors.
   (A) locknuts and bushings.
   (B) conduit clamps.

24. Checking a piece of rigid electrical conduit with a steel scale, you measure the inside diameter as $1\frac{1}{16}''$ and the outside diameter as $1\frac{5}{16}''$. The nominal size of this conduit is

   (A) $\frac{3}{4}''$
   (B) $1''$
   (C) $1\frac{1}{4}''$
   (D) $1\frac{1}{2}''$

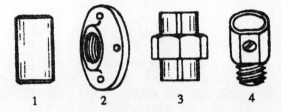

Figure 25

25. In Figure 25, the standard coupling for rigid electrical conduit is

   (A) 1   (C) 3
   (B) 2   (D) 4

26. Where galvanized steel conduit is used, the primary purpose of the galvanizing is to

   (A) increase mechanical strength.
   (B) retard rusting.
   (C) provide a good surface for painting.
   (D) provide good electrical contact for grounding.

27. When a number of insulated wires are being pulled into a run of conduit having several sharp bends between the two pull boxes, the pulling is likely to be hard and the wires are subjected to considerable strain. For these reasons, it is advisable in such a case to

   (A) push the wires into the feed end of the conduit at the same time that pulling is being done.
   (B) pull in only one wire at a time.
   (C) use extra heavy grease.
   (D) pull the wires back a few inches after each forward pull to gain momentum.

28. The six wires shown in Figure 28 are to be properly connected so that the lighting fixture can be controlled by a single-pole on-off switch. The correct connections in accordance with established good practice are

   (A) 1 to 3 and 5; 2 to 4 and 6.
   (B) 1 to 5; 2 to 3; 4 to 6.
   (C) 1 to 3 and 6; 2 to 4 and 5.
   (D) 1 to 3; 4 to 5; 2 to 6.

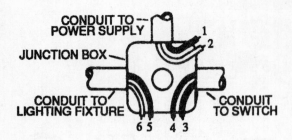

Figure 28

29. Rigid conduit must be so installed as to prevent the collection of water in it between outlets. In order to meet this requirement, the conduit should NOT have a

(A) low point between successive outlets.
(B) high point between successive outlets.
(C) low point at an outlet.
(D) high point at an outlet.

30. One advantage of cutting 1″ rigid conduit with a hacksaw rather than with a 3-wheel pipe cutter is that

(A) the cut can be made with less exertion.
(B) the pipe is not squeezed out of round.
(C) less reaming is required after the cut.
(D) no vise is needed.

31. When a long thread is used on one of two pieces of conduit joined by a coupling secured with a lock nut as indicated in Figure 31, the probable reason for the use of this long thread is that

(A) one piece of conduit has been cut too short.
(B) expansion or contraction of conduit due to temperature changes has to be compensated for.
(C) neither conduit was free to turn when the coupling was made.
(D) the joint has to be firmly anchored in a concrete wall.

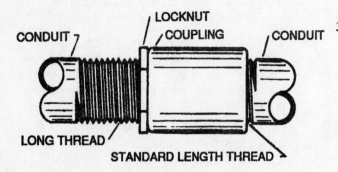

Figure 31

32. If each of the four 90° conduit elbows in Figure 32 has the dimensions shown, the distance S is

(A) 20″   (C) 24″
(B) 22″   (D) 26″

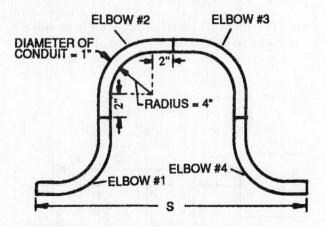

Figure 32

33. Figure 33 shows four standard rigid electrical conduit sizes in cross-section. The one that is nominal $\frac{1}{2}$-inch conduit is No.

(A) 1   (C) 3
(B) 2   (D) 4

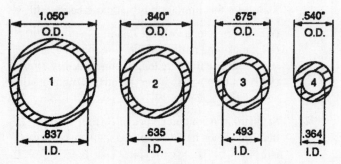

Figure 33

34. The National Electrical Code requires that conduit must be continuous from outlet to outlet, must be mechanically and electrically connected to all fittings, and must be suitably grounded. The reason for having the conduit electrically continuous and grounded is to

(A) provide a metallic return conductor.
(B) shield the wires inside the conduit from external magnetic fields.
(C) make it easy to test wiring connections.
(D) prevent electrical shock that might otherwise result from contact with the conduit.

35. A conduit coupling is sometimes tightened by using a strap wrench rather than by using a Stillson wrench. The strap wrench is used when it is important to avoid

- (A) crushing the conduit.
- (B) stripping the pipe threads.
- (C) bending the conduit.
- (D) damaging the outside finish.

36. A standard pipe thread differs from a standard screw thread in that the pipe thread

- (A) is tapered.
- (B) is deeper.
- (C) requires no lubrication when cutting.
- (D) has the same pitch for any diameter of pipe.

37. Offset nipples are designed to

- (A) connect conduit to a box when the knockout and conduit run do not line up.
- (B) connect conduit to a box when the knockout and conduit run line up.
- (C) terminate conduit runs.
- (D) enlarge vital fittings.

38. Offset nipples may also be used to

- (A) terminate conduit runs.
- (B) enlarge vital fittings.
- (C) connect two boxes side by side when their respective knockouts do not line up.
- (D) connect two boxes side by side when their respective knockouts do line up.

39. No-bolt fixture stems are used with

- (A) hang-on hangers.
- (B) straight nipples.
- (C) offset nipples.
- (D) outlet boxes.

40. Tiger grip locknuts attach a piece of conduit or a connector into a knockout opening in a

- (A) flexible wire mesh.
- (B) metal box.
- (C) sealtite conduit.
- (A) hazardous location.

41. The maximum number of bends allowed with EMT is limited to

- (A) not over 360° of bends between raceway ends.
- (B) less than 100° of bends between raceway ends.
- (C) four in total.
- (D) three at the most.

42. PVC conduit is

- (A) plastic tubing.
- (B) flexible tubing.
- (C) rigid and threaded.
- (D) self-grounding.

ANSWER KEY

1.	A	7.	D	12.	E	19.	D	25.	A	31.	C	37.	A
2.	B	8.	B	13.	D	20.	A	26.	B	32.	D	38.	C
3.	D	9.	A	14.	J	21.	B	25.	A	33.	B	39.	D
4.	D	10.	A	16.	E	22.	D	26.	D	34.	D	40.	B
5.	B	11.	C	17.	K	23.	C	27.	A	35.	D	41.	A
6.	B	12.	B	18.	H	24.	B	30.	C	36.	A	42.	A

LIGHTING AND WIRING

> **DIRECTIONS:** For each question, read all choices carefully. Then select the answer that you consider correct or most nearly correct. Write the letter preceding your best choice next to the question.

1. After a new series lighting circuit has been completely installed but before any lamps are in place, a standard lamp bank is connected across the fuse clips with the fuse out, and the circuit switch is closed. Lamps are then screwed into the sockets of one series, one lamp at a time, starting at the ground end. If there is a ground on any series wire, the lamp bank will light when the

   (A) first lamp is screwed in.
   (B) lamp on the low side of the ground is screwed in.
   (C) lamp on the high side of the ground is screwed in.
   (D) last lamp is screwed in.

2. The grounded leg of a lighting circuit is always connected to the shells of the lighting sockets to

   (A) ground the circuit.
   (B) reduce the possibility of accidental shock.
   (C) simplify the wiring.
   (D) avoid burning out lamps.

3. Light fixtures suspended from chains should be wired so that the

   (A) wires do not support the fixture.
   (B) wires help support the fixture.
   (C) chains have an insulated link.
   (D) chain is not grounded to prevent short circuits.

4. Portable lamp cord is likely to have

   (A) steel armor.
   (B) stranded wires.
   (C) paper insulation.
   (D) No. 8 wire.

5. A test lamp using an ordinary lamp bulb is commonly used to test

   (A) for polarity of a DC power supply.
   (B) whether a power supply is AC or DC.
   (C) whether a circuit is overloaded.
   (D) for grounds on 120-volt circuits.

6. One advantage of DC lighting is

   (A) the ease of locating a burnt-out lamp.
   (B) the possibility of using five-lamp clusters where necessary.

   (C) there is no necessity of providing a special lighting transformer.
   (D) one side of the circuit is grounded.

7. When testing a lighting circuit for grounds, the device that would be LEAST useful is

   (A) a lamp bank.
   (B) a megger.
   (C) an ammeter.
   (D) a voltmeter.

8. One advantage of using series circuits for street lighting is

   (A) lower voltage circuit.
   (B) decreased copper requirement.
   (C) longer lamp life.
   (D) higher lamp efficiency.

9. Five 120-volt lamps are placed in series across a 600-volt circuit and light normally. One of the lamps is then removed and replaced with a good plug fuse. Under these conditions, the total illumination supplied by the remaining four lamps will be

   (A) greater than for the five lamps.
   (B) less than for the five lamps.
   (C) approximately the same as for the five lamps.
   (D) zero because the lamps will burn out almost immediately.

10. In the diagram in Figure 10, the lamps that are lighted with normal brightness are

    (A) 1 and 4 only.
    (B) 1 and 3 only.
    (C) 1 and 2 only.
    (D) only 1.

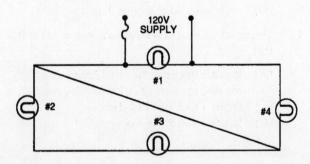

Figure 10

11. Your helper suggests that in order to increase the amount of light on the job you are doing, you should substitute two 100-watt lamps for two of the 40-watt lamps in the 5-lamp bank you are using. If you follow this suggestion, the result will be that (in a 120V circuit connected in parallel)

    (A) all five lamps will burn at normal brightness.
    (B) all five lamps will be very dim.
    (C) the two 100-watt lamps will be dim, and the other three will be very bright.
    (D) the two 100-watt lamps will be very bright, and the other three will be dim.

12. Two 120-volt lamps are connected in series across a 120-volt battery that is ungrounded. The common connection of the lamps is grounded. If the lamp that is connected directly to the negative side of the battery should have a broken filament, a ground fault on the negative side of the battery would be indicated by

    (A) both lamps being dark.
    (B) the good lamp being lighted at full brilliancy.
    (C) the good lamp being short-circuited.
    (D) the good lamp being lighted at approximately half brilliancy.

Questions 13–18 are based on Figure 13, a diagram of portions of two series lighting circuits carried in a single conduit. Refer to this sketch in answering these items.

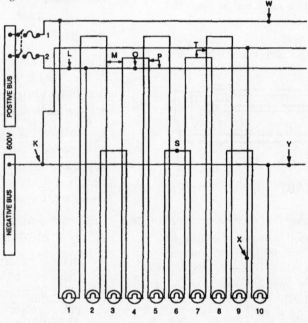

Figure 13

13. One indication of a cross between the two wires at M is that

    (A) the five lamps of circuit No. 1 will be dark.
    (B) the five lamps of circuit No. 2 will be dark.
    (C) only lamp No. 2 will be dark.
    (D) only lamp No. 3 will be dark.

14. One result of a cross between the two wires at P is that

    (A) the fuse of circuit No. 1 will blow out.
    (B) the fuse of circuit No. 2 will blow out.
    (C) lamps 1 and 3 will be dark.
    (D) lamps 1 and 3 will burn out.

15. Of the lamps shown, the fewest will become dark if there is an open circuit at

    (A) K.   (C) S.
    (B) L.   (D) W.

16. Of the lamps shown, the greatest number will be affected by a ground at

    (A) K.   (C) X.
    (B) L.   (D) Y.

17. If the two wires at T become crossed,

    (A) lamps 8 and 10 will become very dim.
    (B) lamp 9 will become very dim.
    (C) the fuse for circuit 2 will burn out.
    (D) the fuse for circuit 1 will burn out.

18. If each lamp takes a current of 0.35 ampere, the current in the wire from X to K, due only to the lamps shown, is

(A) zero.
(B) 0.35 ampere.
(C) 1.75 amperes.
(D) 3.50 amperes.

19. A bank of five similar 120-volt lamps in series was to be used across a 600-volt line to furnish illumination. When connected across the 600-volt source, the first lamp remained dark and the other lamps lit up extra brilliant for a few moments and then went dark. The probable cause of this action was that

(A) the line voltage was too low to light all lamps.
(B) the socket of the first lamp had an open circuit.
(C) all lamps were defective.
(D) the socket of the first lamp was shorted.

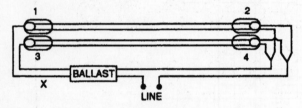

Figure 20

Questions 20–25 refer to the standard lighting fixture in Figure 20 using 72-inch, T-12, "slimline" fluorescent lamps that are fed from a 120-volt, 60-hertz, AC line and are connected as shown in the above sketch. Under normal operating conditions, each lamp takes a current of 425 mA and draws 55 watts, while the ballast loss is 34 watts.

20. The "high voltage" sockets are

(A) 1 and 2.   (C) 2 and 4.
(B) 1 and 3.   (D) 3 and 4.

21. The actual line current taken by the fixture in normal operation is about 1.6 amperes, while the current calculated from the given voltage and wattage is about 1.2 amperes. This difference indicates that the

(A) ballast must require considerable leakage current.
(B) line voltage is usually more than 120 volts.
(C) power factor of the equipment is less than 1.0.
(D) information given is only a rough approximation.

22. If a 0-5 amp. AC ammeter were connected in series with line X, the reading of the meter with the lamps operating would be

(A) 0.43   (C) 1.6
(B) 0.85   (D) 4.25

23. Two wires are connected to each of sockets 2 and 4 in order to provide for

(A) heating of the lamp filaments.
(B) breaking the circuit when the lamps are removed.
(C) operation of the starters.
(D) dependable continuity of service.

24. The highest open-circuit voltage in the type of installation shown is approximately

(A) 200 volts.   (C) 600 volts.
(B) 400 volts.   (D) 800 volts.

25. Of the ten lamps in two adjacent 5-lamp series that are connected to the same circuit, four of the lamps are uniformly bright and the other six are uniformly dim. A possible cause of this condition is that

(A) two sizes of lamp have been used.
(B) one socket in each series is partially short circuited.
(C) there is a cross between the two series.
(D) there is a ground on one of the series.

26. In order to use fluorescent lighting in a building that has only a 110-volt DC supply, it is necessary to use

(A) fluorescent lamps designed for DC.
(B) fluorescent fixtures with an approved DC auxiliary or inductance unit and a series resistance of the correct value.
(C) fluorescent fixtures ordinarily used on AC.
(D) fluorescent fixtures ordinarily used on AC but equipped with a rectifier.

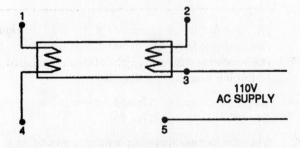

Figure 27

The glow type starter used to operate a fluorescent lamp is designed to act as a time switch that will connect the two filament-type electrodes in each end of the lamp in series with the ballast during the short preheating period when the lamp is first turned on. The starter will then open the circuit to establish the arc.

The following questions, numbered 27 and 28, are to be answered in keeping with the above statement and Figure 27, which is an incomplete diagram of the connections of a fluorescent lamp. *The ballast and starter are not shown.*

27. From the above statement, the competent electrician's helper should know that the starter should be shown connected between points

    (A) 4 and 3.   (C) 4 and 5.

    (B) 1 and 2.   (D) 3 and 5.

28. From the above statement, the competent electrician's helper should know that the choke of the ballast should be shown connected between points

    (A) 4 and 3.   (C) 4 and 5.

    (B) 1 and 2.   (D) 3 and 5.

Questions 29–34 refer to Figure 29 and symbols for an incandescent lighting system installation. Refer to the sketch and symbols in answering these items. Assume a spacing of 10 feet between lighting fixtures, a distance of 75 feet from the lighting panel to the first fixture in each group, and that each circuit will be completely independent.

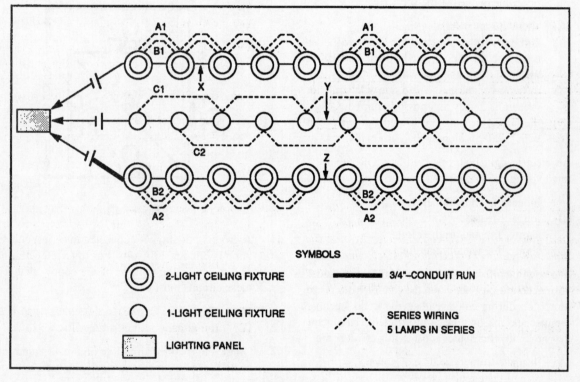

Figure 29

29. The number of standard lengths of conduit required for this job is about

    (A) 24   (C) 51

    (B) 27   (D) 78

30. When the extension is in operation, a ground on a negative wire at "X" will

    (A) blow one circuit fuse.

    (B) blow two circuit fuses.

    (C) cause the series farthest from the panel to be dark.

    (D) have no appreciable effect on the performance of the installation.

31. The number of wires in the conduit at "Z" will be

    (A) 3   (C) 5

    (B) 4   (D) 6

32. The number of switches used to control the extension of the lighting system will be

    (A) 3   (C) 5

    (B) 4   (D) 6

33. When the extension is in operation, a ground on the series wire of circuit C1 at "Y" will

    (A) darken two lamps and cause three to be abnormally bright.
    (B) darken three lamps and cause two to be abnormally bright.
    (C) blow the circuit fuse.
    (D) have no appreciable effect on the performance of the installation.

34. The length of red wire needed for this job is about

    (A) 350 feet.　　(C) 1,200 feet.
    (B) 500 feet.　　(D) 1,750 feet.

35. An unbalanced load of incandescent lamps is connected on a 3-wire DC circuit. If the neutral wire should become opened at the service,

    (A) all the lamps will be extinguished.
    (B) nothing will happen, and the lamps will continue to burn at the same brilliancy as before the neutral became opened.
    (C) the lamps on the less loaded side will burn with greater brilliancy and possibly burn out.
    (D) the lamps on the more loaded side will burn with greater brilliancy than originally.

36. An electric light bulb operated at MORE than its rated voltage will result in a

    (A) longer life and dimmer light.
    (B) longer life and brighter light.
    (C) shorter life and brighter light.
    (D) shorter life and dimmer light.

37. In a bowling alley, the lighting is satisfactory under normal conditions, but when the electric heaters are turned on during cold weather, the lights become dimmer and the lighting is insufficient. The factor that probably contributes most to this effect is the

    (A) distance from the source of power.
    (B) size of the circuit fuses.
    (C) current taken by the lamps.
    (D) size of the circuit conductor.

38. A certain lighting circuit is now wired with No. 14 AWG wire. Additional lamps to be added to the circuit will increase the current beyond the capacity of this size wire, The wire of equal length and the same material required to replace the No. 14 wire will have

    (A) greater weight and lower resistance.
    (B) less weight and lower resistance.
    (C) greater weight and higher resistance.
    (D) less weight and higher resistance.

39. A certain five-lamp series cluster has 36-watt lamps installed. If these lamps are replaced with five 100-watt lamps, the result will be that the

    (A) fuse for the circuit will blow.
    (B) lamps will burn out very quickly.
    (C) amount of light will be increased.
    (D) lamps will be very dim.

40. The five lamps shown in Figure 40 are each rated at 120-volts, 60-watts. If all are good lamps, lamp No. 5 will be

    (A) much brighter than normal.
    (B) about its normal brightness.
    (C) much dimmer than normal.
    (D) completely dark.

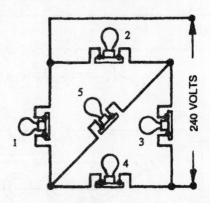

Figure 40

41. A group of 5 lamps is connected in series, and each lamp is rated at 130 volts. For full voltage burning of the lamps, the voltage of the supply that feeds these circuits must be

    (A) 650 volts.　　(C) 130 volts.
    (B) 260 volts.　　(D) 26 volts.

42. On the ungrounded circuit, in Figure 42, lamps connected as shown would normally be used to

    (A) provide a grounded neutral.
    (B) indicate an accidental ground on either line.
    (C) show whether or not the line is alive.
    (D) indicate which line fuse is blown.

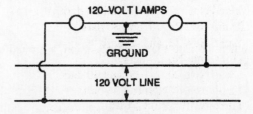

Figure 42

43. Twenty-two lamps are all connected in a single-series circuit that is fed at 600 volts. The voltage rating of each individual lamp in the series must be approximately

(A) 600 volts.   (C) 30 volts.

(B) 120 volts.   (D) 22 volts.

44. The most satisfactory temporary replacement for a 40-watt, 120-volt incandescent lamp, if an identical replacement is not available, is a lamp rated at

(A) 100 watts, 240 volts.

(B) 60 watts, 130 volts.

(C) 40 watts, 32 volts.

(D) 15 watts, 120 volts.

45. If the applied voltage on an incandescent lamp is increased 10 percent, the lamp will

(A) have a longer life.

(B) consume less power.

(C) burn more brightly.

(D) fail by insulation breakdown.

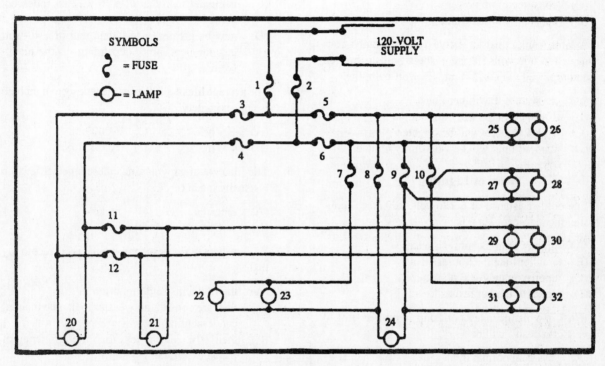

Figure 46

Items 46–54 are based on Figure 46. All of the lamps are normally lighted. The items in Column I are descriptions of abnormal conditions, each of which is caused by one of the faults listed in Column II. For each item in Column I, select the most likely fault from Column II.

ABNORMAL CONDITIONS

COLUMN I

46. Lamp Nos. 24, 27, 28, 31, and 32 dark

47. Lamp Nos. 27, 28, 31, and 32 dark

48. Lamp Nos. 21, 29, and 30 dark

49. Lamp Nos. 22, and 23 dark

50. Only lamp No. 24 dark

51. Lamp Nos. 20, 21, 29, and 30 dark

52. Lamp Nos. 22, 23, and 24 dark

53. Lamp Nos. 22, 23, 24, 25, 26, 27, 28, 31, and 32 dark

54. Only lamp No. 20 dark

FAULTS

COLUMN II

(A) Either fuse No. 11 or fuse No. 12 blown

(B) Fuse No. 9 blown

(C) Fuse No. 10 blown

(D) Lamp burned out

(E) Either fuse No. 9 or fuse No. 10 blown

(H) Either fuse No. 5 or fuse No. 6 blown

(J) Fuse No. 8 blown

(K) Fuse No. 7 blown

(L) Either fuse No. 3 or fuse No. 4 blown

(M) Either fuse No. 1 or fuse No. 2 blown

55. To test whether a 110-volt lighting circuit is alive,

    (A) touch each wire in turn to ground.
    (B) touch the ends of the wires together.
    (C) use a voltmeter across the line.
    (D) use an ammeter across the line.

56. If two identical lamps normally connected in parallel to a 110-volt line are reconnected to be in series across the same line, they will

    (A) give more light.
    (B) give less light.
    (C) consume more power.
    (D) consume the same amount of power.

57. A lamp bank consists of five 100-watt bulbs connected to 600 volts. If one of these bulbs is broken and replaced with a 25-watt, 120-volt bulb, the

    (A) 25-watt bulb will burn out.
    (B) 100-watt bulbs will burn out.
    (C) 100-watt bulbs will be brighter.
    (D) 25-watt bulb will be very dimly lighted.

Types of Lighting

58. The cold resistance of a 120-volt, 100-watt Tungsten incandescent lamp is

    (A) greater than its hot resistance.
    (B) smaller than the hot resistance.
    (C) approximately 100 ohms.
    (D) equal to the hot resistance.

59. If a 120-volt incandescent lamp is burned at 130 volts, the result will be

    (A) less than normal light.
    (B) shorter lamp life.
    (C) a blown circuit fuse.
    (D) decreased lamp efficiency.

60. The resistance of the tungsten filament in any incandescent lamp is

    (A) highest when the lamp is off.
    (B) highest when the lamp is on.
    (C) lowest when the lamp is on.
    (D) approximately the same at all times.

61. With respect to common electric light bulbs, it is correct to state that the

    (A) circuit voltage has no effect on the life of the bulb.
    (B) filament is made of carbon.
    (C) base has a left-hand thread.
    (D) lower wattage bulb has the higher resistance.

62. When an incandescent lamp to be used for general lighting has a mogul base, it is a positive indication that it is rated at over

    (A) 200 watts.   (C) 500 watts.
    (B) 300 watts.   (D) 750 watts.

63. The efficiency in lumens per watt of a 10-watt fluorescent lamp

    (A) is less than that of a 40-watt incandescent lamp.
    (B) is the same as that of a 40-watt incandescent lamp.
    (C) is greater than that of a 40-watt incandescent lamp.
    (D) may be greater or less than that of a 40-watt incandescent lamp, depending on the manufacture.

64. The average life of a 100-watt incandescent light bulb is approximately

    (A) 100 hrs.   (C) 1,000 hrs.
    (B) 400 hrs.   (D) 10,000 hrs.

65. The filament of a regular incandescent electric lamp is usually made of

    (A) tungsten.   (C) nickel.
    (B) carbon.   (D) iron.

66. With respect to fluorescent lamps, it is correct to say that

    (A) the filaments seldom burn out.
    (B) they are considerably easier to handle than incandescent lamps.
    (C) their efficiency is less than the efficiency of incandescent lamps.
    (D) the starters and the lamps must be replaced at the same time.

67. A method that is sometimes used to increase the useful life of incandescent lamps is to

    (A) burn at less than rated voltage.
    (B) burn at more than rated voltage.
    (C) turn the lamps off when not needed.
    (D) prohibit the use of shades.

68. One disadvantage in using fluorescent instead of incandescent lighting is that, compared to incandescent lamps, fluorescent lamps

    (A) are more difficult to handle.
    (B) provide less light for the same power.
    (C) give more glare.
    (D) have shorter lives.

69. Fluorescent lamps compared to incandescent lamps

(A) emit more lumens per watt.
(B) are more adversely affected by vibratory conditions.
(C) are less critical to voltage dips or variations.
(D) cannot be adapted to DC operation.

70. The inert gas present in an incandescent lamp is primarily intended to

(A) increase the luminous output.
(B) decrease filament evaporation.
(C) activate the surface of the filament.
(D) reduce the hazards when the glass is shattered.

71. A fluorescent lamp is a(n)

(A) heat resistance device.
(B) arc-discharge device.
(C) cold gas tube.
(D) hot gas tube.

72. Fluorescent lamps limit current through the glowing tube by using

(A) an inductor. (C) a capacitor.
(B) a resistor. (D) a filament.

73. A pre-heat, or switch start, circuit is used with

(A) incandescent lamps.
(B) instant-start lamps.
(C) mercury lamps.
(D) fluorescent lamps.

74. Duty cycle means

(A) the minimum life expectancy of fluorescent ballasts.
(B) the median life expectancy of fluorescent ballasts.
(C) the maximum life expectancy of fluorescent ballasts.

(D) how often the bulb is turned on and off

75. The unsupported length of liquidtight flex is acceptable at

(A) 3-foot intervals.
(B) terminations.
(C) 6-foot intervals.
(D) 4-to-6 foot intervals.

76. Metal wireways are sheet-metal _____ in which conductors are laid in place after the wireways have been installed in a complete system.

(A) valleys (C) troughs
(B) tubes (D) cable holders

77. Wireways are made in 1,2,3,4,5, and _____- foot standard lengths so no cutting of the duct is necessary.

(A) 20 (C) 50
(B) 30 (D) 10

78. The NEC says that wireway used for circuit conductors for an elevator or escalator may be filled with any number of wires, up to _____ percent of the interior cross section of the wireway.

(A) 10 (C) 40
(B) 20 (D) 50

79. In no case should the distance between supports for wireways exceed

(A) 10 feet. (C) 30 feet.
(B) 20 feet. (D) 40 feet.

80. Round nonmetallic outlet boxes may be used only with

(A) NM cable. (C) PVC.
(B) conduit. (D) rigid conduit.

ANSWER KEY

1.	D	11.	A	21.	C	31.	B	41.	A	51.	L	61.	D	71.	B
2.	B	12.	B	22.	A	32.	D	42.	B	52.	J	62.	B	72.	A
3.	A	13.	D	23.	B	33.	A	43.	C	53.	H	63.	C	73.	D
4.	B	14.	C	24.	C	34.	B	44.	B	54.	D	64.	C	74.	B
5.	D	15.	D	25.	C	35.	C	45.	C	55.	C	65.	A	75.	B
6.	C	16.	B	26.	B	36.	C	46.	B	56.	B	66.	A	76.	C
7.	C	17.	A	27.	B	37.	D	47.	C	57.	A	67.	A	77.	D
8.	B	18.	B	28.	C	38.	A	48.	A	58.	B	68.	A	78.	D
9.	A	19.	D	29.	C	39.	C	49.	K	59.	B	69.	A	79.	A
10.	A	20.	B	30.	D	40.	D	50.	D	60.	B	70.	B	80.	A

WIRING SPECIAL SYSTEMS

DIRECTIONS: For each question, read all choices carefully. Then select the answer that you consider correct or most nearly correct. Write the letter preceding your best choice next to the question.

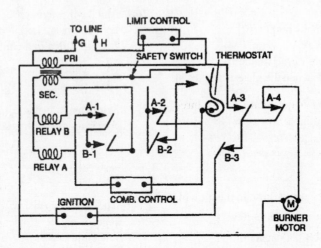

Figure 1

1. When the thermostat in Figure 1 calls for heat,

   (A) relay A is energized, bringing in the motor only.
   (B) relay A is energized, bringing in the ignition only.
   (C) relay A is energized, bringing in the motor and ignition.
   (D) relay B is first energized.

2. Momentary power failure while the burner in Figure 1 is in operation causes

   (A) both relays to drop out.
   (B) relay A to drop out only.
   (C) relay B to drop out only.
   (D) the relay to go out on safety.

3. An interior fire-alarm system best suited to the needs of such buildings as hospitals, public schools, institutions, etc., would be an

   (A) open-circuit, noncode, nonsupervised system.
   (B) closed-circuit, noncode, supervised system.
   (C) closed-circuit, box code, supervised system.
   (D) closed-circuit, box code, presignal, supervised system.

4. Interior fire-alarm systems may be divided into

   (A) two basic groups—pre-signal and dual.
   (B) 1 group only—open-circuit.

   (C) 1 group only—closed-circuit.
   (D) two basic groups—open-circuit and closed-circuit.

5. An open-circuit type of interior fire-alarm system consists of

   (A) vibrating gongs and break-glass stations.
   (B) single-stroke gongs and break-glass stations.
   (C) vibrating gongs and coded stations.
   (D) electrically supervised gongs and boxes.

6. Modem approved closed-circuit fire-alarm systems should have which of the following trouble indicators?

   (A) Trouble light only
   (B) Milliammeter only
   (C) Trouble bell only
   (D) Milliammeter, time limit device, and trouble bell and light

7. An approved closed-circuit type of interior fire alarm should consist of

   (A) mechanical gongs and coded stations.
   (B) vibrating gongs and coded stations.
   (C) electrically supervised gongs and stations and may or may not be coded.
   (D) single-stroke gongs and strap key.

8. The electric energy required to raise the temperature of the water in a pool is 1,000 kWh. The heat losses are 25 percent. The total heating energy required is

   (A) 1,000 kWh.   (C) 1,333 kWh.
   (B) 1,250 kWh.   (D) 1,500 kWh.

9. A 6,000-watt, 3-phase heater composed of three resistance units in delta is connected to a 3-phase, 208-volt supply. The resistance, in ohms, of each resistance unit is most nearly

   (A) 20.8   (C) 83.2
   (B) 41.6   (D) 208

10. Based upon the data given in question 11, if the three heater resistance units are now connected in star (or wye) to a 3-phase, 208-volt supply, the power, in watts, consumed by this heater is most nearly

    (A) 10,400   (C) 3,500
    (B) 6,000   (D) 2,000

11. A resistor is connected across a supply of "E" volts. The heat produced in this resistor is proportional to I^2R. If R is reduced in value, the heat produced in this resistor now

    (A) increases.
    (B) decreases.

   (C) remains the same.
   (D) is indeterminate.

12. An AC current of one ampere RMS flowing through a resistance of 10 ohms has the same heating value as a DC current of

    (A) one ampere flowing through a 10-ohm resistance.
    (B) one ampere flowing through a 5-ohm resistance.
    (C) two amperes flowing through a 10-ohm resistance.
    (A) five amperes flowing through a 1-ohm resistance.

13. The NEC says NM cable, including the sheath, must extend at least _____ inches into every box through a K.O. designed for NM.

    (A) 0.25   (C) 1.0
    (B) 0.50   (D) 1.5

14. NM cable must be clamped to all non-metallic boxes that are not _____ gang boxes.

    (A) double   (C) single
    (B) triple   (D) round

ANSWER KEY

1. C	4. D	7. C	10. D	13. A
2. A	5. A	8. C	11. A	14. C
3. D	6. D	9. A	12. A	

ELECTRIC MOTORS

> **DIRECTIONS:** For each question, read all choices carefully. Then select the answer that you consider correct or most nearly correct. Write the letter preceding your best choice next to the question.

TYPES

General Questions

1. The most common type of motor that can be used with both AC and DC sources is the

   (A) repulsion motor.
   (B) series motor.
   (C) rotary converter.
   (D) shunt motor.

2. One type of electric motor tends to "run away" if it is not always connected to its load. This motor is the

   (A) DC series.
   (B) DC shunt.
   (C) AC induction.
   (D) AC synchronous.

3. A motor that will not operate on DC is the

   (A) series motor.
   (B) shunt motor.
   (C) induction motor.
   (D) compound motor.

Items 4–8 in Column I are various kinds of electrical machines, each with a DC field that is made variable *for one of the specific purposes given in Column II. For each item in Column I, select the specific purpose for which the field is made variable from Column II.*

MACHINES WITH VARIABLE DC FIELDS

SPECIFIC PURPOSES

COLUMN I

4. DC motor
5. Rotary converter
6. Synchronous motor
7. AC generator
8. DC generator

COLUMN II

(A) to change the voltage
(B) to change the speed
(C) to change the power factor
(D) to change the frequency

9. The type of motor that does NOT have a commutator is the

   (A) synchronous.   (C) squirrel cage.
   (B) shunt.   (D) series.

DC, Series, and Shunt Motors

10. The torque of a shunt motor varies as

    (A) the armature current.
    (B) the square of the armature current.
    (C) the cube of the armature current.
    (D) the cube of the field current.

11. If the field of a shunt motor while running under no load opens, the motor will

    (A) stop running immediately.
    (B) continue to run at a very slow speed.

    (C) run away.
    (D) gradually slow down until it stops.

12. In a 5-HP, 220-volt shunt motor rated at 19.2 amperes and 1,500 rpm, the armature resistance is

    (A) smaller than that of the shunt field.
    (B) larger than that of the shunt field.
    (C) the same as that of the shunt field.
    (D) always half as large as that of the shunt field.

13. Comparing the shunt field winding with the series field winding of a compound DC motor, it would be correct to say that the shunt field winding has

    (A) more turns but the lower resistance.
    (B) more turns and the higher resistance.
    (C) fewer turns and the lower resistance.
    (D) fewer turns but the higher resistance.

14. In selecting a starting box for a DC shunt motor, it would be necessary to know the motor

 (A) shunt field resistance and field current.
 (B) armature resistance and full-load current.
 (C) full-load current and speed.
 (D) field current, full-load current, and speed.

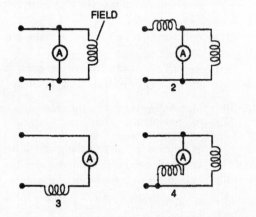

Figure 15

15. Each of the four sketches in Figure 15 shows the proper schematic connections for one kind of DC motor. The one showing the connections for a shunt motor is number

 (A) 1   (C) 3
 (B) 2   (D) 4

16. It is desired to run a DC shunt motor at a speed lower than its rated speed. The most practical way to accomplish this would be to connect a suitable resistance in

 (A) series with the field.
 (B) series with the armature.
 (C) parallel with the field.
 (D) parallel with the armature.

17. If the two line leads of a DC series motor are reversed, the motor will

 (A) not run.
 (B) run backward.
 (C) run the same as before.
 (D) become a generator.

18. In the selection of a direct-current motor,

 (A) a series motor should be chosen where the motor is operated at very light loads.
 (B) a series motor should be used where the required starting torque is low.
 (C) a series motor should be used where the required starting torque is high.

 (D) a shunt motor should be used where the starting torque required is high and it starts under loaded conditions.

19. In the case of a compound-wound DC motor operating at constant voltage with a very light load, increasing the resistance that is in series with the shunt field will

 (A) have no effect on the motor speed.
 (B) cause the motor to slow down.
 (C) cause the motor to either speed up or slow down, depending on the type of load.
 (D) cause the motor to speed up.

20. To change the direction of rotation of a cumulative wound DC motor, you must

 (A) reverse the connections to the armature.
 (B) reverse the connections to the shunt field.
 (C) reverse the connections to the series field.
 (D) do nothing, as it cannot be done.

21. Series-type motors for electrically driven rheostats or governors have a split series field

 (A) for better speed control.
 (B) to change the direction of rotation.
 (C) to produce a greater starting torque.
 (D) for more accurate voltage regulation.

22. To start a 7 1/2-hp, 220-volt, DC motor you should use a(n)

 (A) compensator.
 (B) across-the-line starter.
 (C) suitable starting box.
 (D) "Start-Run" switch.

23. In the DC series motor, when the load torque is decreased, the

 (A) armature rotates at a lower speed.
 (B) armature rotates at a higher speed.
 (C) current through the field is increased.
 (D) current through the armature is increased.

24. Series-type motors for electrically driven rheostats or governors have a split series field to

 (A) obtain low motor speed.
 (B) decrease the current consumption.
 (C) change the direction of rotation.
 (D) produce greater starting torque.

25. In the DC series motor, the field

 (A) has comparatively few turns of wire.
 (B) has comparatively many turns of wire.
 (C) is connected across the armature.
 (D) current is less than the line current.

26. To properly start a 15-hp, DC compound motor, you should use a

    (A) transformer.
    (B) 4-point starting rheostat.
    (C) compensator.
    (D) diverter.

27. The ordinary direct-current series motor does not operate satisfactorily with alternating current. One of the main reasons for this is

    (A) excessive heating due to eddy currents in the solid parts of the field structure.
    (B) that the armature current and field current are out of phase with each other.
    (C) that the field flux lags 120° in time phase with respect to the line voltage.
    (D) excessive heating due to the low voltage drop in the series field.

28. A DC elevator motor on a gearless traction machine has a series field for compounding during the acceleration period. This field is cut out when the motor has reached full speed for the purpose of

    (A) preventing excessive speed.
    (B) reducing the line current.
    (C) providing constant speed over a wide range of load conditions.
    (D) saving the cost of losses in the series field.

29. The temperature of the shunt field of a DC motor increases from 20°C to 60°C after 3 hours' operation. This increase in temperature of the field coils

    (A) will have no effect on the operation of the motor.
    (B) will tend to slow down the motor due to an increase in the resistance of the field coils.
    (C) will tend to speed up the motor due to an increase in resistance of the field coils.
    (D) will tend to slow down the motor due to a decrease in resistance of the field coils.

30. A DC series motor

    (A) cannot be used for driving loads that require high starting torque.
    (B) is a constant speed motor.
    (C) should be directly connected to its load.
    (D) may run away if its field becomes opened.

31. The total developed torque of a DC motor is dependent upon

    (A) the armature current and the flux per pole.
    (B) the speed of the motor.

    (C) the type of armature winding.
    (D) none of the above.

32. Which of the following statements is the most accurate concerning DC motors?

    (A) A lap-wound motor has two brushes regardless of the number of poles.
    (B) A series-wound motor has as many brushes as there are poles.
    (C) A lap-wound motor has as many brushes as there are poles.
    (D) Regardless of the type of armature winding, the number of parallel paths is always two.

33. Interpole windings in direct-current motors are used primarily

    (A) as a means for varying the speed of the motor.
    (B) to reduce armature reaction.
    (C) to increase the efficiency of the motor.
    (D) to compensate for field leakage.

34. The best way to start a large shunt motor is with

    (A) a weak field.
    (B) full voltage on the armature.
    (C) a compensator.
    (D) a strong field.

Induction and Polyphase Motors

35. If two of the three line leads to a three-phase squirrel-cage induction motor are interchanged, the motor will

    (A) reverse its direction of rotation.
    (B) be shorted.
    (C) not run.
    (D) run above synchronous speed.

36. One identifying feature of a squirrel-cage induction motor is that it has no

    (A) windings on the stationary part.
    (B) commutator or slip rings.
    (C) air gap.
    (D) iron core in the rotating part.

37. Large squirrel-cage induction motors are usually started at a voltage considerably lower than line voltage to

    (A) avoid excessive starting current.
    (B) obtain a low starting speed.
    (C) permit starting under full load.
    (D) allow the rotor current to build up gradually.

38. To reverse the direction of rotation of a 3-phase motor, it is necessary to

(A) increase the resistance of the rotor circuit.
(B) interchange all three line connections.
(C) interchange any two of the three line connections.
(D) reverse the polarity of the rotor circuit.

39. To reverse the direction of rotation of a split-phase motor, you would

(A) do nothing, as it cannot be done.
(B) reverse the main lines.
(C) reverse the polarity of all windings.
(D) reverse the polarity of the starting or auxiliary winding.

40. Speed control by a method that requires two wound-rotor induction motors with their rotors rigidly connected together is called speed control by

(A) change of poles.
(B) field control.
(C) concatenation.
(D) voltage control.

41. To properly start a 15-hp, 3-phase induction motor, you should use a

(A) shunt.
(B) 4-point starting rheostat.
(C) compensator.
(D) diverter.

42. To reverse the direction of rotation of a repulsion-induction motor, you should

(A) loosen the set screw and move the rocker arm to its proper place.
(B) interchange the terminal connections.
(C) increase the line voltage.
(D) do nothing, as it cannot be done.

43. Two possible connections, one incorrect, for reversing a wound-rotor, 3-phase induction motor are shown in Figure 43. The contactors are interlocked mechanically. The correct circuit and the proper interlock are given by which of the following items?

(A) Circuit A; both close together
(B) Circuit A; one closed, the other open
(C) Circuit B; both close together
(D) Circuit B; one closed, the other open

Figure 43

Other Types of Motors

44. A certain machine is driven by a 1750-rpm, DC, shunt motor. If the power supply is to be changed to 3-phase, 60-hertz, AC, the most suitable replacement motor would be a

(A) series motor.
(B) repulsion motor.
(C) squirrel-cage induction motor.
(D) capacitor motor.

45. The two small AC motors in Figure 45 are identical, but pinion 2 has twice the diameter of pinion 1. The motors are connected to the same power supply and are wired so that they normally tend to turn in *opposite* directions. When the power is first turned on,

(A) the motors will stall.
(B) both motors will turn at near normal speed in the same direction.
(C) motor 2 will turn in its normal direction, driving motor 1 backward.
(D) motor 1 will turn in its normal direction, driving motor 2 backward.

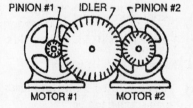

Figure 45

46. The correct method of measuring the power taken by an AC electric motor is to use a

(A) wattmeter.
(B) voltmeter and an ammeter.
(C) power factor meter.
(D) tachometer.

47. To start a $7\frac{1}{2}$ hp., 3-phase, 208-volt AC motor, you should use a(n)

    (A) "4-point" starting box.
    (B) "3-point" starting box.
    (C) M-G set.
    (D) across-the-line starter.

48. A repulsion motor is equipped with

    (A) slip rings.
    (B) a commutator.
    (C) neither a commutator nor slip rings.
    (D) both a commutator and slip rings.

49. The synchronous speed of an old 25 hertz, 10-pole motor is

    (A) 250 rpm.   (C) 150 rpm.
    (B) 600 rpm.   (D) 300 rpm.

50. Increasing the field excitation of a synchronous motor above its normal value when the load remains constant will

    (A) result in a leading power factor.
    (B) result in a lagging power factor.
    (C) result in either a leading or lagging power factor, depending on the kind of load.
    (D) have no effect on the power factor.

51. An advantage of a synchronous motor over a wound-rotor induction motor is that

    (A) its speed may be more readily controlled.
    (B) its speed does not depend on the frequency of the supply.
    (C) it has no brushes to contend with.
    (D) the power factor of the motor may be varied.

52. In a compound motor, the series field as compared with the shunt field

    (A) carries more current.
    (B) has higher resistance.
    (C) has finer wire.
    (D) has more turns of wire.

53. It would be accurate to state that

    (A) opening the series field of a compound motor accelerates the motor.
    (B) increasing the field excitation of a synchronous generator causes the power factor to become less lagging.
    (C) opening the shunt field of a shunt motor accelerates the motor.
    (D) decreasing the field excitation of a synchronous motor causes the power factor to become less lagging.

54. If you tried to start a compound motor in which the series field was open-circuited, the motor

    (A) would not start.
    (B) would blow the fuse.
    (C) would "run away."
    (D) would reverse.

55. The proper way to reverse the direction of rotation of a compound motor is to

    (A) interchange the line leads.
    (B) interchange the armature connections.
    (C) interchange the shunt field connections.
    (A) interchange the series field connections.

56. The NEC requires that branch circuit protection for motor circuits must protect the circuit conductors, the _____ apparatus, and the motor itself against overcurrent due to short circuits or ground.

    (A) branch   (C) switch
    (B) control   (D) motor

57. The Code requires that the 50-hp squirrel-cage motor must be protected at not more than

    (A) 50 A.   (C) 200 A.
    (B) 100 A.   (D) 300 A.

ANSWER KEY

1. B	9. C	16. B	23. B	30. C	37. A	44. C	51. D
2. A	10. A	17. C	24. C	31. A	38. C	45. D	52. A
3. C	11. C	18. C	25. A	32. C	39. D	46. A	53. C
4. B	12. A	19. D	26. B	33. B	40. C	47. B	54. A
5. C	13. B	20. A	27. A	34. D	41. C	48. B	55. B
6. C	14. B	21. B	28. C	35. A	42. A	49. D	56. B
7. A	15. A	22. C	29. C	36. B	43. B	50. A	57. C
8. A							

MOTOR OPERATION

> **DIRECTIONS:** For each question, read all choices carefully. Then select the answer that you consider correct or most nearly correct. Write the letter preceding your best choice next to the question.

Parts, Wiring, and Protective Devices

1. The gears most commonly used to connect two shafts that intersect are usually a form of

   (A) spur gears.
   (B) bevel gears.
   (C) spiral gears.
   (D) herringbone gears.

2. Assume that the field leads of a large, completely disconnected DC motor are not tagged or otherwise marked. You could readily tell the shunt field leads from the series field leads by the

   (A) length of the leads.
   (B) size of wire.
   (C) thickness of insulation.
   (D) type of insulation.

3. The circuit of Figure 3 shows a DC motor starter. One of the features of this starting box is a(n)

   (A) overload release.
   (B) no-field release.
   (C) reverse-current release.
   (D) underload release.

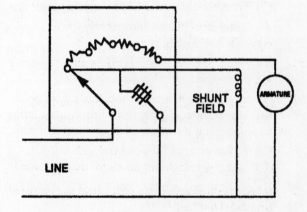

Figure 3

4. On motors with brakes, the brake magnet coil is

   (A) de-energized when current is fed to the motor.
   (B) energized when current is fed to the motor.
   (C) energized after the motor reaches normal speed.
   (D) de-energized after the motor reaches low speed.

5. The commutator bars of a motor are made of

   (A) mica.
   (B) carbon.
   (C) copper.
   (D) phosphor bronze.

6. If the speed of a synchronous motor connected to a 60-hertz power line is 1,200 RPM, the number of poles it must have is

(A) 2   (C) 6
(B) 4   (D) 8

7. Under load, the current in the armature conductors of a DC generator gives rise to an independent excitation that alters both the magnitude and distribution of the flux produced by the field alone. This magnetizing action of the armature is called

(A) armature reaction.
(B) dynamic braking.
(C) field reaction.
(D) radial excitation.

8. Pigtails are used on carbon brushes to

(A) hold the brush in the holder.
(B) supply the proper pressure.
(C) make a good electrical connection.
(D) compensate for wear.

9. When thermal overload relays are used for the protection of polyphase induction motors, their primary purpose is to protect the motors in case of

(A) reversal of phases in the supply.
(B) low line voltage.
(C) short circuit between phases.
(D) sustained overload.

10. The one of the following devices that is commonly used to prevent damage in case of reversal of leads in reconnecting the wiring of three-phase motors is a

(A) reverse-current relay.
(B) reverse-power relay.
(C) reverse-phase relay.
(D) reverse-power factor relay.

11. Motor frames are usually positively grounded by a special connection in order to

(A) remove static.
(B) protect against lightning.
(C) provide a neutral.
(D) protect against shock.

12. The protective device for a motor branch circuit

(A) should have a rating equal to or greater than the starting current of the motor.
(B) should have a rating equal to the full-load current of the motor.
(C) should not be of the instantaneous type.
(D) should have a rating equal to the current capacity of the circuit conductors.

13. When both fuses and thermal cutouts are used in a motor circuit, the

(A) ratings of the fuses should be the same as those of the thermal cuts.
(B) fuses are used to protect against continuous but not large overloads.
(C) thermal cutouts are used to protect against continuous overloading.
(D) thermal cutouts are used to protect against short circuits in the motor and branch circuit.

14. An induction motor circuit would NEVER be protected by

(A) a fuse.
(B) a thermal cutout.
(C) an overload relay.
(D) a reverse-power relay.

15. Most motor starters are provided with either an undervoltage protective device or an undervoltage release device. A starter with an

(A) undervoltage protective device would be used to open a supply circuit upon failure or reduction of voltage and keep it open until manually closed.
(B) undervoltage protective device would be used to open a supply circuit upon failure or reduction of voltage and automatically reclose it upon return of normal voltage.
(C) undervoltage protective device controls the motor voltage and keeps it at a safe value.
(D) undervoltage release device would be used to prevent opening a supply circuit when voltage fluctuations occur in the power system.

16. A polyphase motor may be protected against reversal of rotation by using a

(A) reverse-speed relay.
(B) reverse-power relay.
(C) reverse-phase relay.
(D) reverse-current relay.

Operation and Maintenance

17. A newly installed three-phase induction motor that is to drive a pump is found to be rotating in the wrong direction. This can be corrected by

(A) connecting the motor to the other end of the pump.
(B) interchanging all three leads.
(C) interchanging any two motor leads.
(D) a quick opening and reclosing of the main line switch.

18. To change the direction of rotation of a cumulative compound-wound DC motor and maintain its characteristics, you must reverse the connections to the

   (A) armature.
   (B) shunt field.
   (C) series field.
   (D) armature and the series field.

19. In normal operation, one type of fault that is NOT likely to develop in the armatures of motors and generators is

   (A) short-circuit.
   (B) open-circuit.
   (C) ground.
   (D) reversed coils.

20. If you attempted to start a DC compound motor in which the series field was open-circuited, the motor would

   (A) not start.
   (B) blow the fuse.
   (C) run away.
   (D) start in the reverse direction.

21. To temporarily change the direction of rotation of a single-phase, shaded-pole induction motor, you would

   (A) do nothing since it cannot be done.
   (B) reverse the connections to the starting winding.
   (C) shift the brushes to the opposite neutral.
   (D) reverse the line leads.

22. For maximum safety, the magnetic contactors used for reversing the direction of rotation of a motor should be

   (A) electrically interlocked.
   (B) electrically and mechanically interlocked.
   (C) mechanically interlocked.
   (D) operated from independent sources.

23. Silver electrical contactors are tarnished most readily by

   (A) oxygen.   (C) nitrogen.
   (B) hydrogen.   (D) sulphur.

24. The lubricant used for sleeve bearings on motors is usually

   (A) vaseline.   (C) graphite.
   (B) oil.   (D) grease.

25. The correct method of measuring the power taken by an AC electric motor is to use a

   (A) wattmeter.
   (B) voltmeter and an ammeter.
   (C) power factor meter.
   (D) tachometer.

26. To measure the power taken by a DC electric motor with only a single instrument, you should use a(n)

   (A) voltmeter.
   (B) ammeter.
   (C) wattmeter.
   (D) power factor meter.

27. The speed of a DC shunt motor is generally regulated by means of a

   (A) switch for reversal of the armature supply.
   (B) source of variable supply voltage.
   (C) variable resistance in the armature circuit.
   (D) rheostat in the field circuit.

28. A carbon brush in a DC motor should exert a pressure of about 1 1/2 lbs. per square inch on the commutator. A much lighter pressure would be most likely to result in

   (A) sparking at the commutator.
   (B) vibration of the armature.
   (C) the brush getting out of line.
   (D) excessive wear of the brush holder.

29. New brushes for a motor should be fitted to the commutator by using a

   (A) round file.
   (B) half-round file.
   (C) strip of sandpaper.
   (D) strip of emery cloth.

30. One sure sign that there has been sparking at the brushes of a stopped DC motor would be

   (A) the odor of hot rubber insulation.
   (B) hot bearings.
   (C) grooves worn around the commutator.
   (D) pits on the commutator surface.

31. A common way of reducing the chances of uneven commutator wear is to

   (A) use brushes of different hardness.
   (B) allow some end play in the motor bearings.
   (C) anneal the commutator after assembly.
   (D) turn the commutator down frequently.

32. If an unusual amount of dust is found around the base of a motor that is being inspected, the proper procedure to follow is to

    (A) take no action but report the motor for further inspection.
    (B) remove the dust.
    (C) inspect the bearings for signs of excessive wear.
    (D) lubricate the motor.

33. If one bearing housing of a running motor feels exceptionally hot but there is no unusual vibration, the most logical conclusion is that the

    (A) motor is being overloaded.
    (B) bearing needs lubrication.
    (C) shaft has become worn.
    (D) motor has been running a long time.

34. While a certain DC shunt motor is driving a light load, part of the field winding becomes short circuited. The motor will most likely

    (A) increase its speed.
    (B) decrease its speed.
    (C) remain at the same speed.
    (D) come to a stop.

35. To measure the voltage and current supplied to a DC motor, connect the

    (A) voltmeter across the line and ammeter in series with the motor.
    (B) ammeter across the line and voltmeter in series with the motor.
    (C) voltmeter and ammeter in series with the motor.
    (D) voltmeter and ammeter across the line.

36. A practical method of checking the magnetic polarity of the field poles of a direct-current motor is by the use of

    (A) an iron or steel tool.
    (B) iron filings.
    (C) a magnetic compass.
    (D) a megger.

37. The reason for using oil rings in bearings is to

    (A) increase the bearing surface.
    (B) maintain proper oil level.
    (C) prevent oil leaks.
    (D) lubricate the bearing.

38. A condition that will NOT cause a brush on the collector ring to carry less than its share of the current is

    (A) low brush pressure.
    (B) low resistance of the brush.
    (C) an insulating glaze on the brush face.
    (D) a loose shunt or pigtail.

39. A good practical test to determine whether or not a wetted-down motor has been sufficiently dried out is

    (A) an insulation test.
    (B) an armature resistance test.
    (C) a high-voltage breakdown test.
    (D) a flash-over test.

40. To stop a $7\frac{1}{2}$-hp motor, you should

    (A) overload the motor until you stall it.
    (B) open the line or disconnect switch.
    (C) remove the fuses.
    (D) push the belt off the pulley.

You were sent to see why a DC motor does not run. The motor was connected as indicated in Figure 48.

41. You are running a DC motor, the armature of which has an open coil. You could identify this condition by

    (A) increase in motor speed.
    (B) decrease in motor speed.
    (C) the coil getting excessively hot.
    (D) seeing and hearing a pronounced electric arc under the brushes as the defective coil passed.

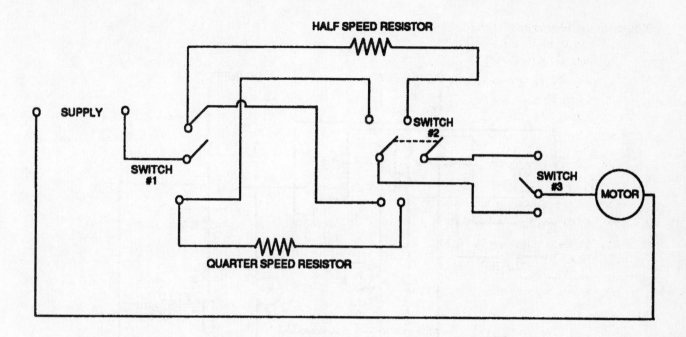

Figure 42

DIRECTIONS: Column I lists various COMBINATIONS OF CLOSED SWITCHES in Figure 42. Each of these combinations will result in one of the MOTOR OPERATING CONDITIONS listed in Column II. Match up Columns I and II. Next to each combination in Column I, write the letter of the resulting operating condition from Column II

COMBINATIONS OF CLOSED SWITCHES

MOTOR OPERATING CONDITIONS

COLUMN I

	Switch 1	Switch 2	Switch 3
42.	up	up	up
43.	up	up	down
44.	up	down	down
45.	down	down	down
46.	down	down	up
47.	down	up	down

COLUMN II

(A) run full speed
(B) run half speed
(C) run quarter speed
(D) not running

You were sent to see why a DC motor does not run. The motor was connected as indicated in Figure 48.

48. After examining the job and the diagram, you came to the conclusion that

(A) the motor will not run; the field circuit is connected incorrectly.

(B) the motor will run if the fuses are good; the job is wired correctly.

(C) the motor will not run; the armature circuit is connected incorrectly.

(D) the motor will not run; the starting box is connected incorrectly.

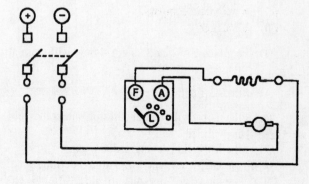

Figure 48

Questions 49–52 refer to Figure 49.

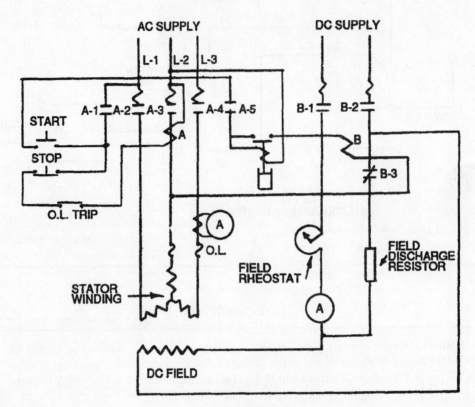

Figure 49

49. Figure 49 represents a starter diagram of a

(A) synchronous motor.
(B) DC series motor.
(C) wound-rotor induction motor.
(D) squirrel-cage induction motor.

50. When the start PB is pressed,

(A) contactor A-1, A-2, A-3, A-4, A-5, B-1, and B-2 will close at once.
(B) contactor A-1, A-2, A-3, A-4, and A-5 will close at once.
(C) contactor A-2, A-3, A-4, and B-3 will close at once.
(D) contactor A-2, A-3, and A-4 only will close at once.

51. After the start button is pressed,

(A) the motor will run but will stop unless the field is energized.
(B) the DC field is energized at once.
(C) the DC field is energized after a definite time.
(D) the motor will not run until the DC field is energized.

52. The field discharge resistor acts to

(A) steady the DC field during the start period.
(B) improve the power factor.
(C) dissipate the energy stored in the field after the DC field supply is cut off.
(D) quench the arc.

53. If, in tracing through an armature winding, all of the conductors are encountered before coming back to the starting point, there is but one closure and the winding is

(A) doubly reentrant.
(B) singly reentrant.
(C) triply reentrant.
(D) quintuply reentrant.

54. If a main unit is operating at full load with a leading power factor for several hours, the part you would expect to become overheated would be the

(A) brushes and rings.
(B) field rheostat.
(C) armature winding.
(D) field winding.

Problems

55. A certain wound-rotor induction motor is equipped with a variable resistor in the rotor circuit for starting purposes only. It is desired to replace this resistor with one that can be used also for motor speed control. Compared with the original resistor, the new resistor should have

(A) higher total resistance.
(B) lower total resistance.
(C) higher current-carrying capacity.
(D) lower current-carrying capacity.

56. If the no-load speed of a squirrel cage-type induction motor connected to a three-phase, 25-cycle line is 373 RPM, the motor has

(A) 2 poles. (C) 6 poles.
(B) 4 poles. (D) 8 poles.

57. The power drawn by a three-phase induction motor that draws 15 amperes at 2,200 volts and power factor of 80 percent is given, in watts, by the product of

(A) $15 \times 2,200 \times .80$
(B) $15 \times 2,200 \times 1.41 \times .80$
(C) $15 \times 2,200 \times 1.73 \times .80$
(D) $15 \times 2,200 \times 3.00 \times .80$

58. It is desired to limit the starting current to the armature of a DC motor taking current from a 120-volt source to 10 amperes. If the armature resistance is 0.2 ohms, the resistance in the armature circuit should be

(A) 118 ohms. (C) 120 ohms.
(B) 11.8 ohms. (D) 20 ohms.

59. When measuring the speed of a DC motor by means of a stopwatch and a revolution counter, the stopwatch was started when the revolution counter read 50. At the end of 80 seconds, the counter read 1,650. The average RPM of the motor during this period was

(A) 200 (C) 1,600
(B) 1,200 (D) 1,700

60. The input to a motor is 16,000 watts and the motor losses total 3,000 watts. The efficiency of the motor is most nearly

(A) 68.4 percent.
(B) 81.25 percent.
(C) 84.21 percent.
(D) 87.5 percent.

61. When a certain motor is started up, the incandescent lights fed from the same circuit dim down somewhat and then return to approximately normal brightness as the motor comes up to speed. This definitely shows that the

(A) starting current of the motor is larger than the running current.
(B) insulation of the circuit wiring is worn.
(C) circuit fuse is not making good contact.
(D) incandescent lamps are too large for the circuit.

62. If a single-phase induction motor draws 10 amperes at 240 volts, the power taken by the motor

(A) will be 2,400 watts.
(B) will be more than 2,400 watts.
(C) will be less than 2,400 watts.
(D) may be more or less than 2,400 watts, depending on the power factor.

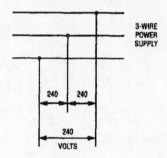

Figure 63

63. In accordance with the voltages shown in Figure 63, the power supply must be

(A) 3-wire DC.
(B) 3-phase AC.
(C) 2-phase AC.
(D) single-phase AC.

64. A coil of wire wound on an iron core draws exactly 5 amperes when connected across the terminals of a 10-volt storage battery. If this coil is now connected across the 10-volt secondary terminals of an ordinary power transformer, the current drawn will be

(A) less than 5 amperes.
(B) more than 5 amperes.
(C) exactly 5 amperes.
(D) more or less than 5 amperes, depending on the frequency.

65. In Figure 63, the 240 volts obtained from the two-wire combinations are

    (A) 2-phase.
    (B) single-phase.
    (C) 3-phase.
    (D) 2-phase and 3-phase.

66. In Figure 63, if the voltages at these points are 240, then the three-phase source must be

    (A) wye-delta.
    (B) wye.
    (C) delta.
    (A) delta-wye.

67. The NEC requires that a wound-rotor, 30 hp motor must be protected at not more than

    (A) 40 A.
    (B) 60 A.
    (C) 80 A.
    (D) 100 A.

68. The Code requires that each 10-hp motor must be protected at not more than

    (A) 45 A.
    (B) 100 A.
    (C) 20 A.
    (D) 30 A.

ANSWER KEY

1. B	10. C	19. D	28. A	37. D	45. D	53. B	61. A
2. B	11. D	20. A	29. C	38. B	46. C	54. C	62. C
3. B	12. C	21. A	30. D	39. A	47. A	55. C	63. B
4. B	13. C	22. B	31. B	40. B	48. C	56. D	64. A
5. C	14. D	23. D	32. B	41. D	49. A	57. C	65. B
6. C	15. A	24. B	33. B	42. B	50. B	58. B	66. B
7. A	16. C	25. A	34. A	43. D	51. C	59. B	67. B
8. C	17. C	26. C	35. A	44. A	52. C	60. B	68. A
9. D	18. A	27. D	36. C				

FUSES

FUSES—THEORY AND PRACTICE

1. The part of a circuit that melts when the current abnormally exceeds the allowable carrying capacity of the conductor is called the

   (A) circuit breaker.
   (B) thermal cutout.
   (C) overload trip.
   (D) fuse.

2. If a fuse becomes hot under normal load, a probable cause is

   (A) rating of the fuse is too high.
   (B) rating of the fuse is too low.
   (C) insufficient pressure at the fuse clips.
   (D) excessive tension in the fuse clips.

3. If it were necessary to replace a 50-ampere fuse with a 65-ampere cartridge fuse of the same voltage rating, it would always be necessary to replace

   (A) all wiring in the protected circuit.
   (B) the renewable link in the fuse.
   (C) the fuse only.
   (D) the cutout and the fuse.

4. When fuses and thermal cutouts are both used in a motor circuit,

   (A) the fuses protect the motor against light overloads.
   (B) the fuses protect the motor and circuit against shorts.
   (C) the thermal cutouts protect the motor and circuit against shorts.
   (D) the thermal cutouts protect the motor against overheating.

5. The one of the following statements about a plug fuse that is most valid is that it should

   (A) always be screwed in lightly to assure easy removal.
   (B) never be used to hold a coin in the fuse socket.
   (C) never be replaced by someone unfamiliar with the circuit.
   (D) always be replaced by a larger size if it burns out frequently.

6. A fuse puller is used in replacing

   (A) plug fuses.   (C) ribbon fuses.
   (B) link fuses.   (D) cartridge fuses.

7. The most important reason for using a fuse puller when removing a cartridge fuse from the fuse clips is to

   (A) prevent blowing of the fuse.
   (B) prevent injury to the fuse element.
   (C) reduce the chances of personal injury.
   (D) reduce arcing at the fuse clips.

8. If a fuse clip becomes hot under normal circuit load, the most probable cause is that the

   (A) clip makes poor contact with the fuse ferrule.
   (B) circuit wires are too small.
   (C) current rating of the fuse is too high.
   (D) voltage rating of the fuse is too low.

9. Before pulling or inserting fuses, it is good practice where possible to

   (A) make sure that the fuses are blown.
   (B) jumper the supply leads.
   (C) remove the power from the circuit by opening the switch.
   (D) ground all leads on both sides of the fuses.

10. The main reason why a blown fuse should not be bridged temporarily by a copper wire is because

    (A) the wire may disrupt violently when a short circuit occurs.
    (B) the circuit may not be adequately protected against overload.
    (C) the wire will maintain an arc when it blows.
    (D) there is danger of electric shock by coming in contact with the wire.

11. The action of a common plug fuse depends on the principle that the

    (A) current develops heat.
    (B) voltage breaks down a thin mica disk.
    (C) current expands and bends a link.
    (D) voltage develops heat.

12. Consumers are warned never to use a coin instead of a spare fuse. The reason for this warning is that

    (A) the protection of the fuse will be lost.
    (B) additional resistance will be placed in the circuit.
    (C) mutilating coins is illegal.
    (D) shock hazard is increased.

Items 13–19 are based on the fuse information given below. Read this information carefully before answering these items

Fuse Information

Badly bent or distorted fuse clips cannot be permitted. Sometimes, the distortion or bending is so slight that it escapes notice, yet it may be the cause for fuse failures through the heat that is developed by the poor contact. Occasionally, the proper spring tension of the fuse clips has been destroyed by overheating from loose wire connections to the clips. Proper contact surfaces must be maintained to avoid faulty operation of the fuse. Electricians should remove oxides that form on the copper and brass contacts, check the clip pressure, and make sure that contact surfaces are not deformed or bent in any way. When removing oxides, use a well-worn file and remove only the oxide film. Do not use sandpaper or emery cloth as hard particles may come off and become embedded in the contact surfaces. All wire connections to the fuse holders should be carefully inspected to see that they are tight.

13. Fuse failure because of poor clip contact or loose connections is due to the resulting

    (A) excessive voltage.
    (B) increased current.
    (C) lowered resistance.
    (D) heating effect.

14. Oxides should be removed from fuse contacts by using

    (A) a dull file.
    (B) emery cloth.
    (C) fine sandpaper.
    (D) a sharp file.

15. One result of loose wire connections at the terminal of a fuse clip is stated in the above paragraph to be

    (A) loss of tension in the wire.
    (B) welding of the fuse to the clip.
    (C) distortion of the clip.
    (D) loss of tension of the clip.

16. Simple reasoning will show that the oxide film referred to is undesirable chiefly because it

    (A) looks dull.
    (B) makes removal of the fuse difficult.
    (C) weakens the clips.
    (D) introduces undesirable resistance.

17. Fuse clips that are bent very slightly

    (A) should be replaced with new clips.
    (B) should be carefully filed.
    (C) may result in blowing of the fuse.
    (D) may prevent the fuse from blowing.

18. From the fuse information paragraph, it would be reasonable to conclude that fuse clips

    (A) are difficult to maintain.
    (B) must be given proper maintenance.
    (C) require more attention than other electrical equipment.
    (D) are unreliable.

19. A safe, practical way of checking the tightness of the wire connection to the fuse clip of a live 120-volt lighting circuit is to

    (A) feel the connection with your hand to see if it is warm.
    (B) try tightening with an insulated screwdriver or socket wrench.
    (C) see if the current works.
    (D) measure the resistance with an ohmmeter.

20. If a cartridge fuse is hot to the touch when you remove it to do some maintenance on the circuit, this most probably indicates that the

    (A) voltage of the circuit is too high.
    (B) fuse clips do not make good contact.
    (C) equipment on the circuit starts and stops frequently.
    (D) fuse is oversized for the circuit.

21. If one end of a cartridge fuse becomes unusually warm, the first action on the part of the electrician should be to

    (A) tighten the fuse clips.
    (B) replace the fuse with a larger one.
    (C) transfer some load to another circuit.
    (D) notify the supervisor.

22. The length of a standard cartridge fuse depends on the circuit

    (A) power.
    (B) amperage.
    (C) voltage.
    (D) type of current (AC or DC).

23. If a fuse of higher than the required current rating is used in an electrical circuit,

    (A) better protection will be afforded.
    (B) the fuse will blow more often since it carries more current.
    (C) serious damage may result to the circuit from overload.
    (D) maintenance of the large fuse will be higher.

ANSWER KEY

1.	D	5.	B	9.	C	13.	D	17.	C	21.	A
2.	C	6.	D	10.	B	14.	A	18.	B	22.	C
3.	D	7.	C	11.	A	15.	D	19.	B	23.	C
4.	B	8.	A	12.	A	16.	D	20.	B		

FUSES—TYPES AND RATINGS

1. In ordering standard cartridge fuses, it is necessary to specify only

    (A) the current capacity.
    (B) the voltage of the circuit.
    (C) the current capacity and the voltage of the circuit.
    (D) the power to be dissipated.

2. The largest size regular plug fuse used is rated at

    (A) 15 amperes.
    (B) 20 amperes.
    (C) 30 amperes.
    (D) 40 amperes.

3. The range of sizes of cartridge fuses with ferrule ends is from

    (A) 0 to 60 amperes.
    (B) 0 to 30 amperes.
    (C) 31 to 50 amperes.
    (D) 61 to 100 amperes.

4. A 600-volt cartridge fuse is most readily distinguished from a 250-volt cartridge fuse of the same ampere rating by comparing the

    (A) insulating materials used.
    (B) shape of the ends.
    (C) diameters.
    (D) lengths.

5. Renewable fuses differ from ordinary fuses in that

    (A) burned out fuse elements can be replaced readily.
    (B) they can carry higher overloads.
    (C) burned out fuses can be located more easily.
    (D) they can be used on higher voltages.

6. A 10-ampere cartridge fuse provided with a navy blue label has a voltage rating, in volts, of

    (A) 220   (C) 550
    (B) 250   (D) 600

7. Knife-blade ends on a cartridge fuse are a positive indication that the fuse is rated at over

    (A) 600 volts.
    (B) 250 volts.
    (C) 100 amperes.
    (D) 60 amperes.

8. In general, the principal factor that determines the current rating of the fuse that should be installed in a lighting circuit is the

    (A) wattage of the individual lamps.
    (B) capacity of the smallest wire in the circuit.
    (C) voltage of the circuit.
    (D) capacity of the largest wire in the circuit.

ANSWER KEY

1. C	3. A	5. A	7. D
2. C	4. D	6. B	8. B

PROBLEMS

1. Testing for a blown cartridge fuse by connecting a lamp from one clip to the other of the suspected fuse will in all cases indicate a

   (A) blown fuse if the lamp remains dark.
   (B) good fuse if the lamp lights up.
   (C) blown fuse if the lamp lights up.
   (D) good fuse if the lamp remains dark.

2. A blown "one-time" fuse is replaced with a good fuse of the same rating. When the switch is closed, the new fuse also blows. In this case,

   (A) a fuse of higher current rating should be used.
   (B) a fuse having a greater time lag should be tried.
   (C) some of the load should be transferred to another circuit.
   (D) the circuit should be checked before trying another fuse.

3. One of the two plug-fuses in a 120-volt circuit blows because of a short circuit. If a 120-volt lamp is screwed into the fuse socket while the circuit is still shorted, the lamp will

   (A) burn dimly.
   (B) remain dark.
   (C) burn out.
   (D) burn normally.

4. Before removing a "blown" 600-volt fuse, it is always desirable to

   (A) open the circuit at another point on the line side.
   (B) shut down the station.
   (C) jumper the fuse.
   (D) ground the circuit.

5. If the 30-ampere fuse is blown frequently on a house lighting circuit,

   (A) check the load and condition of equipment.
   (B) insert a fuse of higher current rating.
   (C) insert a fuse of higher voltage rating.
   (D) check the line voltage.

6. A 120-volt lighting circuit feeding 10 single-lamp, 120-volt fixtures is protected by a 15-ampere fuse. If the same size lamp is used in all 10 fixtures, the largest lamp that can be used without blowing the fuse is

   (A) 100 watts.   (C) 200 watts.
   (B) 150 watts.   (D) 250 watts.

Questions 7 and 8 refer to Figure 7.

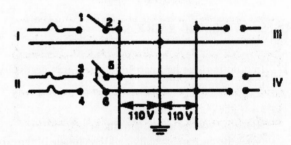

Figure 7

7. Circuit No. I in Figure 7

   (A) is not properly fused since it should have one fuse in each leg.
   (B) supplies 220 volts to the load.
   (C) is grounded if a pair of test lamps light when placed between point 2 and ground.
   (D) supplies 110 volts to the load at the board.

8. Circuit No. II in Figure 7

   (A) is not properly fused since it should have only one fuse in the hot leg.
   (B) supplies 220 volts to the load at the board.
   (C) is grounded if a pair of test lamps light up when placed between points 5 and 6.
   (D) is grounded if, with the switch in the open position, test lamps light up when placed between points 3 and 5.

9. The maximum size of fuse for protecting a 10-HP, 3-phase, 220-volt motor should be

   (A) 20 amperes.   (C) 60 amperes.
   (B) 35 amperes.   (D) 75 amperes.

10. A 115/230-volt, three-wire lighting circuit submain supplies fused branch circuits. It has a grounded neutral and consists of three No. 8 rubber-covered wires. It should be protected at the distribution panel by fuses of not over

    (A)   35 amperes in all three lines.

    (B)   15 amperes in all three lines.

    (C)   35 amperes in the ungrounded lines, with the neutral unfused.

    (D)   15 amperes in the ungrounded lines, with the neutral unfused.

11. When the switch is closed in Figure 11, it is reasonable to expect the blowing of

    (A)   fuse 2 but not fuses 1 and 3.

    (B)   fuses 1 and 2 but not fuse 3.

    (C)   fuses 2 and 3 but not fuse 1.

    (D)   fuses 1, 2, and 3.

12. If the upper fuse in Figure 12 is good and the lower fuse is burned out, the test lamp that will be lighted is

    (A)   1   (C)   3

    (B)   2   (D)   4

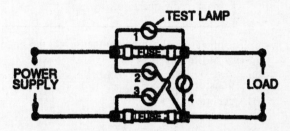

Figure 12

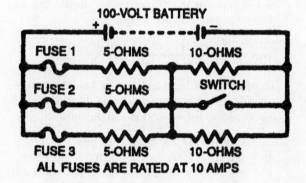

Figure 11

ANSWER KEY

1. C	3. D	5. A	7. D	9. B	11. D
2. D	4. A	6. B	8. B	10. C	12. C

BREAKERS AND BUS BARS

DIRECTIONS: For each question, read all choices carefully. Then select the answer that you consider correct or most nearly correct. Write the letter preceding your best choice next to the question.

1. A piece of electrical equipment that serves the same purpose as a fuse is a

   (A) transformer.
   (B) generator.
   (C) switch.
   (D) circuit breaker.

2. A DC panel-type circuit breaker is adjusted so that the

   (A) arcing tip will open before the main contact.
   (B) main contact will close before the arcing tip.
   (C) main contact will open before the arcing tip.
   (D) arcing tip and main contact will open at the same time.

3. Arcing tips are used on air circuit breakers to

   (A) increase the contact.
   (B) protect the main contacts.
   (C) decrease the arcing time.
   (D) limit the short-circuit current.

4. The reason modern circuit breakers are constructed to be "trip free" is that such breakers

   (A) cannot be held closed when there is an overload.
   (B) can be closed with less effort.
   (C) cannot be opened accidentally.
   (D) can be opened with less arcing.

5. The push buttons used in the control circuits of some remote-controlled lighting switches are required only to make, not break, the control circuit. In such cases, the breaking of the control circuit is generally accomplished by

   (A) a relay on the control panel.
   (B) an auxiliary contact on the lighting switch.
   (C) a blow-out coil on the main contacts of the lighting switch.
   (D) an auxiliary toggle switch on the control panel.

6. A breaker is said to be trip free if

   (A) the closing and tripping operations are independent.
   (B) it will trip on any value of reverse current.
   (C) the tripping devices operate easily.
   (D) it is not latched in position when closed.

7. A trip-free circuit breaker is one that

   (A) is found only in large generating stations.
   (B) cannot be reclosed once it opens.
   (C) rings an alarm when it opens.
   (D) cannot be closed by hand while the abnormal condition that caused it to open exists.

8. The trip-coil of a circuit breaker is connected into a line through a current transformer rated at 200:5 amperes. If normal line current is 120 amperes and the circuit breaker should open at 125 percent normal line current, the trip mechanism should be set to operate when the trip-coil current is

   (A) 6.25 amperes.   (C) 1.94 amperes.
   (B) 3.75 amperes.   (D) 14.1 amperes.

9. To work on a high-voltage bus with remote-controlled switches, after isolating the bus, the safest procedure before working on the bus is to

   (A) short-circuit and ground the bus.
   (B) tag the control switches on the control board.
   (C) notify the shift operator on the control board.
   (D) use rubber gloves and mats.

10. A copper bus bar an inch in diameter has a cross-sectional area of

    (A) 3,141,600 CM.
    (B) 1,000,000 CM.
    (C) 785,400 CM.
    (D) 100,000 CM.

11. Figure A of Figure 11 is the electric circuit, and B is a simplified drawing of the magnetic circuit of the trip mechanism of a DC circuit breaker that opens if the armature drops to the position shown. The circuit beaker remains closed if the load current is zero and the line voltage is normal. It will open if

    (A) both the line voltage and load current are reversed.
    (B) the load current is reversed and line voltage is normal.
    (C) the load current is excessive and line voltage is normal.
    (D) the line voltage is excessive and load current is normal.

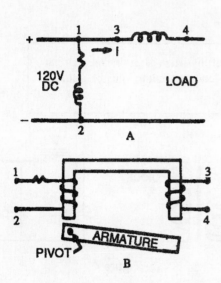

Figure 11

12. In order for a circuit breaker to be remotely opened, it must be equipped with which one of the following tripping devices?

   (A) Shunt trip
   (B) Time-relay trip
   (C) Trip-free mechanism
   (D) Inverse-time trip

13. The reason modem circuit breakers are constructed to be "quick breaking" is that such breakers

   (A) can be operated at more than 100 percent rating.
   (B) cannot be held closed when there is an overload.
   (C) can be opened with less arcing.
   (D) cannot be closed accidentally.

14. The "normal current density" of copper bus is 1,000 amperes per square inch. The number of amperes that a 2 1/2×1/4-inch copper bus may carry under these conditions is

   (A) 625 amperes.
   (B) 1000 amperes.
   (C) 1250 amperes.
   (D) 500 amperes.

15. The weight of a 10-foot section of a 2″×1/8″ copper bus bar that is made of copper having a density of 0.32 lbs. per cubic inch is most nearly

   (A) 0.82 lbs.   (C) 9.6 lbs.
   (B) 7.7 lbs.   (D) 30.0 lbs.

Answer Key

1. D	4. A	7. D	10. B	13. C
2. C	5. B	8. B	11. B	14. A
3. B	6. A	9. A	12. A	15. C

RECTIFIERS

> **DIRECTIONS:** For each question, read all choices carefully. Then select the answer that you consider correct or most nearly correct. Write the letter preceding your best choice next to the question.

1. A bake-out is generally considered necessary for a rectifier if [older type equipment]

   (A) it has been subjected to a heavy overload.
   (B) it has been operating at light load for a long period.
   (C) more than three months have elapsed since previous bake-out.
   (D) it has been open to atmosphere for a long period.

2. The possibility of an arc-back in a rectifier is increased by [on older type equipment]

   (A) operating the rectifier at less than rated capacity.
   (B) the presence of mercury vapor in the rectifier tank.
   (C) the absence of non-condensible gases in the rectifier tank.
   (D) operating the rectifier at more than rated capacity [older type equipment].

3. A commonly used method of controlling the DC voltage of a rectifier is by [older type equipment]

   (A) inserting a rheostat in the main positive lead.
   (B) varying the tank pressure.
   (C) controlling the potential of the anode grids.
   (D) increasing or decreasing the interphase transformer ratio.

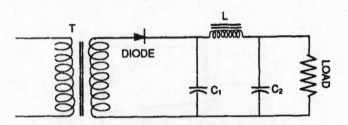

Figure 4

4. In order to furnish DC for the operation of relays and control circuits where only a source of AC is available and the use of batteries is not convenient, diodes are used extensively as rectifiers. The schematic diagram shown in Figure 4 represents a typical

   (A) full-wave rectifier.
   (B) push-pull rectifier.
   (C) bridge rectifier.
   (D) half-wave rectifier.

5. In reference to the sketch in Figure 4, the circuit element marked L together with C_1 and C_2 acts to

   (A) smooth the voltage across the load.
   (B) change the frequency across the load.
   (C) rectify the incoming AC.
   (D) maintain the factor cos θ intact.

ANSWER KEY

| 1. D | 2. D | 3. C | 4. D | 5. A |

RHEOSTATS—RELAYS

1. Burnt or pitted contact studs on a synchronous generator-field rheostat should be

   (A) dressed with a file.
   (B) smoothed with emery cloth.
   (C) restored with a burnishing tool.
   (D) resurfaced by brazing.

2. If an open circuit is discovered in an exciter shunt-field rheostat between two contact points, the exciter

   (A) must be left out of service until the open coil or grid is replaced.
   (B) can be operated if the open coil or grid is short-circuited.
   (C) must be operated at low loads with reduced field.
   (D) can be operated without the field rheostat by exciting the field from the exciter bus.

3. Series-type motors for electrically driven rheostats or governors have a split-series field to

   (A) obtain low motor speed.
   (B) decrease the current consumption.
   (C) change the direction of rotation.
   (D) produce greater starting torque.

4. A relay coil with a resistance in series is connected in parallel with a contactor coil to a battery. If the current is 5 amperes in the relay coil, 5 amperes in the resistor, and 3 amperes in the contactor coil, the battery current is

   (A) 13 amperes.
   (B) 2 amperes.
   (C) 5 amperes.
   (D) 8 amperes.

5. The electrical device occasionally connected across relay contacts to minimize arcing when the contacts open is a(n)

   (A) capacitor.
   (B) resistor.
   (C) inductance coil.
   (D) carbon tip.

6. An induction-type overcurrent relay usually

   (A) operates instantaneously.
   (B) has a constant time delay for all settings.
   (C) has increased time delay with an increase in current.
   (D) has decreased time delay with an increase in current.

7. An electrical helper notices that a certain relay does not pick up promptly when its control circuit is closed. Of the following faults, the only one that could be the cause of this delayed operation is a

   (A) control wire broken off one of the relay terminals.
   (B) burned out fuse.
   (C) burned out relay coil.
   (D) fuse making poor contact.

8. Differential relays are installed to protect against

   (A) overcurrents.
   (B) reverse currents.
   (C) internal faults.
   (D) no voltage.

9. A hesitating relay is

   (A) to allow for momentary impulse-type closing control.
   (B) to provide a definite time for tripping an overload.
   (C) one that stops halfway unless interlock circuits are clear.
   (D) an AC relay with insufficient shading.

10. An induction-type overcurrent relay

    (A) operates quicker with large currents than with small ones.
    (B) operates quicker with small currents than with large ones.
    (C) operates in the same time with any overload current.
    (D) operates eventually even on currents less than the trip-setting value.

11. An induction overcurrent relay has its time setting adjusted by means of an index lever, which is moved over a scale with graduations numbered 1 to 10. Moving the lever from 10 toward 1

    (A) increases the time of operation on large overloads only when the maximum current connection is used.
    (B) decreases the time of operation on large overloads only when the maximum current connection is used.
    (C) decreases the time of operation on large overloads only when the minimum current connection is used.
    (D) decreases the time of operation on large overloads when any current connection is used.

12. In relay testing, a cycle counter is used to

    (A) measure the frequency of the system voltage.
    (B) determine the number of operations of a relay in a 24-hour period.
    (C) check the current required to operate a relay.
    (D) check the time of operation of a relay.

13. Series-type motors for electrically driven rheostats have a split-series field to

    (A) change the direction of rotation.
    (B) decrease the current consumption.
    (C) obtain low motor speed.
    (D) produce greater starting torque.

14. A photoelectric relay system could NOT be used for which one of the following applications?

    (A) Controlling the temperature of a furnace
    (B) Amplifying audio frequencies
    (C) Sorting objects of different sizes
    (D) Counting moving objects without physical contact

15. A relay circuit is connected to a 120-volt, 60-hertz AC supply as shown in Figure 15. The current flowing in the circuit is

    (A) 20 amperes.
    (B) 15 amperes.
    (C) 12 amperes.
    (D) 8.57 amperes.

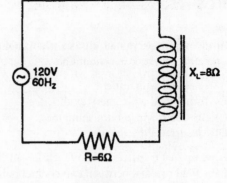

Figure 15

16. In the circuit in Figure 16, the capacitive reactance is equal to the inductive reactance. Under these conditions, the current is

    (A) a minimum.
    (B) 10 amperes.
    (C) 6 amperes.
    (D) 4 amperes.

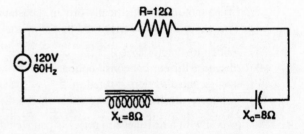

Figure 16

ANSWER KEY

1. A	3. C	5. A	7. D	9. A	11. D	13. A	15. C
2. B	4. D	6. D	8. C	10. A	12. D	14. B	16. B

ROTARY CONVERTERS—COMMUTATORS

1. The speed of a rotary converter in normal operation is governed by the frequency of the AC supply and the

   (A) DC load.
   (B) number of poles.
   (C) AC voltage.
   (D) shunt-field current.

2. When a rotary converter is started on reduced AC voltage (from the AC side), if the polarity of the rotary is reversed, the operator should

   (A) shut the machine down and restart.
   (B) close the field switch "down" until correct polarity is indicated then close it in the "up" position.
   (C) close the field switch "down" and leave it in that position.
   (D) open the oil switch momentarily and then reclose it.

3. The power factor of a synchronous converter in normal operation will change from lag to lead if the

   (A) load increases to a high value.
   (B) load drops to a low value.
   (C) field current is reduced to a low value.
   (D) DC bus voltage drops suddenly.

4. The overspeed device on a rotary converter is usually arranged so that when it operates, it will open the rotary

   (A) positive breaker or switch.
   (B) oil switch.
   (C) negative breaker or switch.
   (D) oil switch and positive breaker or switch.

5. One purpose for having dampers or amortisseur windings on rotary converter pole faces is to

   (A) equalize the field strength.
   (B) provide a compound field.
   (C) minimize hunting.
   (D) improve admission of cooling air.

6. When an induction motor is mounted on the shaft of a rotary converter for starting purposes, the motor usually has two fewer poles than the rotary. It is constructed this way

   (A) to simplify the stator winding.
   (B) so that its synchronous speed is higher than the speed of the rotary.
   (C) because it is smaller than the rotary.
   (D) to keep the starting current at a low value.

7. The most likely cause for overspeed on a rotary in service is

   (A) loss of AC power.
   (B) loss of DC power.
   (C) low AC frequency.
   (D) loss of field.

8. When rotary brushes are properly adjusted, the contact pressure of the brushes on the commutator will be

   (A) greatest at the top brushes.
   (B) the same for all brushes.
   (C) smallest at the side brushes.
   (D) smallest at the bottom brushes.

9. Weakening the field of a rotary operating in parallel with other rotaries will cause the

   (A) brushes to spark.
   (B) DC output to increase.
   (C) speed to decrease.
   (D) DC output of this rotary to decrease.

10. In case of a short circuit in the windings of a rotary converter, the device that limits the duration of the excessive AC current is the

    (A) overload relay.
    (B) overspeed device.
    (C) transformer.
    (D) reverse-current relay.

11. The simplest way to check the bearing of a rotary for excessive heating is by

    (A) a thermometer.
    (B) feeling the housing.
    (C) noting discoloration of the housing.
    (D) detecting odors.

12. The purpose of having the armature of a rotary converter oscillate is so that the

    (A) brushes will wear evenly.
    (B) area of contact between brushes and commutator will be increased.
    (C) armature will be better ventilated.
    (D) commutator will wear evenly.

13. The interpole (commutating) field winding of a rotary converter is usually connected

    (A) in series with the armature on the negative side.
    (B) in series with the armature on the positive side.
    (C) in parallel with the armature.
    (D) in parallel with the shunt field.

14. A 3,000-kW rotary converter operating at full load with a DC voltage of 625 volts would deliver a direct current of

    (A) 1,875 amperes.
    (B) 2,083 amperes.
    (C) 3,625 amperes.
    (D) 4,800 amperes.

15. A piece of No. $\frac{1}{9}$ emery cloth should be used to grind the commutator of a DC motor

    (A) whenever there is sparking at the brushes.
    (B) under no condition.
    (C) when the commutator is rough or worn.
    (D) when the brushes do not make good contact.

16. A simple method of checking a commutator for tightness is to

    (A) feel the surface for uneven spots.
    (B) check one of the V-ring bolts with a wrench.
    (C) tap it lightly with a small hammer.
    (D) measure the diameter at several points.

17. If high mica develops on a commutator, it is corrected by

    (A) undercutting.
    (B) stoning.
    (C) shimming the copper.
    (D) smoothing with sandpaper.

18. Mica is commonly used in electrical construction for

    (A) commutator bar separators.
    (B) switchboard panels.
    (C) strain insulators.
    (D) heater cord insulation.

ANSWER KEY

1. B	4. A	7. A	10. A	13. A	16. C
2. B	5. C	8. B	11. B	14. D	17. A
3. B	6. B	9. D	12. D	15. B	18. A

Note: Rotary converters have, in general, been replaced by electronics. Absence of moving parts and long life without maintenance are the great attractions for electronic conversion of electrical power. Questions and answers concerning rotary converters are included here because some local tests have not been updated, and you may still encounter questions similar to these.

CAPACITORS—EXCITERS REACTORS—ALTERNATORS

CAPACITORS—EXCITERS REACTORS—ALTERNATORS

1. It is suspected that a capacitor is short-circuited. In order to test the capacitor, it is put in series with a 120-volt test lamp across 120 volts DC. If the capacitor is short-circuited, the lamp should

---

CAPACITORS—EXCITERS REACTORS—ALTERNATORS

1. It is suspected that a capacitor is short-circuited. In order to test the capacitor, it is put in series with a 120-volt test lamp across 120 volts DC. If the capacitor is short-circuited, the lamp should

   (A) flash on and then become and remain dark.
   (B) flash on and off intermittently.
   (C) give off normal light.
   (D) remain dark.

2. A one-microfarad capacitor is connected in series with a one-half microfarad capacitor. The resulting capacity of the combination is

   (A) one-half microfarad.
   (B) one-third microfarad.
   (C) one and one-half microfarad.
   (D) one microfarad.

3. The reason for connecting a capacitor across relay contacts that make and break frequently is to

   (A) make the relay slow acting.
   (B) make the relay quick acting.
   (C) reduce pitting of the contacts.
   (D) raise the power factor of the circuit.

4. An alternator in parallel with other alternators, all having automatic voltage regulators, is to be taken off the bus. The usual procedure before opening the alternator switch is to

   (A) do nothing.
   (B) reduce the power feed to the prime mover.
   (C) reduce the alternator field.
   (D) increase the alternator field.

5. Two alternators operating in parallel are driven by governor-regulated turbines. They supply a unity power factor load, and each has been individually adjusted to unity power factor. Increasing the field current of one

   (A) increases the frequency.
   (B) causes its power factor to become leading.
   (C) causes its current to decrease.
   (D) causes its power factor to become lagging.

6. An alternator is supplying load in parallel with one or more machines of considerably larger rating. In order to increase its load,

   (A) power factor is increased.
   (B) field current is decreased.
   (C) speed is decreased.
   (D) prime mover power input is increased.

7. The rating of an alternator, as given on its nameplate, is 800-kW, 0.8 power factor. The significance of this rating is that the alternator

   (A) always operates at 0.8 power factor.
   (B) can supply an 800-kW, 0.8 lagging power factor load at rated voltage.
   (C) can supply a 1,000 kVa load, any power factor, at rated voltage.
   (D) is fully loaded at 800 kW, any power factor.

8. You have just wired up two 3-phase alternators. You have checked the frequency and voltage of each. They are the same. Before you would connect these alternators in parallel, you would

   (A) check the steam pressure.
   (B) check the speed of the turbine.
   (C) check the phase rotation.
   (D) lubricate everything.

9. When exciter brushes are properly adjusted, the contact pressure of the brushes on the commutator will be

   (A) greatest at the top brushes.
   (B) smallest at the side brushes.
   (C) smallest at the bottom brushes.
   (D) the same for all brushes.

ANSWER KEY

1. C	3. C	5. D	7. B	9. D
2. B	4. B	6. D	8. C	

TRANSFORMERS

THEORY, USE, PARTS, AND WIRING

1. The primary and secondary coils of a transformer always have

    (A) the same size of wire.
    (B) a common magnetic circuit.
    (C) separate magnetic circuits.
    (D) a different number of turns.

2. The maximum load a power transformer can carry is limited by its

    (A) temperature rise.
    (B) insulation resistance.
    (C) oil's dielectric strength.
    (D) voltage ratio.

3. The transformer is based on the principle that energy may be effectively transferred by induction from one set of coils to another by a varying magnetic flux, provided both sets of coils

    (A) are not on a common magnetic circuit.
    (B) have the same number of turns.
    (C) are on a common magnetic circuit.
    (D) do not have the same number of turns.

4. In a transformer, the induced emf per turn in the secondary winding is

    (A) equal to the induced emf per turn in the primary winding.
    (B) not equal to the induced emf per turn in the primary winding.
    (C) equal to the induced emf per turn in the primary winding multiplied by the ratio $N - 1/N - 2$.
    (D) equal to the induced emf per turn in the primary winding divided by the ratio $N - 1/N - 2$.

5. Transformer cores can be composed of laminated sheet metal rather than solid metal and as a result,

    (A) eddy currents are reduced.
    (B) less insulation is needed on the windings.
    (C) oil penetrates the core more easily.
    (D) the voltage ratio is higher than the turn ratio.

6. Compared to the secondary of a loaded step-down transformer, the primary has

    (A) higher voltage and lower current.
    (B) lower voltage and higher current.
    (C) lower voltage and current.
    (D) higher voltage and current.

7. Current transformers for meters and relays usually have

    (A) five ampere secondaries.
    (B) ten ampere secondaries.
    (C) a ten-to-one ratio.
    (D) a hundred-to-one ratio.

8. An auto-transformer is used in preference to a two-winding transformer

    (A) where it is desired to isolate two circuits.
    (B) where the ratio of transformation is low.
    (C) where neither the primary nor secondary is over 250 volts.
    (D) because the auto-transformer is safer to operate.

9. When a step-up transformer is used, it increases the

    (A) voltage.
    (B) current.
    (C) power.
    (D) frequency.

10. For a given 3-phase transformer, the connection giving the highest secondary voltage is

    (A) wye primary, delta secondary.
    (B) delta primary, delta secondary.
    (C) wye primary, wye secondary.
    (D) delta primary, wye secondary.

11. The purpose of laminating the core of a power transformer is to keep the

    (A) hysteresis loss at a minimum.
    (B) eddy current loss at a minimum.
    (C) copper losses at a minimum.
    (D) friction losses at a minimum.

12. An isolating transformer is used in the rectifier control circuit to

   (A) prevent the possibility of high voltage being impressed on the low voltage AC supply.
   (B) obtain full wave rectification.
   (C) lower the voltage.
   (D) obtain single-phase power from the three-phase supply.

13. A booster transformer is a transformer connected

   (A) in such a manner as to increase the load on the line by a fixed percentage.
   (B) as a delta-connected bank.
   (C) as an auto-transformer to raise the line voltage by a fixed percentage.
   (D) in such a manner as to raise the frequency by a fixed percentage.

Answer Key

1. B	4. A	6. A	8. B	10. D	12. A
2. A	5. A	7. A	9. A	11. B	13. C
3. C					

OPERATION AND MAINTENANCE

1. In the operation of dry-type transformers, the accumulation of dust on the windings and core is objectionable mainly because it

   (A) may short-circuit the windings.
   (B) tends to corrode the metal.
   (C) absorbs oil and grease.
   (D) reduces the dissipation of heat.

2. The terminals of the secondary winding of a current transformer in whose primary winding current is flowing and whose secondary winding is open-circuited must never be

   (A) connected to the current coil of a wattmeter.
   (B) short-circuited.
   (C) connected to an ammeter.
   (D) touched with your hands.

3. The relative polarity of the windings of a transformer is determined by

   (A) an open-circuit test.
   (B) phasing out.
   (C) a short-circuit test.
   (D) a polarimeter test.

4. The secondary of a single-phase transformer consists of two similar coils, and it is required to place them in parallels. A common procedure is to connect any two terminals and impress not more than the normal voltage upon either coil. With a voltmeter, measure the voltage across the other two terminals. The coils are correctly connected in parallel if the voltmeter reads

   (A) twice the impressed voltage.
   (B) zero.
   (C) one-half the impressed voltage.
   (D) a fraction of the impressed voltage.

5. Connecting up power transformer windings requires

   (A) knowledge of the frequency.
   (B) an open-circuit test.
   (C) a short-circuit test.
   (D) phasing out of the leads.

6. The common cause of contamination by water of oil in transformers located indoors is

   (A) electrolytic action of high voltage on air.
   (B) condensation of moisture from air in the upper part of the tank.
   (C) decomposition of organic matter in the oil.
   (D) the use of filter blotters that have absorbed moisture from the air.

7. The secondary of a current transformer whose primary is connected in a high-voltage line and whose primary current is normal should never be

   (A) subjected to too high a secondary current overload.
   (B) short-circuited.
   (C) grounded.
   (D) open-circuited.

8. If three single-phase transformers are connected delta to delta, and the secondary of one develops short circuits between coils, the load may be partially carried by

    (A) disconnecting the damaged secondary, leaving the primaries all connected in delta.
    (B) short-circuiting the damaged section.
    (C) removing the damaged transformer from the circuit entirely.
    (D) no method with the two remaining transformers.

9. From your knowledge of electrical equipment you know that the part of a transformer that is most subject to damage from high temperature is the

    (A) iron core.
    (B) copper winding.
    (C) winding insulation.
    (D) frame or case.

10. Before disconnecting an ammeter or relay from an energized current transformer circuit, the

    (A) circuit should be opened.
    (B) fuse should be removed.
    (C) current transformer secondary should be shorted.
    (D) current transformer primary circuit should be shorted.

11. In general, the most important point to watch in the operation of transformers is the

    (A) primary voltage.
    (B) exciting current.
    (C) core loss.
    (D) temperature.

12. A common use for autotransformers in electrical power work is as

    (A) starting compensators for induction motors.
    (B) current-limiting reactors.
    (C) instrument current transformers.
    (D) insulating transformers.

13. A single-phase AC potential of 60 volts is required for test purposes. A 440-volt AC source and two identical transformers with 440-volt primary windings and 120-volt secondary windings are available. For this purpose, the transformers should be connected with

    (A) primaries in parallel, secondaries in parallel.
    (B) primaries in series, secondaries in series.
    (C) primaries in parallel, secondaries in series.
    (D) primaries in series, secondaries in parallel.

14. The secondary of a current transformer in whose primary winding current is flowing should

    (A) always be short-circuited.
    (B) not be connected to the current coil of a watt-meter.
    (C) not be open-circuited.
    (D) not be short-circuited.

15. Oil is used in many large transformers to

    (A) lubricate the core.
    (B) lubricate the coils.
    (C) insulate the coils.
    (D) insulate the core.

16. Almost all transformers used to supply rotary converters have primary winding taps. Changing tap connections on these transformers would have the direct effect of changing the

    (A) rotary DC voltage.
    (B) rotary speed.
    (C) setting of the rotary overload relays.
    (D) load capacity of the rotary.

17. A rotary converter is supplied through a bank of three single-phase air-blast transformers. During operation one of the transformers is found to be considerably hotter than normal while the other two transformers are at normal temperature. A probable cause for this condition would be

    (A) low air pressure.
    (B) overload on rotary.
    (C) dampers not opened on the one transformer.
    (D) rotary operated at low power factor.

18. Transformers can be

    (A) 100 percent efficient.
    (B) 10 percent efficient.
    (C) 99 percent efficient.
    (D) 90 percent efficient.

19. Iron core transformers use the _____ principle to transfer power between primary and secondary windings.

    (A) capacitive reactance
    (B) inductive reactance
    (C) mutual inductance
    (D) self-inductance

20. A good example of an autotransformer used in industry is the buck and _____ transformer.

    (A) boost   (C) break
    (B) beat   (D) induce

21. Hysteresis in a transformer

    (A) is another of its advantages.
    (B) is another of its losses.
    (C) is used to step up current.
    (D) is used to step down voltage.

22. Copper losses in a transformer can be minimized by

    (A) using smaller wire sizes.
    (B) using correct wire sizes.
    (C) using larger cores.
    (D) using laminated cores.

23. What type of oil is no longer allowed in a transformer?

    (A) Mineral
    (B) PCB
    (C) Lubricating
    (D) Machine

24. Transformers are made for a number of loads and

    (A) wattages.
    (B) currents.
    (C) resistances.
    (D) voltages.

25. Autotransformers are designed to completely control light intensity by controlling the _____ applied to the lamps.

    (A) voltage
    (B) current
    (C) resistance
    (D) inductance

ANSWER KEY

1. D	6. B	10. C	14. C	18. C	22. B
2. D	7. D	11. D	15. C	19. C	23. B
3. B	8. C	12. A	16. A	20. A	24. D
4. B	9. C	13. D	17. C	21. B	25. A
5. D					

TRANSFORMER PROBLEMS

> **DIRECTIONS:** For each question, read all choices carefully. Then select the answer that you consider correct or most nearly correct. Write the letter preceding your best choice next to the question.

1. A 10-to-1 step-down transformer has 44,000 volts on the primary and 4,400 on the secondary. If the taps are changed to reduce the number of turns in the primary by 2.5 percent, then the secondary voltage will be most nearly

   (A) 4,290 volts.
   (B) 4,390 volts.
   (C) 4,410 volts.
   (D) 4,510 volts.

2. If the input to a 10-to-1 step-down transformer is 15 amperes at 2,400 volts, the secondary output would be nearest to

   (A) 1.5 amperes at 24,000 volts.
   (B) 150 amperes at 240 volts.
   (C) 1.5 amperes at 240 volts.
   (D) 150 amperes at 24,000 volts.

3. If the input to a 10-to-1 step-down transformer is 25 amperes at 1,200 volts, the secondary output would be nearest to

   (A) 2.5 amperes at 12,000 volts.
   (B) 250 amperes at 120 volts.
   (C) 2.5 amperes at 120 volts.
   (D) 250 amperes at 12,000 volts.

4. When the input to a 6-to-1 step-up transformer is 12 amperes at 120 volts, the output is approximately

   (A) 72 amperes at 20 volts.
   (B) 2 amperes at 20 volts.
   (C) 2 amperes at 720 volts.
   (D) 72 amperes at 720 volts.

5. If the input to a 5-to-1 step-down transformer is 100 amperes at 2,200 volts, the output will be nearly

   (A) 100 amperes at 440 volts.
   (B) 500 amperes at 440 volts.
   (C) 20 amperes at 11,000 volts.
   (D) 500 amperes at 2,200 volts.

6. Three single-phase transformers are connected in delta on both the primary and secondary sides. If one of the transformers burns out, the system can continue to operate, but its capacity, in terms of the capacity of the original arrangement, is reduced to

   (A) $66\frac{2}{3}$ percent.
   (B) 57.8 percent.
   (C) 115 percent.
   (D) 100 percent.

7. On the transformer in Figure 7, the dimension marked "X" is

   (A) $9\frac{7}{8}''$
   (B) $14''$
   (C) $18\frac{1}{8}''$
   (D) $19\frac{1}{8}''$

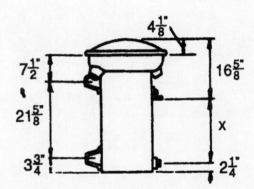

Figure 7

8. If the secondary of a 10-to-1 step-up transformer is connected to the primary of a 2-to-1 step-up transformer, the total step-up of both transformers combined is

   (A) 20 to 1
   (B) 12 to 1
   (C) 8 to 1
   (D) 5 to 1

9. An autotransformer whose primary is bd is connected across a 100-volt AC supply as shown in Figure 9. The load of 5 ohms is connected across points c and d. If it is assumed that $N_1 = N_2$, (that is, point c is the midpoint of the winding) current I_1, in amperes, is approximately equal to

(A) 5
(B) 10
(C) 15
(D) 20

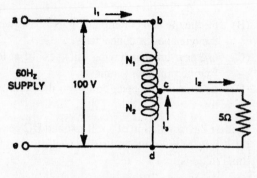

Figure 9

10. In Figure 9, current I_2, in amperes, is approximately equal to

(A) 5
(B) 10
(C) 15
(D) 20

11. In Figure 9, current I_3, in amperes, is approximately equal to

(A) 5
(B) 10
(C) 15
(D) 20

12. A wye-delta transformer bank of 3 single-phase transformers is to be used for step-down operation between circuits with voltages between lines of 23,000 and 2,300. The ratio of each individual transformer should be approximately

(A) 5.8 : 1
(B) 7.05 : 1
(C) 10 : 1
(D) 14.1 : 1

13. A single-phase AC potential of 60 volts is required for test purposes. A 600-volt AC source and two identical transformers with 600-volt primary windings and 120-volt secondary windings are available. For this purpose, the transformers should be connected with

(A) primaries in parallel, secondaries in parallel.
(B) primaries in series, secondaries in parallel.
(C) primaries in parallel, secondaries in series.
(D) primaries in series, secondaries in series.

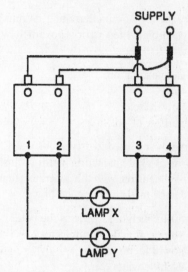

Figure 14

14. The sketch in Figure 14 shows two stepdown transformers with 120-volt secondaries connected in a phasing test with two 120-volt lamps to determine which connections to make for paralleling the secondaries. If leads 1 and 3 are of the same polarity, then

(A) lamp X will be bright and lamp Y dark.
(B) lamp Y will be bright and lamp X dark.
(C) both lamps will be bright.
(D) both lamps will be dark.

ANSWER KEY

1. D	4. C	7. C	10. B	13. B
2. B	5. B	8. A	11. A	14. C
3. B	6. B	9. A	12. A	

GENERATORS AND BATTERIES

> **DIRECTIONS:** For each question, read all choices carefully. Then select the answer that you consider correct or most nearly correct. Write the letter preceding your best choice next to the question.

GENERATORS

1. The frequency of the alternating current generated by a synchronous generator is governed by the speed and the

   (A)   field excitation.
   (B)   load.
   (C)   power factor.
   (D)   number of poles.

2. A leather belt is used to drive a 3-kW DC generator by a 5-hp, 3-phase induction motor. Adjustments for proper belt tension, with the generator running at full load, can be made with the aid of a

   (A)   50-lb. weight as wide as the belt.
   (B)   voltmeter and an ammeter.
   (C)   power factor meter.
   (D)   3-phase wattmeter.

3. Compound DC generators are usually wound so as to be somewhat overcompounded. The degree of compounding is usually regulated by

   (A)   shunting more or less current from the series field.
   (B)   shunting more or less current from the shunt field.
   (C)   connecting it short-shunt.
   (D)   connecting it long-shunt.

4. With reference to a shunt-wound DC generator, if the resistance of the field is increased to a value exceeding its critical field resistance, the generator

   (A)   output may exceed its nameplate rating.
   (B)   may burn out when loaded to its nameplate rating.
   (C)   output voltage will be less than its nameplate rating.
   (D)   cannot build up.

5. A DC shunt generator has developed some trouble. You find that there is an open armature coil. As a temporary measure, you should

   (A)   use new brushes having a thickness of at least three commutator segments.

   (B)   bridge the two commutator bars across which the open coil is connected.
   (C)   use new brushes having thickness of at least four commutator segments.
   (D)   disconnect the open coil from the commutator.

6. If, after the installation of a self-excited DC generator it fails to build up on its first trial run, the first thing to do is

   (A)   increase the field resistance.
   (B)   check the armature insulation resistance.
   (C)   reverse the connections to the shunt field.
   (D)   decrease the speed of the prime mover.

7. In reference to question 6, if the generator still fails to build up, you should make sure that the

   (A)   resistance of the field rheostat is all in.
   (B)   diverter is in series with the armature.
   (C)   resistance of the field circuit is sufficiently small.
   (D)   diverter is in parallel with the armature.

8. In reference to questions 6 and 7, if the generator still fails to build up now, you most probably would have to separately excite the

   (A)   field for a few minutes with the battery.
   (B)   armature for a few minutes with the battery.
   (C)   armature with AC current.
   (D)   field with AC current.

9. The output of a 6-pole DC generator is 360 amperes at 240 volts. If its armature is simplex lap-wound, the current per path, in amperes, through the armature is

   (A)   52.5
   (B)   60
   (C)   105
   (D)   210

10. In reference to question 9, the voltage per path, in volts, is

    (A) 120
    (B) 420
    (C) 60
    (D) 240

11. In reference to question 9, the kilowatt rating of the machine is approximately

    (A) 86
    (B) 50
    (C) 14
    (D) 7

12. A probable cause for a turbogenerator tripping out on overspeed is a sudden

    (A) loss of field excitation.
    (B) large increase in load.
    (C) total loss of load.
    (D) loss of steam pressure.

13. Except for the power limitation of the turbine, the maximum load carried by a generator is limited by the

    (A) relay settings.
    (B) generator voltage.
    (C) field current.
    (D) temperature rise.

14. Differential relays are used on generators to guard against

    (A) unbalanced phase currents.
    (B) an open in the ground neutral.
    (C) large load fluctuations.
    (D) reactive currents.

15. A 60-hertz synchronous generator will run at the greatest possible speed if it is wired for

    (A) 8 poles.
    (B) 6 poles.
    (C) 4 poles.
    (D) 2 poles.

16. Equalizer connections are required when paralleling two

    (A) synchronous generators.
    (B) series generators.
    (C) shunt generators.
    (D) compound generators.

17. A six-pole DC generator has developed an open circuit in one of its six shunt field coils. To locate the defective coil, the field is connected across a 120-volt source and voltmeter readings taken across each coil. The defective coil will be the one across whose ends the voltage is

    (A) 120
    (B) 100
    (C) 20
    (D) 0

18. The frequency of the alternating current generated by a synchronous generator is governed by the speed and the

    (A) field excitation.
    (B) load.
    (C) power factor.
    (D) number of poles.

ANSWER KEY

1.	D	5.	B	9.	B	13.	D	16.	D
2.	D	6.	C	10.	D	14.	A	17.	A
3.	A	7.	C	11.	A	15.	D	18.	D
4.	D	8.	A	12.	C				

BATTERIES

1. The term "ampere-hours" is associated with

   (A) motors.
   (B) transformers.
   (C) electromagnets.
   (D) storage batteries.

2. In an installation used to charge a storage battery from a motor-generator, you would *least* expect to find a(n)

   (A) rectifier.
   (B) rheostat.
   (C) voltmeter.
   (D) ammeter.

3. Lead is the metal commonly used for

   (A) transformer cores.
   (B) storage battery plates.
   (C) knife-switch blades.
   (D) power station panel boards.

4. When the liquid in a lead-acid storage cell is low, it is usually proper to

   (A) add a special weak acid solution.
   (B) add only distilled water.
   (C) empty out the cell and replace the solution.
   (D) do nothing until the voltage has dropped in half.

5. In a storage battery installation consisting of twenty 2-volt cells connected in series, a leak develops in one of the cells and all the electrolyte runs out of it. The terminal voltage across the twenty cells will now be

   (A) 40
   (B) 38
   (C) 2
   (D) 0

6. It is objectionable to leave a lead-acid storage battery in a discharged state for a long time mainly because the

   (A) terminals will corrode.
   (B) acid will evaporate.
   (C) electrolyte will attack the container.
   (D) plates will become sulphated.

7. When completing the charging of a lead-acid battery, the charging rate should be lowered to prevent violent gassing. The main reason for this is because

   (A) violent gassing tends to loosen the active material on the positive plates.

   (B) the gases given off are explosive.
   (C) evaporation of the acid weakens the electrolyte.
   (D) the cell containers are subjected to excessive gas pressure.

8. Routine specific gravity readings taken of a lead-acid storage battery pilot cell are usually corrected for electrolyte temperature. The main reason for doing this is to

   (A) allow the readings to be "rounded off" to the nearest 0.001.
   (B) lower the value of the specific gravity if the temperature is too high.
   (C) minimize the effect of errors in taking readings.
   (D) permit a true comparison of the reading with other readings.

9. When mixing sulphuric acid and water to prepare new electrolyte for a lead-acid battery, the acid should be poured into the water to avoid

   (A) making the initial mixture too strong.
   (B) corrosion of the mixing vessel.
   (C) generation of excessive heat.
   (D) the use of too much concentrated acid.

10. Sediment that collects at the bottom of a lead-acid battery cell is mainly due to

    (A) precipitation from the electrolyte.
    (B) dust particles from the atmosphere.
    (C) active material dropped from the plates.
    (D) disintegration of the container.

11. Overcharging a storage battery will NOT cause

    (A) water loss.
    (B) excessive gassing.
    (C) overtemperature.
    (D) sulphation of the plates.

12. A partially discharged lead storage battery may be brought back to full charge by recharging with

    (A) sulphuric acid.
    (B) distilled water.
    (C) direct current.
    (D) alternating current.

13. An accumulation of hard salts blocking the valve in the filler cap of a storage cell might result in

    (A) bulging of the case.
    (B) limiting the charge to less than a full charge.

(C)   buckling of the plates.

(D)   corrosion of the terminals.

14.   A battery is "floating" on the battery bus when the

(A)   battery is supplying all the load.

(B)   battery voltage is higher than the bus voltage.

(C)   charger is shut down.

(D)   battery voltage is equal to the charger voltage.

15.   The advantage a storage battery has over a dry cell is that the storage battery

(A)   is cheaper.

(B)   is easier to use.

(C)   can be recharged.

(D)   can be portable.

16.   During discharge, the internal resistance of a storage battery

(A)   increases.

(B)   remains the same.

(C)   decreases.

(D)   is negative.

17.   The terminal voltage of eight cells connected in series is

(A)   the product of the voltages of each cell.

(B)   the sum of the voltages of each cell.

(C)   the difference between the largest and smallest individual voltages.

(D)   the same as the voltage of any cell.

18.   Of the following, the best indication of the condition of the charge of a lead acid battery is the

(A)   specific gravity.

(B)   open circuit cell voltage.

(C)   level of the electrolyte.

(D)   temperature of the electrolyte.

19.   Cable connections to lead acid storage batteries can be most economically kept free from corrosion by

(A)   the application of petroleum jelly.

(B)   frequent cleaning with a wire brush.

(C)   painting with lacquer.

(D)   continuous charging.

20.   The plates of a lead acid storage battery are most likely to be short circuited if

(A)   the electrolyte evaporates.

(B)   the battery is charged too slowly.

(C)   sediment collects on the bottom of the battery.

(D)   too much water is added.

21.   The active materials on the positive and negative plates of a fully charged acid storage cell in good condition are, respectively,

(A)   lead peroxide and pure lead.

(B)   pure lead and lead sulphate.

(C)   lead peroxide and lead sulphate.

(D)   pure lead and pure lead.

22.   In an ungrounded control battery circuit, an accidental ground on one leg should be removed as soon as possible because, while this condition exists,

(A)   the battery is supplying a heavy load.

(B)   a ground on the other leg would short the battery.

(C)   the closing and trip coils of OCBs will not function.

(D)   difficulty will be experienced in charging the battery.

23.   In connection with storage batteries, water is decomposed forming an explosive mixture of hydrogen and oxygen when a battery is

(A)   left standing while fully charged.

(B)   discharging.

(C)   being charged.

(D)   left standing while completely discharged.

24.   A lead cell storage battery having a 75 ampere-hour capacity is $\frac{1}{3}$ charged. After this battery has been charged at an average rate of 10 amperes for $2\frac{1}{2}$ hours, it will be approximately

(A) $\frac{2}{5}$ charged.

(B) $\frac{1}{2}$ charged.

(C) $\frac{2}{3}$ charged.

(D) $\frac{3}{4}$ charged.

25.   The number of fresh dry cells that should be connected in series to obtain 12 volts is

(A)   2

(B)   6

(C)   8

(D)   12

26. The maximum voltage obtainable from a dry cell series connection is

    (A) 100
    (B) 200
    (C) 300
    (D) 400

27. An advantage of nickel-cadmium cells is their

    (A) ability to be recharged.
    (B) inability to be discharged.
    (C) cost.
    (D) size.

28. Alkaline cells have all but replaced the carbon-zinc cell because

    (A) they cost less.
    (B) they are safer to use.
    (C) they last longer.
    (D) they are rechargeable.

29. Lithium cells are useful in

    (A) medical devices such as pacemakers.
    (B) automobile starter circuits.
    (C) automobile light circuits.
    (D) running personal computers.

ANSWER KEY

1. D	6. D	11. D	16. A	21. A	26. C
2. A	7. A	12. C	17. B	22. B	27. A
3. B	8. D	13. A	18. A	23. C	28. C
4. B	9. C	14. D	19. A	24. C	29. A
5. D	10. C	15. C	20. C	25. C	

QUESTIONS ON BASIC ELECTRONICS

The modern electrician is expected to be knowledgeable in the area of basic electronics. Today there are many pieces of equipment in almost every industrial or commercial location that require the electrician to have a basic knowledge of electronics. The electrician is usually called upon to identify a problem and to isolate a piece of equipment for further work by an electronics technician. By studying these questions and by having the answers at your fingertips, you may be able to obtain the job over someone else with a similar background who does not know the terms and how they are used.

It is to the advantage of every apprentice electrician, electrician's helper, and electrician to have a fundamental knowledge of electronics.

1. An autotransformer

    (A) has many coils.
    (B) has 2 coils.
    (C) has only 1 coil.
    (D) is used on autos only.
    (E) has low efficiency.

2. A 10-microfarad capacitor is charged to one time constant so its stored energy is equal to

    (A) 63.2 percent of maximum.
    (B) 77.1 percent of maximum.
    (C) 99.3 percent of maximum.
    (D) 85.6 percent of maximum.
    (E) 50.0 percent of maximum.

3. Impedance is measured in

    (A) volts.
    (B) amps.
    (C) ohms.
    (D) hertz.
    (E) farads.

4. Which of these has the LEAST influence on the strength of the emf induced in an induction coil?

    (A) Strength of current in primary
    (B) Number of turns on secondary as compared to turns on primary
    (C) Size of wire of primary and secondary coils
    (D) Rate of field variations
    (E) Material of the core

5. In a 100 percent efficient step-down transformer of 100 watts (volt-amperes) connected to 100 volts, how many amps at 10 volts will the secondary deliver?

    (A) 1,000
    (B) 100
    (C) 10
    (D) 1.0
    (E) 0.5

6. A device that automatically causes the current to stop flowing when too much current goes through it is called a

    (A) relay.
    (B) electromagnet.
    (C) fuse.
    (D) circuit stopper.
    (E) solenoid.

7. In a parallel circuit consisting of these elements, which would get the *hottest* when power is applied?

    (A) A long thin copper wire
    (B) A short thick copper wire
    (C) A long thin nichrome wire
    (D) A short thick nichrome wire
    (E) A short thick iron wire

8. Electric motors transform electrical energy into

    (A) magneto energy.
    (B) potential energy.
    (C) static energy.
    (D) physical energy.
    (E) mechanical energy.

9. Which of these is NOT true about the d'Arsonval movement?

    (A) Detects presence of electric current
    (B) Determines direction of the current
    (C) Measures its strength
    (D) Coil is fixed
    (E) Can be used as an ohmmeter

10. Electricity is defined as the flow of which of these through a conductor?

    (A) Resistance
    (B) Volts
    (C) Ohms
    (D) Protons
    (E) Electrons

11. The voltmeter is always connected

 (A) in series with the ammeter.
 (B) across the load.
 (C) across the ammeter.
 (D) in series with the load.
 (E) directly in the line.

12. In a series circuit, the unit that is the same in all parts of the circuit is the

 (A) voltage.
 (B) resistance.
 (C) wattage.
 (D) current.
 (E) power.

13. A picture of the variations in amplitude of an electric current is called

 (A) sine wave.
 (B) graph.
 (C) amperage.
 (D) wave form.
 (E) envelope.

14. An inductance has a reactance of 10,000 ohms at 10,000 hertz. At 20,000 hertz its inductive reactance equals

 (A) 500 ohms.
 (B) 1,000 ohms.
 (C) 628,000 ohms.
 (D) 20,000 ohms.
 (E) 10,000 ohms.

15. An alternating current sine wave whose peak amplitude gradually and continuously decreases for each hertz is called a

 (A) continuous wave.
 (B) damped wave.
 (C) carrier wave.
 (D) DC.
 (E) fluctuating DC.

16. The primary coil is always the

 (A) smallest coil.
 (B) largest coil.
 (C) input coil.
 (D) output coil.
 (E) coil on the left.

17. Generally, an RF coil has a(n)

 (A) copper core.
 (B) solid iron core.
 (C) air dielectric.
 (D) dielectric core.
 (E) lead core.

18. In order for one ampere to flow through a 3-ohm resistor, you must connect

 (A) a 6-volt battery.
 (B) three dry cells in parallel.
 (C) two dry cells in series.
 (D) one dry cell.
 (E) one large battery.
 (Note: Dry cells have 1.5 volts)

19. With two resistances connected in parallel,

 (A) the current through each must be the same.
 (B) the voltage across each must be the same.
 (C) their combined resistance equals the sum of the individual values.
 (D) each must have the same resistance value.
 (E) the total resistance is equal to four times one resistance.

20. When a capacitor is charged,

 (A) both plates are negatively charged.
 (B) both plates are positively charged.
 (C) one plate is positively charged and the other is negatively charged.
 (D) the dielectric has a positive charge.
 (E) both plates get smaller.

21. The plate of a capacitor connected to the positive terminal of a battery will

 (A) have a surplus of electrons.
 (B) have a shortage of electrons.
 (C) have a neutral charge.
 (D) have a very high voltage.
 (E) not operate properly.

22. A battery connected across an inductance in series with a switch

 (A) can produce induced voltage as the current decreases when the switch is opened.
 (B) cannot produce induced voltage because the current has only one polarity.
 (C) must supply at least 500 volts to produce any induced voltage.
 (D) produces more induced voltage when the switch is closed than when it is open.
 (E) has no effect on the circuit with the switch closed.

23. In a 60-hertz AC circuit with 90 ohms resistance in series with 90-ohms X_L, the phase angle equals

 (A) 0 degrees.
 (B) 30 degrees.
 (C) 45 degrees.
 (D) 90 degrees.
 (E) 180 degrees.

24. The number of amperes flowing in a circuit can best be measured by using a(n)

    (A) ohmeter.
    (B) voltmeter.
    (C) wattmeter.
    (D) galvanometer.
    (E) ammeter.

25. The DC resistance of a device can be measured by using a(n)

    (A) ohmeter.
    (B) voltmeter.
    (C) wattmeter.
    (D) galvanometer.
    (E) ammeter.

26. A 16-millihenry inductance has a reactance of 1,000 ohms. If two of these are connected in series without any mutual coupling, their total reactance equals

    (A) 500 ohms.
    (B) 1,000 ohms.
    (C) 1,600 ohms.
    (D) 2,000 ohms.
    (E) 0.016 ohms.

27. When testing an unknown source of power, first you should connect across it at

    (A) a low range on the ammeter.
    (B) a high range on the ammeter.
    (C) a low range on the voltmeter.
    (D) a high range on the voltmeter.
    (E) a low range on the wattmeter.

28. The smallest whole unit of an element like uranium is called a(n)

    (A) atom.
    (B) molecule.
    (C) electron.
    (D) proton.
    (E) ion.

29. Static electricity

    (A) operates a radio.
    (B) is moving.
    (C) is stored.
    (D) runs motors.
    (E) can't do any work.

30. To connect a basic meter movement so that it will safely measure larger current, you should add a

    (A) high resistance in parallel.
    (B) high resistance in series.
    (C) low resistance in parallel.

    (D) low resistance in series.
    (E) battery in series.

31. A coil has 1,000 henrys and 5 ohms of internal resistance. Its time constant equals

    (A) 0.005 second.
    (B) 5 seconds.
    (C) 200 seconds.
    (D) 1,000 seconds.
    (E) 5,000 seconds.

32. In a series LC circuit, at the resonant frequency, the

    (A) current is minimum.
    (B) voltage across C is minimum.
    (C) impedance is maximum.
    (D) current is maximum.
    (E) voltage across L is minimum.

33. At resonance, the phase angle equals

    (A) 0 degrees.
    (B) 90 degrees.
    (C) 180 degrees.
    (D) 270 degrees.
    (E) 360 degrees.

34. In a parallel LC circuit, at the resonant frequency, the

    (A) line current is maximum.
    (B) inductive branch current is minimum.
    (C) total impedance is minimum.
    (D) total impedance is maximum.
    (E) capacitive branch current is minimum.

35. To make the best permanent magnet, you should use

    (A) hard steel.
    (B) soft iron.
    (C) brass.
    (D) zinc.
    (E) copper.

36. The best conductor of magnetic lines of force is

    (A) brass.
    (B) wood.
    (C) air.
    (D) aluminum.
    (E) soft iron.

37. The difference between a magnetized and unmagnetized bar of iron is that the magnetized bar

    (A) is heavier.
    (B) is lighter.
    (C) is softer.
    (D) is harder.
    (E) has its molecules aligned.

38. In the carbon-zinc dry cell, the negative terminal is made of

(A) lead oxide.
(B) copper.
(C) carbon.
(D) sponge lead.
(E) zinc.

39. The property of a coil that tends to oppose any change of current through it is called

(A) inductance.
(B) oscillation.
(C) henry.
(D) mutual inductance.
(E) resonance.

40. When either L or C is increased, the resonant frequency of the LC circuit

(A) increases.
(B) decreases.
(C) remains the same.
(D) is determined by the resistance.
(E) is determined by pi (π).

41. The resonant frequency of a 10-henry and a 10-microfarad coil and capacitor is

(A) 15.9 Hz.
(B) 15.9 KHz.
(C) 15.9 MHz.
(D) 159 Hz.
(E) 1590 Hz.

42. In a 60-hertz sine wave AC circuit with X_L and R in series, the

(A) voltages across R and X_L are in phase.
(B) voltages across R and X_L are 180 degrees out of phase.
(C) voltage across R lags the voltage across X_L by 90 degrees.
(D) voltage across R leads the voltage across X_L by 90 degrees.
(E) voltages add up to a 360-degree phase shift.

43. For a series or parallel LC circuit, resonance occurs when

(A) X_L is 10 times X_C.
(B) X_C is 10 times X_L.
(C) $X_L = X_C$.
(D) the phase angle of the current in the circuit is 90 degrees.
(E) the phase angle of the current in the circuit is 180 degrees.

44. In a standard home, the lights and convenience outlets are connected in

(A) parallel.
(B) series.
(C) rotation.
(D) series-parallel.
(E) None of the above

45. In which of the following circuits will the voltage source produce the most current?

(A) 10 volts across 10 ohms' resistance
(B) 10 volts across two 10-ohm resistors in series
(C) 10 volts across two 10-ohm resistors in parallel
(D) 1,000 volts across a one-meg resistance
(E) 100 volts across 1,000 ohms

46. A potential difference applied across a one-meg resistor produces 1 mA of current. The applied voltage is

(A) 1 millivolt.
(B) 1 microvolt.
(C) 1 kilovolt.
(D) 1,000,000 volts.
(E) 10 kilovolts.

47. According to Kirchhoff's laws, the sum of the currents entering a point in the circuit is equal to the

(A) sum of the currents leaving that point.
(B) constant-current source in the circuit.
(C) sum of the voltages around the loop.
(D) sum of the applied voltages.
(E) constant-voltage source in the circuit.

48. According to Kirchhoff's laws, the algebraic sum of the voltages around any closed loop is equal to

(A) the highest voltage.
(B) zero.
(C) the magnitude of the constant-current source.
(D) the Thelvin voltage source.
(E) the magnitude of the constant-voltage source.

49. When a changing current in one coil causes a changing current in a nearby coil, it is known as

(A) mutual-induction.
(B) self-induction.
(C) resonance.
(D) oscillation.
(E) transformation.

50. The resonant frequency of a tuned circuit depends on the inductance and the

(A) detector.
(B) reproducer.
(C) capacitance.
(D) ground.
(E) battery.

51. In parallel banks with three unequal branch resistances, the

(A) current is highest in the highest R.
(B) current is equal in all the branches.
(C) voltage is highest across the lowest R.
(D) current is highest in the lowest R.
(E) voltage is highest across the highest R.

52. In a series voltage divider, the

(A) lowest R has the highest voltage.
(B) highest R has the highest voltage.
(C) lowest R has the most current.
(D) highest R has the most current.
(E) lowest R has a zero voltage.

53. If a parallel circuit has one of its three branches open, the current

(A) is zero in all the branches.
(B) is zero in the open branch and increases in all the other branches.
(C) is zero in the open branch and decreases in all the other branches.
(D) in the line decreases.
(E) in the line increases.

54. The plates of the automobile storage battery are usually made of

(A) rubber.
(B) lead.
(C) iron.
(D) brass.
(E) aluminum.

55. A negative particle of electricity is called a(n)

(A) atom.
(B) molecule.
(C) electron.
(D) proton.
(E) ion.

56. The average voltage of the common carbon-zinc dry cell is

(A) 1.5 volts.
(B) 0.5 volt.
(C) 1.0 volt.

(D) 2.0 volts.
(E) 2.5 volts.

57. A dry cell produces electrical energy from

(A) mechanical energy.
(B) chemical energy.
(C) frictional energy.
(D) kinetic energy.
(E) potential energy.

58. The center, or core, of an atom is called the

(A) nucleus.
(B) axis.
(C) proton.
(D) molecule.
(E) electron.

59. The strongest part of a magnet is at its

(A) center.
(B) ends.
(C) inside.
(D) outside.
(E) top.

60. Larger cell plates in a battery

(A) increase voltage.
(B) decrease voltage.
(C) increase amperage.
(D) decrease amperage.
(E) have no effect.

61. Which of the following will have minimum eddy current losses?

(A) Iron core
(B) Laminated core
(C) Powdered iron core
(D) Copper core
(E) Steel core

62. In a sine wave AC circuit with 40 ohms R in series with 30 ohms X_L, the total impedance equals

(A) 30 ohms.
(B) 40 ohms.
(C) 50 ohms.
(D) 70 ohms.
(E) 17 ohms.

63. Two 250-millihenry chokes in series have a total inductance of

(A) 60 mH.
(B) 125 mH.
(C) 250 mH.
(D) 500 mH.
(E) 1,000 mH.

64. When two resistances are connected in series,

(A) they must both have the same resistance value.
(B) the voltage across each must be the same.
(C) they must have different resistance values.
(D) there is only one path for current through both resistances.
(E) they are equal in value.

65. Three carbon-zinc dry cells connected in series to a 1.5-ohm resistor would force how much current to flow?

(A) 0.75 amperes
(B) 1.00 amperes
(C) 2 amperes
(D) 3 amperes
(E) 0.5 amperes

66. With a 10,000-ohm resistance in series with a 2,000-ohm resistance, the total R_T equals

(A) 2K.
(B) 8K.
(C) 10K.
(D) 12K.
(E) 1.65K.

67. In a capacitive circuit,

(A) a decrease in applied voltage makes a capacitor charge.
(B) a steady value of applied voltage causes discharge.
(C) an increase in applied voltage makes a capacitor discharge.
(D) an increase in applied voltage makes a capacitor charge.
(E) an increase in applied voltage changes the capacitance.

68. In a sine wave AC circuit with a resistive branch and capacitive branch in parallel, the

(A) voltage across the capacitance lags the voltage across the resistance by 90 degrees.
(B) resistive branch current is 90 degrees out of phase with the capacitive branch current.
(C) resistive and capacitive branch currents have the same phase.
(D) resistive and capacitive branch currents are 180 degrees out of phase.
(E) resistive and capacitive branch currents are 270 degrees out of phase.

69. Which of these has NOTHING to do with the resistance of a conductor?

(A) Length
(B) Diameter
(C) Voltage
(D) Material
(E) Temperature

70. In a sine wave AC circuit with 90 ohms resistance in series with 90 ohms capacitive reactance, the phase angle is

(A) –90 degrees.
(B) –45 degrees.
(C) zero.
(D) 90 degrees.
(E) 45 degrees.

71. Which of these is NOT true of the induction rotor?

(A) External current is fed to the rotor.
(B) Current is induced in the rotor.
(C) Interaction between the induced current in the rotor and the air gap flux causes the rotor to turn.
(D) Its speed is determined by the frequency of the AC.
(E) It may be wound several ways.

72. With two equal resistances in series across a 90-volt battery, the voltage across each resistance equals

(A) 30 volts.
(B) 45 volts.
(C) 90 volts.
(D) 180 volts.
(E) 15 volts.

73. The material having the highest electrical conductivity is

(A) nichrome.
(B) tungsten.
(C) zinc.
(D) copper.
(E) silver.

74. The current in every part of a series circuit is

(A) different.
(B) opposite.
(C) equal to the resistance.
(D) equal.
(E) alternating.

75. In a parallel circuit of lamps, the most current will flow in the branch whose lamp

(A) burns dimmest.
(B) has the least resistance.
(C) has the most resistance.
(D) is frosted.
(E) has the least wattage.

76. The sum of series I × R voltage drops

    (A)   is less than the smallest voltage drop.
    (B)   equals the average value of all the voltage drops.
    (C)   equals the applied voltage.
    (D)   is usually more than the applied voltage.
    (E)   is the same voltage across each resistor.

77. R_1 and R_2 are in series with an applied voltage of 90 volts. If the voltage of V_1 is 30 volts, then V_2 must be

    (A)   30 volts.   (D)   60 volts.
    (B)   90 volts.   (E)   15 volts.
    (C)   45 volts.

78. When one resistance in a series string is open, the

    (A)   current is maximum in the normal resistance.
    (B)   current is zero in all the resistances.
    (C)   voltage is zero across the open resistance.
    (D)   current increases in the voltage source.
    (E)   current decreases by the amount of the resistance that is open.

79. With a 4-ohm resistance and a 2-ohm resistance in series across a 6-volt battery, the current in

    (A)   the larger resistance is 1.33 amperes.
    (B)   the smaller resistance is 3 amperes.
    (C)   both resistors is 1 ampere.
    (D)   both resistors is 2 amperes.
    (E)   both resistors is 3 amperes.

80. The resistance of an open series string is

    (A)   zero.
    (B)   equal to the normal resistance of the string.
    (C)   about double the normal resistance of the string.
    (D)   infinite.
    (E)   about six times the normal resistance of the string.

81. A 250-pF capacitor is in series with a one-meg-ohm resistor across a 100-volt battery. The voltage equals 63 volts across the

    (A)   capacitor after 250 microseconds.
    (B)   resistor after 250 microseconds.
    (C)   capacitor after 1,250 microseconds.
    (D)   resistor after 1,250 microseconds.
    (E)   capacitor after 63 milliseconds.

82. The voltage applied across a 20-ohm and a 30-ohm resistor in series is 100 volts. The voltage drop across R_1 is 40 volts. The current through the other resistor is

    (A)   5 amperes.
    (B)   3.33 amperes.
    (C)   1.33 amperes.
    (D)   2 amperes.
    (E)   2.5 amperes.

83. A 0.2-microfarad capacitance will have a reactance of 1,000 ohms at the frequency of

    (A)   795.77 Hz.
    (B)   1 Khz.
    (C)   1 MHz.
    (D)   79.577 Hz.
    (E)   10 MHz.

84. The relay

    (A)   transforms a small current to a large one.
    (B)   opens a closed circuit only.
    (C)   acts as an electrically operated switch.
    (D)   reduces the resistance in a long telegraph line.
    (E)   replaces a battery.

85. With steady DC voltage from a battery applied to a capacitance after it charges to the battery voltage, the current in the circuit

    (A)   depends on the current rating of the battery.
    (B)   is greater for larger values of capacitance.
    (C)   is smaller for larger values of capacitance.
    (D)   is zero for any capacitance value.
    (E)   is maximum for any capacitance value.

86. With 50 volts of RMS applied across 100 ohms of capacitance reactance, the RMS current in the circuit equals

    (A)   0.5 ampere.
    (B)   0.637 ampere.
    (C)   0.707 ampere.
    (D)   1.414 amperes.
    (E)   5.0 amperes.

87. Four carbon-zinc dry cells connected in series would have a total voltage of

    (A)   1.5 volts.
    (B)   8.0 volts.
    (C)   4.5 volts.
    (D)   6 volts.
    (E)   3 volts.

88. A coil of wire that has electricity through it acts the same as if it were a

    (A)   generator.
    (B)   magneto.
    (C)   magnet.
    (D)   starter.
    (E)   transformer.

89. Wherever electricity flows through a wire, around that wire you will find

(A) moisture.
(B) lightning.
(C) an electromagnetic field.
(D) static.
(E) radio waves.

90. Current is directly proportional to the voltage and inversely proportional to the

(A) wattage.
(B) amperes.
(C) resistance.
(D) volts.
(E) distance.

91. The best of these conductors of electricity is

(A) gold.
(B) silver.
(C) lead.
(D) aluminum.
(E) copper.

92. Two 1,000-ohm X_C in parallel have a combined reactance of

(A) 500 ohms.
(B) 707 ohms.
(C) 1,000 ohms.
(D) 2,000 ohms.
(E) 1,414 ohms.

93. The unit of electrical resistance is the

(A) volt.
(B) ohm.
(C) henry.
(D) ampere.
(E) watt.

94. Two 1,000-ohm X_C values in series have a total reactance of

(A) 500 ohms.
(B) 707 ohms.
(C) 1,000 ohms.
(D) 2,000 ohms.
(E) 1,414 ohms.

95. The capacitive reactance of a 0.1-microfarad capacitor at 1,000 Hz equals

(A) 1,592 ohms.
(B) 159.2 ohms.

(C) 628 ohms.
(D) 3,200 ohms.
(E) 15,920 ohms.

96. Which of these describes a short circuit?

(A) A small piece of wire
(B) A very low resistance across a power source
(C) A short wire of high resistance
(D) A current flowing for a very short time
(E) An open circuit

97. At one frequency, larger capacitance results in

(A) more reactance.
(B) less reactance.
(C) less reactance if the voltage amplitude decreases.
(D) more reactance if the voltage amplitude increases.
(E) the same reactance.

98. In an AC circuit with resistance but no reactance,

(A) two 1,000-ohm resistances in series total 1,414 ohms.
(B) two 1,000-ohm resistances in series total 2,000 ohms.
(C) two 1,000-ohm resistances in parallel total 707 ohms.
(D) 1,000 ohms in series with 400 ohms totals 600 ohms.
(E) 1,000 ohms in parallel with 400 ohms totals 1,400 ohms.

99. Alternating current in an inductive circuit produces maximum induced voltage when the current has its

(A) maximum value.
(B) maximum change in magnetic flux.
(C) minimum change in magnetic flux.
(D) RMS value of $0.707 \times$ peak.
(E) RMS value of $1,414 \times$ peak.

100. A magnet *will* pick up

(A) wood.
(B) iron.
(C) rubber.
(D) glass.
(E) paper.

101. In a resonant parallel LC circuit,

(A) $X_L = X_C$

(B) $f_r = \sqrt{LC}$

(C) $f_r = 2\pi\sqrt{LC}$

(D) $X_L = \sqrt{X_C}$

(E) $X_C = 2\pi\sqrt{LC}$

102. The symbol for impedance is

(A) X

(B) Z

(C) X_L

(D) C

(E) R

103. Impedance is measured in

(A) voltage.

(B) resistance.

(C) ohms.

(D) amperes.

(E) current.

104. When $X_L = X_C$ in a series RCL circuit, the only opposition is provided by the

(A) inductor.

(B) capacitor.

(C) resistor.

(D) capacitance.

(E) inductance.

ANSWER KEY

1. C	19. B	37. E	55. C	73. E	91. A
2. A	20. C	38. E	56. A	74. D	92. A
3. C	21. B	39. A	57. B	75. B	93. B
4. C	22. A	40. B	58. A	76. C	94. D
5. C	23. C	41. A	59. B	77. D	95. A
6. C	24. E	42. C	60. C	78. B	96. B
7. B	25. A	43. C	61. B	79. C	97. B
8. E	26. D	44. A	62. C	80. D	98. B
9. D	27. D	45. C	63. D	81. A	99. A
10. E	28. A	46. C	64. D	82. D	100. B
11. B	29. C	47. A	65. D	83. A	101. A
12. D	30. C	48. B	66. D	84. C	102. B
13. D	31. C	49. A	67. D	85. D	103. C
14. D	32. D	50. C	68. B	86. A	104. C
15. B	33. A	51. D	69. C	87. D	
16. C	34. D	52. B	70. B	88. C	
17. C	35. B	53. D	71. A	89. C	
18. C	36. E	54. B	72. B	90. C	

THE INDUSTRIAL ELECTRICIAN

Electricians are in demand wherever industry relies on electricity for its power and operation. Without electricity, we would be back in the Dark Ages. For people to have a decent modern standard of living, there must be a source of energy to take the place of muscle labor. The most economical source of this energy is electricity. It has been made to accomplish the menial tasks that bore people. Through electricity, space travel, television, radio, and computers have been made possible. Heavy labor has almost been eliminated by an inexpensive servant—the electric motor.

Control of this servant is most important in an industrialized society. Many devices have been designed to control the electric motor and to increase its applications and efficiency. Some of these are electromechanical; others are solid state electronics. The control of electricity, however, is not without its problems. That is where you, the industrial electrician, come in. You will see to it that electricity is safely controlled wherever it is needed.

This chapter has been prepared to help you master some of the information you will need to be a successful industrial electrician with a motor control specialty. The emphasis of the questions is on the most important knowledge and information expected in this specialty. You should obtain a good textbook on Motor Controls to update you on the latest developments in this field.

Once you have mastered the terminology, you should be able to carry on a conversation with skilled people working in this trade. You should be able to put some of this information to immediate use. The basic principles of electricity can be helpful to a person who wants to branch out and specialize in electronic controls. Everything you learn will be helpful to you should you decide to specialize in some aspect of electronics in addition to electricity.

DIRECTIONS: Complete the following statements by filling in the blanks.

---

1. There are three types of motors when classified into larger groups. They are the AC, DC, and _____ motors.

   (A) universal
   (B) shaded pole
   (C) capacitor start
   (D) synchronous

2. In a DC motor, there is always a _____ emf developed.

   (A) counterclockwise
   (B) clockwise
   (C) counter
   (D) central

3. The three categories of DC motors are the series, shunt, and _____.

   (A) differential
   (B) compound
   (C) noncompound
   (D) cumulative

4. A _____ motor is connected with the field windings in parallel with the armature windings.

   (A) series
   (B) shunt
   (C) compound
   (D) cumulative

5. Split-phase motors are designed to use inductance, capacitance, or _____ to develop a starting torque.

   (A) resistance
   (B) slip
   (C) counter emf
   (D) cumulative surges

6. Speed of a squirrel-cage motor depends on the frequency of the power source and the number of _____ the motor has.

   (A) armatures
   (B) poles
   (C) capacitors
   (D) inductors

7. Torque of a motor is measured in _____.

   (A) pound-feet
   (B) inch-ounces
   (C) foot-pounds
   (D) pound-inches

8. It takes _____ watts of electrical energy to equal one horsepower.

   (A) 1000
   (B) 100
   (C) 746
   (D) 146

9. Classes of motor insulation are indicated by a _____.

   (A) number
   (B) letter
   (C) number and letter
   (D) stroke mark

10. Timers are broken down into three categories: dash-pot, _____ clock, and electronic timers.

    (A) asynchronous
    (B) synchronous
    (C) nonsynchronous
    (D) bi-synchronous

11. The solid state timer is more accurate and _____ and is becoming the standard of the industry.

    (A) versatile
    (B) variable
    (C) variant
    (D) volume oriented

12. Thumbwheel switches are utilized on many electronic devices to allow for the setting of time or _____.

    (A) cycles
    (B) sequences
    (C) processes
    (D) counts

13. Sensors are the _____ of the motor control system.

    (A) foundation
    (B) basis
    (C) heart
    (D) eyes

14. Force, pressure, temperature, and tactile sensors all respond to _____.

    (A) light
    (B) magnetism
    (C) noncontact
    (D) contact

15. LEDs are available in four basic color bands: infra-red, red, green, and _____.

    (A) blue
    (B) black
    (C) orange
    (D) yellow

16. BCD stands for binary _____ decimal.

    (A) class
    (B) controlled
    (C) coded
    (D) colored

17. Proximity switches are designed for _____ environments in places in which it is required to sense the presence of metal objects without touching them.

    (A) industrial
    (B) outdoor
    (C) indoor
    (D) enclosed

18. The retroreflective type photoelectric switch is ideal for transparent _____ detection.

    (A) plastic
    (B) cup
    (C) jar
    (D) bottle

19. The RF system uses radio frequency to transmit data from an RF tag whenever it passes an _____.

    (A) antenna
    (B) object
    (C) article
    (D) UII

20. Identification, location, and sorting of objects by _____ recognition is possible with the utilization of video imagery and computer technology.

    (A) article
    (B) pattern
    (C) programmed
    (D) object

21. A solenoid that is long in comparison to its diameter has a field intensity at its end approximately one half of that at the _____.

    (A) center
    (B) top
    (C) bottom
    (D) core

22. The presence of a low, barely audible _____ is normal when a coil is energized.

   (A) hum
   (B) noise
   (C) chatter
   (D) chirp

23. Electric motors are designed to deliver their best overall performance when operated at the _____ voltage show on the nameplate.

   (A) excess
   (B) low
   (C) high
   (D) design

24. One of the most important parts of the electric motor is the _____ mechanism.

   (A) brake
   (B) run
   (C) stop
   (D) start

25. The stator of a split-phase motor has two types of coils; one is called the run winding, and the other is called the _____ winding.

   (A) stop
   (B) start
   (C) bucking
   (D) aiding

26. The direction of rotation of the split-phase motor can be changed by reversing the _____ winding leads.

   (A) run
   (B) start
   (C) bucking
   (D) aiding

27. The stator of the _____ motor is constructed very much like that of a split-phase or capacitor-start motor.

   (A) repulsion
   (B) induction
   (C) shaded pole
   (D) repulsion-induction

28. Most motors classified as reversible while running will reverse with a _____ type load.

   (A) noninertial
   (B) inertial
   (C) static
   (D) flexible

29. The PSC motor has a _____ capacitor in series with the start winding.

   (A) standard
   (B) stop
   (C) start
   (D) run

30. Autotransformer starters provide reduced voltage starting at the motor terminals through the use of a tapped, _____ autotransformer.

   (A) three-phase
   (B) single-phase
   (C) two-phase
   (D) bucking

31. Part winding starters are the _____ expensive reduced voltage controller.

   (A) least
   (B) most
   (C) more
   (D) non

32. Wye-delta or star-delta starters are used with delta-wound squirrel-cage motors that have all leads brought out to facilitate a wye connection for reduced _____ starting.

   (A) current
   (B) resistance
   (C) capacitance
   (D) voltage

33. Multi-speed starters are designed for the automatic control of two-speed squirrel-cage motors of either the _____ pole or separate winding types.

   (A) shaded
   (B) sequence
   (C) consequent
   (D) constant

34. When one _____ of a part-winding motor is energized, the torque produced is about 50 percent of "both winding" torque.

   (A) armature
   (B) winding
   (C) pole
   (D) starter

35. The shaded-pole induction motor is a _____ -phase motor.

   (A) single
   (B) three
   (C) two
   (D) four

36. The _____ of some of the currents in the windings of a consequent pole motor has the same effect as physically increasing or decreasing the number of poles.

(A) increasing
(B) reducing
(C) shorting
(D) reversal

SOLID-STATE REDUCED-VOLTAGE STARTERS

Electromechanical devices have been used for years and are still reliable and working in many installations. They are used to provide sequencing and interlocking tasks. They are simple in construction, flexible in use, and have many contact combinations. They can also handle large currents and break the circuit as required.

Solid-state devices have no moving parts and no contacts to clean, replace, or adjust. They use transistors, triacs, diacs, and SCRs to do the switching. These logic elements can perform the same functions in a solid-state system as do relays in the electromechanical system.

The solid-state control device has many advantages that make it desirable for the various environments in which it has to operate. It has no contacts to become dirty or to malfunction when they are needed to control a critical sequence of operations. Solid-state control devices are more reliable than electromechanical devices. They come in sealed-in modules that can be plugged into a rack and can be replaced as a unit if anything goes wrong with the circuitry. As you can see, this is a different approach to trouble shooting than that which was previously utilized. This type of electrical work requires the electrician to have a working knowledge of solid-state switching devices.

Reduced-voltage starting can be accomplished in a number of ways. In solid-state circuitry, however, starting is somewhat simpler than what was described previously. The exact details of the circuit functions are somewhat more complex than those of the electromechanical system; however, a complete understanding of solid-state physics and/or electronics is not necessary in order to grasp the workings of the simple devices utilized to perform the operations of solid-state switching and motor control.

> **DIRECTIONS:** Complete the following statements by selecting the correct word and filling in the blanks.

37. Solid-state devices use transistors, triacs, diacs, and _____ to do the switching.

(A) SCRs
(B) relays
(C) diodes
(D) LEDs

38. The proper name for the SCR is _____.

(A) solid control rectifier
(B) thyrister
(C) thermistor
(D) thermocouple

39. Once an SCR is turned on or _____, it does not stop forward current flow.

(A) off

(B) biased
(C) switched
(D) gated

40. The _____ is basically a diac with a gate terminal.

(A) triac
(B) SCR
(C) transistor
(D) diode

41. Diacs are used in the control of motors and in _____ detectors.

(A) light
(B) proximity
(C) radiation
(D) random

42. A _____ can be used to trigger a triac.

    (A) diac
    (B) SCR
    (C) diode
    (D) transistor

43. When reverse biased, the LED is _____.

    (A) glowing
    (B) sensitive
    (C) nonconducting
    (D) conducting

44. The purpose of a surge suppressor is to limit voltage noise and _____ spikes produced by the starter coil when the coil circuit is opened.

    (A) current
    (B) overvoltage
    (C) undervoltage
    (D) resistance

45. Suppressors are for use with relays, timers, AC contactors, and _____.

    (A) diacs
    (B) LEDs
    (C) SCRs
    (D) starters

46. Surge suppressors are made up of a combination consisting of a capacitor and a _____.

    (A) LED
    (B) resistor
    (C) diode
    (D) triac

MOTOR CONTROL AND MONITORING

47. The difference in speed for any given load between synchronous and load speed is called the _____ of the motor.

    (A) slip
    (B) slide
    (C) efficiency
    (D) braking

48. To make a synchronous motor self-starting, a squirrel-cage winding is usually placed on the _____.

    (A) frame
    (B) stator
    (C) armature
    (D) rotor

49. In addition to a DC winding on the field, synchronous motors are generally provided with a damper or _____ winding.

    (A) amortisseur
    (B) squirrel-cage
    (C) rotor
    (D) stator

50. If the motor is to operate at high starting torque, it is common practice to use a full-line starting voltage in connection with a time-delay _____ relay.

    (A) overcurrent
    (B) undercurrent
    (C) overvoltage
    (D) undervoltage

51. Synchronous motors may be used for power factor correction; for constant-speed, constant-load drives; and for voltage _____.

    (A) increasing
    (B) regulation
    (C) correction
    (D) reduction

52. Magnetic starters are built to _____ motor speed, start the motor, and set the speed of the motor.

    (A) regulate
    (B) increase
    (C) decrease
    (D) vary

53. Frequency speed control is accomplished by varying the frequency of the power source from 2 to _____ hertz.

(A) 50
(B) 100
(C) 120
(D) 60

54. A _____ generator allows accurate monitoring of machine operating speeds.

(A) tachometer
(B) DC
(C) AC
(D) PDC

MOTOR CONTROL AND PROTECTION

55. Motors must be started, stopped, and _____, and their speed must be controlled.

(A) controlled
(B) regulated
(C) reversed
(D) protected

56. Jogging, or _____, is defined by NEMA as the momentary operation of a motor from rest for the purpose of accomplishing small movements of the driven machine.

(A) jolting
(B) inching
(C) jarring
(D) crawling

57. Plugging is defined by the NEMA as a system of _____ in which the motor connections are reversed so that the motor develops a counter torque.

(A) jolting
(B) jogging
(C) inching
(D) braking

58. Electronic braking is commonly known as _____ braking.

(A) quick
(B) slow
(C) instant
(D) dynamic

59. Brakes are selected by the amount of _____ required for the particular application.

(A) magnetism
(B) pressure
(C) leverage
(D) torque

60. Surge protection and _____ are two of the factors to be considered when protecting motors used to power pumps.

(A) backspin
(B) slip
(C) chatter
(D) pressure

61. A magnetically operated _____ time current overload relay can be used in the protection of AC or DC motors.

(A) inverse
(B) reverse
(C) converse
(D) inverted

THREE-PHASE CONTROLLERS

62. Three-phase squirrel cage motors can be used in _____ different locations and for various applications, including rotary compressors, machine tools, large fans, light conveyors, milling machines, agitators, elevators, hoists, punch presses, centrifugal pumps, and blowers.

    (A) all
    (B) any
    (C) some
    (D) many

63. The synchronous motor is made for power correction and for exact slow-speed drives and maximum efficiency on continuous loads above _____ horsepower.

    (A) 75
    (B) 100
    (C) 25
    (D) 50

64. The purpose of _____ is to have the motor operate only as long as the button is held down.

    (A) braking
    (B) jolting
    (C) plugging
    (D) jogging

65. On _____ motor controllers, the controller operates first one motor and then the other on successive closings of the pilot device.

    (A) duplex
    (B) full-voltage
    (C) two-speed
    (D) medium-voltage

66. Motor _____ centers are used in a wide variety of industrial and commercial applications, such as pulp and paper mills, sawmills, building products, food processing, can plants, waste water treatment plants, coal and bulk handling, chemical plants, and oil and gas production.

    (A) control
    (B) plugging
    (C) jogging
    (D) dynamic

67. _____ voltage usually refers to the range from 2200 to 7200 volts.

    (A) Very high
    (B) High
    (C) Low
    (D) Medium

68. The _____ voltage, primary reactor, squirrel-cage motor controller permits the starting of motors without the high inrush currents and voltage variations associated with full voltage starting.

    (A) reduced
    (B) increased
    (C) high
    (D) medium

69. Programmable controllers are used in a variety of applications to replace conventional _____ devices.

    (A) control
    (B) loop
    (C) circuit
    (D) timer

70. The triac can conduct in _____.

    (A) both directions
    (B) one direction only
    (C) forward direction only
    (D) backward direction only

71. The advantage of all thyristors is that small _____ currents can control large load currents.

    (A) forward
    (B) reverse
    (C) gate
    (D) anode

72. The SCR (Silicon Controlled Rectifier) is basically a _____.

    (A) capacitor
    (B) transistor
    (C) coil
    (D) rectifier

73. The NEC requires that the control transformer in the motor starter must be on the _____ side of the disconnect.

    (A) load
    (B) left
    (C) right
    (D) top

74. The Code says that a 3-pole switch, circuit breaker, or motor starter may be used in a 3-phase motor circuit derived from a 3-phase, 3-wire, corner-grounded _____ system—with the grounded phase leg switched with the hot legs.

    (A) delta-wye
    (B) delta
    (C) wye
    (D) wye-delta

ANSWER KEY

1. D	14. D	27. D	39. D	51. B	63. A
2. C	15. D	28. A	40. A	52. A	64. D
3. B	16. C	29. D	41. B	53. C	65. A
4. B	17. A	30. A	42. A	54. A	66. A
5. A	18. D	31. A	43. C	55. C	67. D
6. B	19. A	32. D	44. B	56. B	68. A
7. A	20. B	33. C	45. D	57. D	69. A
8. C	21. A	34. B	46. B	58. D	70. A
9. B	22. A	35. A	47. A	59. D	71. C
10. B	23. D	36. D	48. D	60. A	72. D
11. A	24. B	37. A	49. A	61. A	73. A
12. D	25. B	38. B	50. A	62. D	74. B
13. A	26. B				

PART THREE

Previous Examinations for Practice

PREVIOUS EXAM 1 — ELECTRICIAN'S HELPER

DIRECTIONS: Each question has four suggested answers, lettered (A), (B), (C), and (D). Decide which is the best answer and underline it. You may check your answers with the answer key that appears at the end of the test. Do not do so until you have completed the entire test.

TIME ALLOWED: 3.5 HOURS

1. Which of the following is a unit of inductance?

   (A) Millihenry
   (B) Microfarad
   (C) Kilohm
   (D) Weber

2. Of the following, the best conductor of electricity is

   (A) aluminum.
   (B) copper.
   (C) silver.
   (D) iron.

3. A voltage of 1,000 microvolts is the same as

   (A) 1,000 volts.
   (B) 0.100 volt.
   (C) 0.010 volt.
   (D) 0.001 volt.

4. The function of a rectifier is similar to that of a(n)

   (A) inverter.
   (B) relay.
   (C) commutator.
   (D) transformer.

5. A 9-ohm resistor rated at 225 watts is used in a 120-volt circuit. In order not to exceed the rating of the resistor, the maximum current, in amperes, that can flow through the circuit is

   (A) 2
   (B) 3
   (C) 4
   (D) 5

6. The number of circular mils in a conductor 0.036 inch in diameter is

   (A) 6
   (B) 36
   (C) 72
   (D) 1,296

7. The color of the label on most commercially available 250-volt cartridge fuses of 15-amperes-or-less capacity is

   (A) green.
   (B) blue.
   (C) red.
   (D) yellow.

8. Assume that a two-microfarad capacitor is connected in parallel with a 3-microfarad capacitor. The resulting capacity, in microfarads, is

   (A) $\frac{2}{3}$

   (B) $\frac{6}{5}$

   (C) $\frac{3}{2}$

   (D) 5

9. The speed of the rotating magnetic field in a 12-pole, 60-Hz stator is

   (A) 1,800 rpm.
   (B) 1,200 rpm.
   (C) 720 rpm.
   (D) 600 rpm.

10. The transformer connection generally used to convert from 3-phase to 2-phase by means of two transformers is the

    (A) Scott or T.
    (B) V or open delta.
    (C) wye-delta.
    (D) delta-wye.

11. The conductance, in ohms, of a circuit whose resistance is one ohm is

    (A) $\frac{1}{10}$

    (B) 1
    (C) 10
    (D) 100

12. Assume that a 220-volt, 25-Hz, AC emf is impressed across a circuit consisting of a 25-ohm resistor in series with a 30-microfarad capacitor. The current in this circuit, in amperes, is most nearly

    (A) 0.5
    (B) 0.8
    (C) 1.0
    (D) 1.5

13. An ammeter has a full-scale deflection with a current of 0.010 ampere and an internal resistance of 20 ohms. In order for the ammeter to have a full-scale deflection with a current of 10 amperes and not damage its movement, a shunt should be used having a value of

    (A) 10 ohms.
    (B) 0.2 ohms.
    (C) 0.02 ohms.
    (D) 0.01 ohms.

14. American Wire Gage (AWG) wire size numbers are set so that the resistance of wire per 1,000 feet doubles with every increase of

    (A) one gage number.
    (B) two gage numbers.
    (C) three gage numbers.
    (D) four gage numbers.

15. In an ideal transformer for transforming or "stepping down" the voltage from 1,200 volts to 120 volts, the turns ratio is

    (A) 10:1
    (B) 12:1
    (C) 1:12
    (D) 1:10

16. When a lead-acid battery is fully charged, the negative plate consists of

    (A) lead peroxide.
    (B) lead sponge.
    (C) lead sulfate.
    (D) lead dioxide.

17. Improving the commutation of a DC generator is most often done by using

    (A) a rheostat in series with the equalizer.
    (B) an equalizer alone.
    (C) a compensator.
    (D) interpoles.

18. In a wave-wound armature, the minimum number of commutator brushes necessary is

    (A) two times the number of poles.
    (B) two, regardless of the number of poles.
    (C) one-half times the number of poles.
    (D) four, regardless of the number of poles.

19. A three-phase induction motor runs hot with all stator coils at the same temperature. The trouble that would cause this condition is that

    (A) the motor is running single-phase.
    (B) the motor is overloaded.
    (C) a part of the motor windings is inoperative.
    (D) the rotor bars are loose.

20. Where constant speed is required, the one of the following motors that should be used is a

    (A) wound-rotor motor.
    (B) series motor.
    (C) compound motor.
    (D) shunt motor.

21. To reverse the direction of rotation of a 3-phase induction motor,

    (A) the field connections should be reversed.
    (B) the armature connections should be reversed.
    (C) any two line leads should be interchanged.
    (D) the brushes should be shifted in the direction opposite to that of the armature rotation.

22. The speed of a wound-rotor motor may be increased by

    (A) decreasing the resistance in the secondary circuit.
    (B) increasing the resistance in the secondary circuit.
    (C) decreasing the shunt field current.
    (D) increasing the series field resistance.

23. The one of the following methods that can be used to increase the slip of the rotor in a single-phase, shaded-pole motor is the

    (A) reversal of the leads of the field winding.
    (B) addition of capacitors in series with the starting winding.
    (C) reduction of the impressed voltage.
    (D) addition of more capacitors in parallel with the starting winding.

24. The direction of rotation of a single-phase AC repulsion motor may be reversed by

    (A) interchanging the two line leads to the motor.
    (B) interchanging the leads to the main winding.

(C) interchanging the leads to the starting winding.

(D) moving the brushes to the other side of the neutral position.

25. The torque developed by a DC series motor is

(A) inversely proportional to the square of the armature current.

(B) proportional to the square of the armature current.

(C) proportional to the armature current.

(D) inversely proportional to the armature current.

26. Of the following, the one that is most commonly used to clean a commutator is

(A) an emery cloth.

(B) graphite.

(C) a smooth file.

(D) fine-grit sandpaper.

27. The type of motor that requires both AC and DC for operation is the

(A) compound motor.

(B) universal motor.

(C) synchronous motor.

(D) squirrel-cage motor.

28. Compensators are used for starting large

(A) shunt motors.

(B) series motors.

(C) induction motors.

(D) compound motors.

29. The device most frequently used to correct low-lagging power factor is a(n)

(A) solenoid.

(B) induction regulator.

(C) induction motor.

(D) synchronous motor.

30. Of the following motors, the one with the highest starting torque is the

(A) compound motor.

(B) series motor.

(C) shunt motor.

(D) split-phase motor.

31. The approximate efficiency of a 60-Hz, 6-pole induction motor running at 1,050 rpm and having a synchronous speed of 1,200 rpm is

(A) 67.0 percent.

(B) 78.5 percent.

(C) 87.5 percent.

(D) 90.0 percent.

32. The main contributing factor to motor starter failures usually is

(A) overloading.

(B) dirt.

(C) bearing trouble.

(D) moisture.

33. The neutral or grounded conductors in branch circuit wiring must be identified by being colored

(A) black or brown.

(B) black with white traces.

(C) white with black traces.

(D) white or natural gray.

34. The smallest radius for the inner edge of any field bend in a 1-inch rigid or flexible conduit when type R wire is being used is

(A) 3 inches.

(B) 5 inches.

(C) 6 inches.

(D) 10 inches.

35. Thermal cutouts used to protect a motor against overloads may have a current rating of not more than

(A) the starting current of the motor.

(B) 125 percent of the full-load current rating of the motor.

(C) the full-load current of the motor.

(D) the current-carrying capacity of the branch circuit conductors.

36. The maximum size of EMT is

(A) 4 inches.

(B) $3\frac{1}{2}$ inches.

(C) 3 inches.

(D) 2 inches.

37. The type of equipment that is defined in the Code as a set of conductors originating at the load side of the service equipment and supplying the main and/or one or more secondary distribution centers is a

(A) subfeeder.

(B) feeder.

(C) main.

(D) service cable.

38. The smallest size rigid conduit that may be used in wiring is

    (A) ³⁄₈ inch.

    (B) ¹⁄₂ inch.

    (C) ³⁄₄ inch.

    (D) 1 inch.

39. An enclosed 600-volt cartridge fuse must be of the knife-blade contact type if its ampere rating is

    (A) 20
    (B) 40
    (C) 60
    (D) 80

40. An insulated ground for fixed equipment should be color coded

    (A) yellow.
    (B) green or green with a yellow stripe.
    (C) blue or blue with a yellow stripe.
    (D) black.

41. Of the following, the meter that CANNOT be used to measure AC voltage is the

    (A) electrodynamic voltmeter.
    (B) electrostatic voltmeter.
    (C) D'Arsonval voltmeter.
    (D) thermocouple voltmeter.

42. Of the following, an instrument frequently used to measure high insulation resistance is

    (A) a tong-test ammeter.
    (B) a megger.
    (C) an ohmmeter.
    (D) an electrostatic voltmeter.

43. When using a voltmeter in testing an electric circuit, the voltmeter should be placed in

    (A) series with the circuit.
    (B) parallel with the circuit.
    (C) parallel or in series with a current transformer, depending on the current.
    (D) series with the active element.

44. The minimum number of wattmeters necessary to measure the power in the load of a balanced 3-phase, 4-wire system is

    (A) 1
    (B) 2
    (C) 3
    (D) 4

45. An instrument that measures electrical energy is the

    (A) current transformer.
    (B) watthour meter.
    (C) dynamometer.
    (D) wattmeter.

46. Of the following items, the one that can be used to properly test an armature for a shorted coil is a

    (A) neon light.
    (B) megger.
    (C) growler.
    (D) pair of series test lamps.

47. The instrument that measures loads at the load terminals averaged over specified time periods is the

    (A) coulomb meter.
    (B) wattmeter.
    (C) demand meter.
    (D) var-hour meter.

48. A multiplier is usually used to increase the range of a

    (A) voltmeter.
    (B) watthour meter.
    (C) Wheatstone bridge.
    (D) Nernst bridge.

49. The instrument used to indicate the phase relation between the voltage and the current of an AC circuit is called a

    (A) power factor meter.
    (B) synchroscope.
    (C) phase indicator.
    (D) var-hour meter.

50. Except where busways are entering or leaving service or distribution equipment, the bottom of the busway enclosure for all horizontal busway runs should be kept at a minimum height above the floor of

    (A) 4 feet.
    (B) 6 feet.
    (C) 8 feet.
    (D) 10 feet.

51. The lubricant commonly used to make it easier to pull braid-covered cable into a duct is

    (A) soapstone.
    (B) soft soap.
    (C) heavy grease.
    (D) light oil.

52. Of the following, the conductor insulation that may be used in wet locations is type

    (A) RH.
    (B) RHH.
    (C) RHW.
    (D) RUH.

53. Assume that at a certain distribution point, you, an electrician's helper, notice that among several of the conductors entering the same raceway, some have a half-inch band of yellow tape while the others do not. The conductors with the yellow tape are all

    (A) grounded.
    (B) ungrounded.
    (C) AC.
    (D) DC.

54. Conductors of the same length, the same circular mil area, and the same type of insulation may be run in multiple

    (A) under no circumstances.
    (B) if each conductor is 4 or larger.
    (C) if each conductor is 2 or larger.
    (D) if each conductor is 1/0 or larger.

55. In order to keep conduits parallel where several parallel runs of conduit of varying size are installed through 45- or 90-degree bends, it is best to

    (A) bend conduit on the job.
    (B) use standard factory-made elbows.
    (C) use flexible connectors to adjust runs.
    (D) bend conduit at the factory.

56. The best way to join two lengths of conduit that cannot be turned is to

    (A) use a split adapter.
    (B) use a conduit union ("Erickson").
    (C) cut running threads on one end of one length of the conduit.
    (D) cut running threads on the ends of both lengths of conduit.

57. When an electrical splice is wrapped with both rubber tape and friction tape, the main purpose of the friction tape is to

    (A) protect the rubber tape.
    (B) provide additional insulation.
    (C) build up the insulation to the required thickness.
    (D) increase the strength of the splice.

58. Assume that explosion-proof wiring is required in a certain area. Conduits entering an enclosure in this area, which contains apparatus that may produce arcs, sparks, or high temperature, shall be provided with

    (A) a cable terminator.
    (B) an approved sealing compound.
    (C) couplings with three full threads engaged.
    (D) insulated bushings.

59. If installed in dry locations, wireways may be used for circuits of not more than

    (A) 208 volts.
    (B) 440 volts.
    (C) 600 volts.
    (D) 1,100 volts.

60. An interior wiring circuit has two conductors, one white and one black. Assume that it becomes necessary to add a third conductor as a switch leg. The color of the third conductor should be

    (A) blue.
    (B) red.
    (C) green.
    (D) natural gray.

61. Keyless lampholders rated at 1,500 watts have bases that are classed as

    (A) intermediate.
    (B) medium.
    (C) mogul.
    (D) admedium.

62. In precast cellular-concrete-floor raceways, the largest conductor that may be installed, except by special permission, is

    (A) No. 2
    (B) No. 0
    (C) No. 00
    (D) No. 000

63. The conductor insulation that may be used for fixture wire is type

    (A) TF.
    (B) TW.
    (C) TA.
    (D) RW.

64. Multiple fuses are permissible

    (A) under no circumstances.
    (B) for conductors longer than 1/0.
    (C) for conductors larger than 2/0.
    (D) for conductors larger than 4/0.

65. In loosing a nut, a socket wrench with a ratchet handle should be used in preference to other types of wrenches if

(A) the nut is out of reach.
(B) the turning space for the handle is limited.
(C) the nut is worn.
(D) greater leverage is required.

66. Solders used for electrical connections are alloys of

(A) tin and lead.
(B) tin and zinc.
(C) lead and zinc.
(D) tin and copper.

67. Another name for a pipe wrench is a

(A) crescent wrench.
(B) torque wrench.
(C) Stillson wrench.
(D) monkey wrench.

68. The tool used to cut raceways is a hacksaw with fine teeth, commonly called a

(A) crosscut saw.
(B) keyhold saw.
(C) rip saw.
(D) tube saw.

69. Lead expansion anchors are most commonly used to fasten conduit to a

(A) wooden partition wall.
(B) plaster wall.
(C) solid concrete wall.
(D) gypsum wall.

70. The use of "running" threads when coupling two sections of conduit is

(A) always good practice.
(B) good practice only when installing enameled conduits.
(C) good practice only if it is impossible to turn one of the conduits.
(D) always poor practice.

71. A quick-break knife switch is often used rather than a standard knife switch of the same rating because the quick-break knife switch

(A) resists burning due to arcing at the contact points.
(B) is easier to install and align.
(C) is simpler in construction.
(D) can carry a higher current without overheating.

72. The tip of a soldering iron is made of copper because

(A) copper is a very good conductor of heat.
(B) solder will not stick to other metals.
(C) it is the cheapest metal available.
(D) the melting point of copper is very high.

73. Good practice requires that cartridge fuses be removed from their clips by using a fuse puller rather than the bare hand. The reason for using the fuse puller is that the

(A) bare hand may be burned or otherwise injured.
(B) fuse is less likely to break.
(C) fuse clips may be damaged when pulled.
(D) use of the bare hand slows down the removal of the fuse and causes arcing.

74. The frame of a portable electric tool should be grounded in order to

(A) reduce leakage from the winding.
(B) prevent short circuits.
(C) reduce the danger of overheating.
(D) prevent the frame from becoming alive to ground.

75. Small cuts or injuries should be

(A) cared for immediately because infection may result.
(B) ignored because they are seldom important.
(C) cared for at the end of the day.
(D) ignored unless they are painful.

76. The least desirable device for measuring the dimensions of an electrical equipment cabinet containing live equipment is a

(A) wooden yardstick.
(B) 6-foot folding wooden ruler.
(C) 12-inch plastic ruler.
(D) 6-foot steel tape.

77. A commonly recommended safe distance between the foot of an extension ladder and the wall against which it is placed is

(A) 3 feet for ladders less than 18 feet in height.
(B) between 3 feet and 6 feet for ladders less than 18 feet in length.
(C) 1/8 the length of the extended ladder.
(D) 1/4 the length of the extended ladder.

78. The first thing to do when a person gets an electric shock and is still in contact with the supply is to

(A) treat the person for burns.
(B) start artificial respiration.

(C) remove the victim from the contact by using a dry stick or dry rope.

(D) cut the power if it can be done in 5 or 6 minutes.

79. When applying the back pressure-arm lift (Holger-Nielsen) method of artificial respiration, the victim should first be placed

(A) in a face-down position.
(B) on his or her back.
(C) in a sitting position.
(D) on his or her left side.

80. The best type of fire extinguisher for electrical fires is the

(A) dry chemical extinguisher.
(B) foam extinguisher.
(C) carbon monoxide extinguisher.
(D) baking soda-acid extinguisher.

81. The conductance, in ohms, of a circuit whose resistance is one ohm is

(A) 0.1
(B) 1
(C) 10
(D) 100

82. Assume that a 220-volt, 25 Hz, AC, emf is impressed across a circuit consisting of a 25-ohm resistor in series with a 30 microfarad capacitor. The current in this circuit, in amperes, is most nearly

(A) 0.5
(B) 0.8
(C) 10
(D) 1.5

83. When a lead-acid battery is fully charged, the negative plate consists of

(A) lead peroxide.
(B) lead sponge.
(C) lead sulfate.
(D) lead dioxide.

84. Improving the commutation of a DC generator is most often done by using

(A) a rheostat in series with the equalizer.
(B) an equalizer alone.
(C) a compensator.
(D) interpoles.

85. In a wave-wound armature, the minimum number of commutator brushes necessary is

(A) two times the number of poles.
(B) two, regardless of the number of poles.
(C) one-half times the number of poles.
(D) four, regardless of the number of poles.

86. The speed of a wound-rotor motor may be increased by

(A) decreasing the resistance in the secondary circuit.
(B) increasing the resistance in secondary circuit.
(C) decreasing the shunt field current.
(D) increasing the series field resistance.

87. Of the following methods, the one that can be used to increase the slip of the rotor in a single-phase, shaded-pole motor is the

(A) reversal of the leads of the field winding.
(B) addition of capacitors in series with the start winding.
(C) reduction of the impressed voltage.
(D) addition of more capacitors in parallel with the start winding.

88. Compensators are used for starting large

(A) shunt motors.
(B) series motors.
(C) induction motors.
(D) compound motors.

89. The device most frequently used to correct low-lagging power factor is a(n)

(A) solenoid.
(B) induction regulator.
(C) induction motor.
(D) synchronous motor.

90. Of the following motors, the one with the highest starting torque is the

(A) compound motor.
(B) series motor.
(C) shunt motor.
(D) split-phase motor.

91. An insulated ground for fixed equipment should be color coded

    (A) yellow.
    (B) green or green with a yellow stripe.
    (C) blue or blue with a yellow stripe.
    (D) black.

92. Of the following, an instrument frequently used to measure high insulation resistance is

    (A) a tong-test ammeter.
    (B) a megger.
    (C) an ohmmeter.
    (D) an electrostatic voltmeter.

93. When using a voltmeter in testing an electric circuit, the voltmeter should be placed in

    (A) series with the circuit.
    (B) parallel with the circuit.
    (C) parallel or in series with a current transformer, depending on the current.
    (D) series with the active element.

94. The minimum number of wattmeters necessary to measure the power in the load of a balanced 3-phase, 4-wire system is

    (A) 1
    (B) 2
    (C) 3
    (D) 4

95. Six resistors of 20 ohms each are connected in series and across a 120-volt power source. The current through each resistor is 1 ampere. The voltage across each resistor would be

    (A) 20 volts.
    (B) 120 volts.

(C) 1200 volts.
(D) 6 volts.

96. Three ammeters are inserted in series with three 40-ohm resistors that have been placed in parallel with one another across a power source. Each ammeter reads 3 amperes. The voltmeter placed across any of the resistors would read

    (A) 40 volts.
    (B) 60 volts.
    (C) 120 volts.
    (D) 80 volts.

97. Three resistors of 30 ohms each are placed in parallel, and two 10-ohm resistors are added in series with the two parallel 30-ohm resistors. The total resistance of the circuit is

    (A) 10 ohms.
    (B) 20 ohms.
    (C) 30 ohms.
    (D) 110 ohms.

98. Forced ventilation is generally an inherent design feature of

    (A) induction motors.
    (B) DC motors.
    (C) synchronous motors.
    (D) hysteresis motors.

ANSWER KEY

1. A	21. C	41. C	61. C	81. B
2. C	22. A	42. B	62. B	82. C
3. D	23. C	43. B	63. A	83. B
4. C	24. D	44. A	64. A	84. D
5. D	25. B	45. B	65. B	85. B
6. D	26. D	46. C	66. A	86. A
7. B	27. C	47. C	67. C	87. C
8. D	28. C	48. A	68. D	88. C
9. D	29. D	49. A	69. C	89. D
10. A	30. B	50. C	70. D	90. B
11. B	31. C	51. A	71. A	91. B
12. C	32. B and D	52. C	72. A	92. B
13. C	33. D	53. D	73. A	93. B
14. C	34. C	54. D	74. D	94. A
15. A	35. B	55. A	75. A	95. A
16. B	36. A	56. B	76. D	96. C
17. D	37. B	57. A	77. D	97. C
18. B	38. B	58. B	78. C	98. A
19. B	39. D	59. C	79. A	
20. D	40. B	60. B	80. A	

PREVIOUS EXAM 2—ELECTRICIAN'S HELPER

> **DIRECTIONS:** Each question has four suggested answers, lettered (A), (B), (C), and (D). Decide which is the best answer and underline it. You may check your answers with the answer key that appears at the end of the test. Do not do so until you have completed the entire test.

TIME ALLOWED: 2.5 HOURS.

1. The property of an electric circuit tending to prevent the flow of current and at the same time causing electric energy to be converted into heat energy is called

    (A) conductance.
    (B) inductance.
    (C) resistance.
    (D) reluctance.

2. If a certain length of copper wire is elongated by stretching and its volume does not change, it then can be said that for a fixed volume the resistance of this conductor varies directly in proportion to

    (A) the square of its length.
    (B) its length.
    (C) the cube of its length.
    (D) the square root of its length.

3. The property of a circuit or of a material that tends to permit the flow of an electric current is called

    (A) conductance.
    (B) inductance.
    (C) resistance.
    (D) reluctance.

4. The equivalent resistance in ohms of a circuit having four resistances, 1, 2, 3, and 4 ohms, respectively, in parallel, is

    (A) 14.8
    (B) 10
    (C) 4.8
    (D) 0.48

5. The area in square inches of one circular mil is

    (A) $(\pi/4)(0.001)^2$
    (B) $4\pi(.01)$
    (C) $(0.001)^2$
    (D) $(0.01)^2$

6. The current through a field rheostat is 5 amperes, and its resistance is 10 ohms. The power lost as heat in the rheostat is approximately

    (A) 500 watts.
    (B) 250 watts.
    (C) 125 watts.
    (D) 50 watts.

7. A DC motor takes 30 amperes at 220 volts and has an efficiency of 80 percent. The horsepower available at the pulley is approximately

    (A) 10
    (B) 7
    (C) 5
    (D) 2

8. A tap is a tool commonly used to

    (A) remove broken screws.
    (B) cut internal threads.
    (C) cut external threads.
    (D) smooth the ends of conduit.

9. Lead covering is used on conductors for

    (A) heat prevention.
    (B) explosion protection.
    (C) grounding.
    (D) moisture proofing.

10. The one of the following tools that is run through a conduit to clear it before wire is pulled through is a(n)

    (A) auger.
    (B) borer.
    (C) stop.
    (D) mandrel.

11. A pothead as used in the trade is a

    (A) pot to heat solder.
    (B) cable terminal.
    (C) protective device used for cable splicing.
    (D) type of fuse.

12. Resistance measurements show that an electromagnet coil consisting of 90 turns of wire having an average diameter of 8 inches is shorted. The length of wire in feet required to rewind this coil is approximately

    (A) 110
    (B) 190
    (C) 550
    (D) 2,280

13. An inexpensive and portable instrument commonly used for detecting the presence of static electricity is the

    (A) neon-tube electrical circuit tester.
    (B) gauss meter.
    (C) photoelectric cell.
    (D) startometer.

14. A coil of wire is connected to an AC source of supply. If an iron bar is placed in the center of this coil, it will affect the magnetic circuit in such a way that the

    (A) inductance of the coil will increase.
    (B) power taken by the coil will increase.
    (C) coil will draw more current.
    (D) impedance of the coil will decrease.

15. The electrolyte used with the Edison nickel-iron-alkaline cell is

    (A) sulphuric acid.
    (B) nitric acid.
    (C) potassium hydroxide.
    (D) lead peroxide.

16. The D'Arsonval galvanometer principle used in sensitive current-measuring instruments is nothing more than

    (A) the elongation of a wire due to the flow of current.
    (B) two coils carrying current reacting with one another.
    (C) the dynamic reaction of an aluminum disc due to eddy currents.
    (D) a coil turning in a magnetic field.

17. With reference to armature windings, lap windings are often called

    (A) series windings.
    (B) cascade windings.
    (C) multiple or parallel windings.
    (D) ring windings.

18. With reference to armature windings, wave windings are often called

    (A) series windings.
    (B) cascade windings.
    (C) multiple or parallel windings.
    (D) ring windings.

19. Polarization in a dry cell causes the reduction in the current capacity of the cell after it has delivered current for some time. A remedy for polarization is to bring oxidizing agents into intimate contact with the cell cathode. A chemical agent commonly used for this purpose is

    (A) potash.
    (B) manganese dioxide.
    (C) lead carbonate.
    (D) acetylene.

20. The emf induced in a coil is greatest where the magnetic field within the coil is

    (A) constant.
    (B) increasing.
    (C) decreasing.
    (D) changing most rapidly.

21. The brightness of incandescent lamps is commonly rated in

    (A) foot candles.
    (B) kilowatts.
    (C) lumens.
    (D) watts.

22. The effect of eddy currents in AC magnetic circuits may be reduced by

    (A) laminating the iron used.
    (B) making the magnet core of solid steel.
    (C) making the magnet core of solid cast iron.
    (D) inserting brass rings around the magnet core.

23. The direction of rotation of a single-phase repulsion induction motor can be reversed by

    (A) reversing two supply leads.
    (B) shifting the position of the brushes.
    (C) changing the connections to the field.
    (D) changing the connections to the armature.

24. Underexciting the DC field of a synchronous motor will cause it to

    (A) slow down.
    (B) speed up.
    (C) draw lagging current.
    (D) be unable to carry full normal load.

25. A certain 6-pole, 60-Hz induction motor has a slip of 5 percent when operating at a certain load. The actual speed of this motor under these conditions is most nearly

- (A) 1200 rpm.
- (B) 1140 rpm.
- (C) 570 rpm.
- (D) 120 rpm.

26. The direction of rotation of a 3-phase, wound-rotor induction motor can be reversed by

- (A) interchanging the connections to any two rotor terminals.
- (B) interchanging the connections to any two stator terminals.
- (C) interchanging the connections to the field.
- (D) shifting the position of the brushes.

27. A 10″ pulley revolving at 950 rpm is belted to a 20″ pulley. The rpm of the 20″ pulley is most nearly

- (A) 1,900
- (B) 1,425
- (C) 950
- (D) 475

28. A battery composed of 5 cells each having an emf of 1.5 volts and an internal resistance of .1 ohm is connected to a .5-ohm resistance. If the cells are all in parallel, the current in amperes drawn from the battery is most nearly

- (A) 2.88
- (B) 3.00
- (C) 12.50
- (D) 14.50

29. The maximum power delivered by a battery is obtained when the external resistance of the battery is made

- (A) two times as large as its internal resistance.
- (B) one half as large as its internal resistance.
- (C) one quarter as large as its internal resistance.
- (D) equal to its internal resistance.

30. A voltmeter is connected across the terminals of a certain battery. The difference between the open-circuit voltage and the voltage when current is taken from the battery is the

- (A) internal voltage drop in the battery.
- (B) external voltage drop of the battery.
- (C) emf of the battery.
- (D) drop in voltage across the load resistance.

Questions 31 and 32 relate to the following information:

According to the National Electrical Code, the number of wires running through or terminating in an outlet or junction box shall be limited according to the free space within the box and the size of the wires. For combinations NOT found in a table provided for the selection of junction boxes, the Code gives the following table:

Size of Conductor	Free Space Within Box for Each Conductor
no. 14	2 cubic inches
no. 12	2.25 cubic inches
no. 10	2.5 cubic inches
no. 8	3 cubic inches

31. In accordance with the above information, the minimum size of box, in inches, for 9 No. 12 wires is

- (A) $1\frac{1}{2} \times 4$ square.
- (B) $1\frac{1}{2} \times 3$ square.
- (C) 2×3 square.
- (D) 2×4 square.

32. With reference to the above information, the minimum size of box, in inches, for 4 No. 8 wires and 4 No. 10 wires is

- (A) $1\frac{1}{2} \times 4$ square.
- (B) $1\frac{1}{2} \times 3$ square.
- (C) 2×3 square.
- (D) 2×4 square.

Questions 33–36 refer to the diagram below.

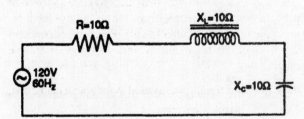

33. The value of the impedance, in ohms, of the above circuit is most nearly

- (A) 30
- (B) 10
- (C) 3.33
- (D) 1.73

34. The current, in amperes, flowing in the above circuit is most nearly

(A) 4
(B) 6
(C) 12
(D) 18

35. The power, in watts, consumed in the above circuit is most nearly

(A) 480
(B) 635
(C) 720
(D) 1,440

36. The voltage drop across the 10-ohm resistance is most nearly

(A) 10V.
(B) 40V.
(C) 60V.
(D) 120V.

37. The current, in amperes, drawn from a battery cell having an emf of 3 volts and an internal resistance of 0.02 ohm when connected to an external resistance of 0.28 ohm is most nearly

(A) 5
(B) 10
(C) 15
(D) 20

Questions 38–41 are to be answered in accordance with the paragraph below.

Persons engaged in industrial electrical work have a *significant* responsibility and opportunity for service in securing the success of industrial undertakings. Viewed in this light, industrial people from top to bottom have *inherent* importance that should inspire *maximum* cooperation with other departments and with the executive branches.

38. The word *significant,* as used in the above paragraph, means

(A) important.
(B) accidental.
(C) meaningless.
(D) doubtful.

39. The word *inherent,* as used in the above paragraph, means

(A) separable.
(B) alienable.

(C) loose.
(D) natural.

40. The word *maximum,* as used in the above paragraph, means

(A) steepest.
(B) lowest.
(C) greatest.
(D) sharpest.

41. The above paragraph means most nearly that

(A) industrial undertakings are the concern of executives only.
(B) the success of industrial undertakings is affected to an important degree by industrial electrical workers.
(C) executives rarely cooperate with industrial workers.
(D) industrial electrical workers are of little importance.

42. The term *open circuit* means that

(A) the wiring is exposed.
(B) the fuse is located outdoors.
(C) the circuit has one end exposed.
(D) all parts of the circuit (or path) are not in contact.

43. A form of metal suitable for carrying electrical current, such as a wire or cable, is called a(n)

(A) raceway.
(B) trough.
(C) conductor.
(D) appliance.

44. In accordance with the National Electrical Code, the minimum size of the wire used on a 15-ampere circuit is

(A) No. 16
(B) No. 14
(C) No. 12
(D) No. 10

45. In cutting conduit, the pressure applied on a hacksaw should be on

(A) the forward stroke only.
(B) the return stroke only.
(C) the forward and return strokes equally.
(D) either the forward or return stroke, depending on the material.

46. To measure the diameter of wire most accurately, it is best to use a

    (A) wire gage.
    (B) depth gage.
    (C) micrometer.
    (D) microtome.

47. To measure the speed of an armature directly in rpm, it is best to use a

    (A) tachometer.
    (B) chronometer.
    (C) bolometer.
    (D) manometer.

48. The primary purpose for the use of oil in certain transformers is

    (A) for lubrication.
    (B) to reduce the permeability.
    (C) to provide insulation and aid in cooling.
    (D) as a rust inhibitor.

49. Of the following tools, the one most commonly used to cut holes in masonry is the

    (A) star drill.
    (B) auger.
    (C) router.
    (D) reamer.

50. Resistance coils having a small resistance temperature coefficient are made with a wire of a metal alloy called

    (A) mallacca.
    (B) massicot.
    (C) manganin.
    (D) malachite.

51. For lead-acid type storage batteries, the normal battery potential is calculated on the basis of

    (A) 12 volts per cell.
    (B) 6 volts per cell.
    (C) 3 volts per cell.
    (D) 2 volts per cell.

52. Fluorescent lamps, while designed for alternating-current operation, can be used on a direct-current circuit if a specially designed DC auxiliary and

    (A) parallel capacitor of correct value are employed.
    (B) series capacitor of correct value are employed.
    (C) parallel resistance of correct value are employed.
    (D) series resistance of correct value are employed.

53. A transformer bank composed of three single-phase transformers is to be connected delta-delta. The primary side is first connected, but before making the last secondary connection, the transformer should be

    (A) tested for an open circuit.
    (B) tested for a grounded circuit.
    (C) tested for a cross circuit.
    (D) tested for the proper phase relation.

54. As a safety measure, water should not be used to extinguish fires involving electrical equipment. The main reason is that water

    (A) is ineffective on electrical fires.
    (B) may transmit current and shock to the user.
    (C) may destroy the insulation property of wire.
    (D) may short-circuit the equipment.

55. The smallest number of wires necessary to carry 3-phase current is

    (A) 2 wires.
    (B) 3 wires.
    (C) 4 wires.
    (D) 5 wires.

56. A 5-ampere DC ammeter may be safely used on a 50-ampere circuit provided the

    (A) correct size current transformer is used.
    (B) proper size shunt is used.
    (C) proper circuit series resistance is used.
    (D) proper size multiplier is used.

57. As used in the National Electrical Code, the term *device* refers to

    (A) an electrical appliance that does not have moving parts.
    (B) a unit of an electrical system other than a conductor that is intended to carry but not consume electrical energy.
    (C) current-consuming equipment.
    (D) an accessory that is intended primarily to perform a mechanical rather than an electrical function.

58. The difference of electrical potential between two wires of a circuit is its

    (A) voltage.
    (B) resistance.
    (C) amperage.
    (D) wattage.

59. On long, straight horizontal conduit runs it is good practice to use

    (A) expansion joints.
    (B) universal joints.

(C) isolation joints.

(D) insulation joints.

60. A set of conductors originating at the load side of the service equipment and supplying the main and/or one or more secondary distribution centers is commonly called a

(A) circuit.

(B) line.

(C) cable.

(D) feeder.

61. A 5-microfarad capacitor is charged by putting 100 volts DC across its terminals. If this capacitor is now placed across another capacitor that has the same capacity rating and is identical in every other respect, the new voltage across these two capacitors is most nearly

(A) 100

(B) 75

(C) 50

(D) 25

62. A synchronous capacitor, so far as construction and appearance are concerned, closely resembles a(n)

(A) electrolytic capacitor.

(B) synchronous motor.

(C) synchroscope.

(D) wound-rotor induction motor.

63. In an electric spot-welding machine, the primary winding contains 200 turns of No. 10 wire and the secondary contains one turn made up of laminated copper sheeting. When the primary current is 5 amperes, the current, in amperes, passing through the metal to be welded is approximately

(A) 100

(B) 200

(C) 500

(D) 1,000

64. With reference to an electric spot-welding machine, the metal best suited to be united by spot welding is

(A) copper.

(B) zinc.

(C) lead.

(D) iron.

65. Two steel bars "G" and "H" have equal dimensions, but one of them is a magnet and the other an ordinary piece of soft steel. In order to find out which one of the two bars is the magnet, you would touch the point midway between the ends of bar "G" with one end of bar "H." Then if bar "H" tends to

(A) pull bar "G," bar "H" is not the magnet.

(B) pull bar "G," bar "H" is the magnet.

(C) repel bar "G," bar "H" is the magnet.

(D) repel bar "G," bar "H" is not the magnet.

66. The *main* purpose of a cutting fluid used in threading electrical conduits is to

(A) prevent the formation of electrolytic pockets.

(B) improve the finish of the thread.

(C) wash away the chips.

(D) prevent the eventual formation of rust.

67. If a certain electrical job requires 212 feet of $\frac{1}{2}''$ rigid conduit, the number of lengths that you should requisition is

(A) 16

(B) 18

(C) 20

(D) 22

68. The number of threads per inch commonly used for $\frac{1}{2}''$ electrical conduit is

(A) 15

(B) 14

(C) 13

(D) 12

69. For mounting a heavy pull box on a hollow tile wall, it is best to use

(A) lag screws.

(B) masonry nails.

(C) toggle bolts.

(D) expansion shields.

70. For mounting an outlet box on a concrete ceiling, it is best to use

(A) ordinary wood screws.

(B) masonry nails.

(C) expansion screw anchors.

(D) toggle bolts.

71. The National Electrical Code states that "Incandescent lamps shall not be equipped with medium bases if above 300 watts rating nor mogul bases if above 1,500 watts. Special approved bases or other devices shall be used." In accordance with the above statement, the lamp base that you should use for a 750-watt incandescent lamp is the

(A) medium base.

(B) candelabra base.

(C) intermediate base.

(D) mogul base.

72. In order to remove rough edges after cutting, all ends of conduit should be

    (A) filed.
    (B) sanded.
    (C) reamed.
    (D) honed.

73. Where a conduit enters a box, in order to protect the wire from abrasion, you should use an approved

    (A) coupling.
    (B) close nipple.
    (C) locknut.
    (D) bushing.

74. The maximum number of No. 10-type R conductors permitted in a $\frac{3}{4}''$ conduit is

    (A) 8
    (B) 6
    (C) 4
    (D) 2

75. A large switch that opens automatically when the current exceeds a predetermined limit is called a

    (A) disconnect.
    (B) contactor.
    (C) circuit breaker.
    (D) limit switch.

76. The flux commonly used for soldering electrical wires is

    (A) rosin.
    (B) borax.
    (C) zinc chloride.
    (D) tallow.

77. The cost of the electrical energy consumed by a 50-watt lamp burning for 100 hours as compared to that consumed by a 100-watt lamp burning for 50 hours is

    (A) four times as much.
    (B) three times as much.
    (C) twice as much.
    (D) the same.

78. Pneumatic tools are run by

    (A) electricity.
    (B) steam.
    (C) compressed air.
    (D) oil.

79. It is required to make a right-angle turn in a conduit run in which there are already three quarter-bends following the last pull box. The fitting best suited to properly do this is a(n)

    (A) cross.
    (B) tee.
    (C) union.
    (D) ell.

80. A 10,000-ohm resistance in an electronic timing switch burned out and must be replaced. The service manual states that this resistance should have an accuracy of 5 percent. This means that the value of the new resistance should differ from 10,000 ohms by not more than

    (A) 50 ohms.
    (B) 150 ohms.
    (C) 300 ohms.
    (D) 500 ohms.

ANSWER KEY

1. C	17. C	33. B	49. A	65. B
2. A	18. A	34. C	50. C	66. B
3. A	19. B	35. D	51. D	67. D
4. D	20. D	36. D	52. D	68. B
5. A	21. C	37. B	53. D	69. C
6. B	22. A	38. A	54. B	70. C
7. B	23. B	39. D	55. B	71. D
8. B	24. C	40. C	56. B	72. C
9. D	25. B	41. B	57. B	73. D
10. D	26. B	42. D	58. A	74. C
11. B	27. D	43. C	59. A	75. C
12. B	28. A	44. B	60. D	76. A
13. A	29. D	45. A	61. C	77. D
14. A	30. A	46. C	62. B	78. C
15. C	31. A	47. A	63. D	79. D
16. D	32. A	48. C	64. D	80. D

PREVIOUS EXAM 3—ELECTRICIAN

DIRECTIONS: Each question has four suggested answers, lettered (A), (B), (C), and (D). Decide which is the best answer and underline it. You may check your answers with the answer key that appears at the end of the test. Do not do so until you have completed the entire test.

TIME ALLOWED: 3.5 HOURS

1. Five 100-watt, 120-volt lamps connected in series across a 600-volt circuit will draw a current, in amperes, of most nearly

   (A) 4.2
   (B) 0.8
   (C) 0.6
   (D) 0.4

2. For a given level of illumination in a certain lighting installation, the cost of electrical energy using fluorescent lighting fixtures as compared with incandescent lighting fixtures is

   (A) more.
   (B) less.
   (C) the same.
   (D) dependent on the load.

3. Assume that three 20.8-ohm resistances are connected in delta across a 208-volt, 3-phase circuit. The line current in amperes will be most nearly

   (A) 20.8
   (B) 17.3
   (C) 10.4
   (D) 8.6

4. Assume that three 10-ohm resistances are connected in wye across a 208-volt, 3-phase circuit. The power in watts dissipated in this resistance load will be most nearly

   (A) 4,320
   (B) 1,440
   (C) 2,160
   (D) 720

5. A tungsten incandescent lamp has its greatest resistance when the lamp is

   (A) cold.
   (B) burning at full brilliance.
   (C) burning at half brilliance.
   (D) burning at one-quarter brilliance.

6. Direct current can be converted to alternating by means of a(n)

   (A) inverter.
   (B) rectifier.
   (C) filter.
   (D) selsyn.

7. The direction of rotation of a DC shunt motor can be reversed by

   (A) interchanging the line terminals.
   (B) reversing the field and armature current.
   (C) reversing the field or armature current.
   (D) reversing the current in any one of the commutating pole windings.

8. The insulation resistance of the conductors of an electrical installation is measured or tested with a(n)

   (A) strobe.
   (B) ammeter.
   (C) Q-meter.
   (D) megger.

9. In dealing with electrician's helpers, it is most important that the electrician be

   (A) stern.
   (B) fair.
   (C) blunt.
   (D) chummy.

10. If an electrician does not understand the instructions that are given by the supervisor, the best thing to do is to

   (A) work out the solution to the problem himself or herself.
   (B) do the job the way he or she thinks is best.
   (C) get one of the other electricians to do the job.
   (D) ask that the instructions be repeated and clarified.

11. Assume that a group of DC shunt motors is 500 feet from a power panel and is supplied by two 350,000-c.m. conductors with a maximum load for this circuit of 190 amps. If the resistance of 1,000 feet of 350,000-c.m. conductor is 0.036 ohm, and the voltage at the power panel is 230 volts, the voltage at the load will be most nearly

    (A) 217
    (B) 220
    (C) 223
    (D) 229

12. The power in a 3-phase, 3-wire circuit is measured by means of the 2-watt meter method. When the reading of one watt meter is exactly the same as the reading of the other watt meter, the power factor will be

    (A) 1
    (B) 0.866
    (C) 0.5
    (D) 0

13. Assume that a fluorescent lamp blinks "on" and "off." This may

    (A) in time result in injury to the ballast.
    (B) cause a fuse to blow.
    (C) be due to a shorted switch.
    (D) be caused by an abnormally high voltage.

14. Of the following troubles, the one that is NOT a cause of sparking at the commutator of a DC motor is

    (A) a short-circuited armature coil.
    (B) an open-circuited armature coil.
    (C) vibration of the machine.
    (D) running below rated speed.

15. The current in amperes of a 220-volt, 10-hp DC motor having an efficiency of 90 percent is approximately

    (A) 37.6
    (B) 34
    (C) 28.6
    (D) 40.5

16. The grid-controlled gas-type electronic tube most often used in motor control circuits is the

    (A) ignitron.
    (B) thyratron.
    (C) strobostron.
    (D) magnetron.

17. With reference to electronic control work, the vacuum tube element or electrode that is placed in the electron stream and to which a control voltage may be applied is the

    (A) plate.
    (B) grid.
    (C) filament.
    (D) cathode.

18. Full-wave rectifiers

    (A) may be built with one tungar bulb.
    (B) produce AC current that contains some DC.
    (C) are used to change DC current to AC.
    (D) must have at least two tungar bulbs.

19. Assume that two batteries are connected in multiple. If the voltage and internal resistance of one battery are 6 volts and 0.2 ohms respectively, and the voltage and internal resistance of the other battery are 3 volts and 0.1 ohm respectively, the circulating current, in amperes, will be approximately

    (A) 2
    (B) 5
    (C) 10
    (D) 30

20. In a single-phase motor, the temporary production of a substitute for a 2-phase current so as to obtain a makeshift rotating field in starting is commonly called

    (A) phase splitting.
    (B) phase spread.
    (C) phase transformation.
    (D) phantom circuit.

21. If a solenoid is grasped in the right hand so that the fingers point in the direction in which the current is flowing in the wires, the thumb extended will point in the direction of the

    (A) negative pole.
    (B) positive pole.
    (C) south pole.
    (D) north pole.

22. The junction of two dissimilar metals produces a flow of current when the junction is

    (A) wet.
    (B) heated.
    (C) highly polished.
    (D) placed in a DC magnetic field.

23. The active material in the positive plates of a charged lead-acid storage battery is

    (A) lead carbonate.
    (B) lead acetate.
    (C) lead peroxide.
    (D) sponge lead.

24. The negative plates of a charged lead-acid storage battery are composed of

    (A) lead carbonate.
    (B) lead acetate.
    (C) lead peroxide.
    (D) sponge lead.

25. A constant-horsepower, two-speed, squirrel-cage induction motor may be made to run at the higher speed by

    (A) changing the connections to make it an eight-pole motor.
    (B) decreasing the rotor resistance.
    (C) changing the connections so that the motor has the lesser number of poles.
    (D) changing the connections so that the motor has the greater number of poles.

26. A constant-horsepower, two-speed, squirrel-cage induction motor has its stator coils and the line wires connected so as to form a series-delta connection. Assume that the connections of the stator coils and the lines are now changed so as to form a parallel-wye connection. Under these conditions, the motor will now have

    (A) fewer poles and higher speed.
    (B) fewer poles and lower speed.
    (C) more poles and higher speed.
    (D) more poles and lower speed.

27. Assume that a circuit carrying 8 amperes of DC current and 6 amperes of AC current is connected to a hot-wire ammeter. The reading, in amperes, of this meter will be most nearly

    (A) 16
    (B) 14
    (C) 12
    (D) 10

28. To start a 20-hp, 3-phase, 208-volt plain-induction motor it is good practice to use a

    (A) compensator.
    (B) 3-point box.
    (C) rotor box.
    (D) 4-point box.

29. A 25-ampere, 50-millivolt DC shunt has a resistance, in ohms, of approximately

    (A) 0.002
    (B) 0.02
    (C) 0.5
    (D) 5

30. When a relay coil is energized by applying the rated voltage across its terminals, a certain time, in seconds, must elapse from the moment the circuit is completed before the current attains approximately $\frac{2}{3}$ of its full strength. This elapsed time is

    (A) entirely dependent on the coil resistance.
    (B) entirely dependent on the coil inductance.
    (C) proportional to the coil resistance divided by the coil inductance.
    (D) proportional to the coil inductance divided by the coil resistance.

31. For proper operation, all gas discharge lamps require

    (A) a series resistor.
    (B) a parallel resistor.
    (C) some sort of ballast.
    (D) a starter.

32. To obtain proper short-circuit protection for a service, one should use a

    (A) limiting resistor.
    (B) time-delay breaker.
    (C) time-delay relay.
    (D) current-limiting fuse.

33. A neon test lamp can be used by an electrician to test

    (A) the phase rotation of a source of supply.
    (B) the power factor of a source of supply.
    (C) a source of supply to see if it is AC or DC.
    (D) the field intensity of a relay magnet.

34. A DC milliammeter may be adapted for AC measurements by using with it a(n)

    (A) paper condenser.
    (B) instrument shunt.
    (C) instrument transformer.
    (D) selenium rectifier.

35. A static capacitor used for power-factor correction is connected to the line in

    (A) parallel with a machine drawing lagging current.
    (B) series with a machine drawing lagging current.

(C) parallel with a machine drawing leading current.

(D) series with a machine drawing leading current.

36. To start a squirrel-cage induction motor with an across-the-line starter without undue disturbance to the line voltage, the capacity of the motor in HP should NOT exceed

(A) 100
(B) 75
(C) 50
(D) 5

37. The type of AC motor most commonly used where considerable starting torque is required is the

(A) squirrel-cage induction motor.
(B) wound-rotor induction motor.
(C) shunt motor.
(D) synchronous motor.

38. On direct-current controllers where it is necessary to remove or replace blow-out coils, it is important to

(A) see that the positive pole is facing down.
(B) see that the negative pole is facing up.
(C) insert the blow-out coils to give the proper polarity.
(D) cross the coil leads before connecting them.

39. The size of the fuse to be used in a circuit depends upon the

(A) connected load.
(B) size of wire.
(C) voltage of the line.
(D) size and rating of the switch.

40. Assume that a DC contactor coil has two turns short-circuited. In operation, it will

(A) burn out.
(B) hum excessively.
(C) continue to operate at reduced efficiency.
(D) vibrate due to the high induced current.

41. The primary purpose of oil in an oil circuit breaker is to

(A) quench the arc.
(B) lubricate the contacts.
(C) reduce the reluctance of the core.
(D) lubricate between windings and the case.

42. Assume that an autotransformer has a ratio of 2:1. With a primary voltage of 100 volts, 60 Hz AC and a secondary load of 5 ohms, the current in the load is most nearly

(A) 20
(B) 15
(C) 10
(D) 5

43. Assume that an autotransformer has a ratio of 2:1 with a primary voltage of 100 volts, 60 Hz AC and a load of 5 ohms placed across the secondary. Under the above conditions, the current in the secondary coil of the autotransformer is most nearly

(A) 20
(B) 15
(C) 10
(D) 5

44. In fire extinguishers used to fight electrical fires, the chemical used as the fire extinguishing agent is

(A) H_2O
(B) K_0H
(C) CO_2
(D) CCl_4

45. At a frequency of 60 Hz, the reactance in ohms of a capacitor having a capacitance of 10 microfarads is most nearly

(A) 26.6
(B) 37.7
(C) 266
(D) 377

46. Transformation of 3-phase to 2-phase systems can be obtained by using two special transformers. The common method used for connecting these transformers is called a(n)

(A) open-delta.
(B) zig-zag.
(C) differential y on z.
(D) Scott or T.

47. The electrolyte for a lead-acid storage battery is properly prepared by pouring the

(A) sulphuric acid into the water.
(B) water into the sulphuric acid.
(C) potassium hydroxide into the water.
(D) water into the potassium hydroxide.

48. The full-wave rectifier has a ripple frequency that is

(A) one half that of the half-wave rectifier.
(B) double that of the half-wave rectifier.
(C) four times that of the half-wave rectifier.
(D) equal to that of the half-wave rectifier.

49. Of the following, the one type of resistance wire that has an extremely low temperature coefficient of resistance is known as

    (A) replevin.
    (B) ribbon.
    (C) maganin.
    (D) bifilar.

50. In the AC dynamometer-type voltmeter, the deflections depend upon the square of the voltage. It can correctly be said that this instrument reads

    (A) average values.
    (B) peak values.
    (C) effective values.
    (D) maximum values.

51. The Dobrowolsky method used for three-wire generator systems is a very efficient means of obtaining a(n)

    (A) neutral.
    (B) V or open-delta.
    (C) two-phase system.
    (D) three-phase system.

52. Direct-current armatures wound with coils having fractional-pitch windings have

    (A) a coil span that is less than the pole pitch.
    (B) a coil span that is greater than the pole pitch.
    (C) more than 4 poles.
    (D) less than 4 poles.

53. To measure the current in a conductor without breaking into the conductor, you would use an

    (A) ampback.
    (B) amprobe.
    (C) ampule.
    (D) ampclip.

54. If two identical coils each having an inductance of one henry are connected in series aiding, the combined inductance, in henrys, is

    (A) exactly two.
    (B) greater than two.
    (C) exactly one.
    (D) less than one.

55. In a simplex lap winding, there are as many paths through the armature as there are

    (A) armature slots.
    (B) poles.
    (C) commutator segments.
    (D) armature coils.

56. In a wave winding, the minimum number of commutator brushes required is

    (A) four.
    (B) two.
    (C) depedent on the number of commutator segments.
    (D) dependent on the armature coils.

57. Some electricians have the faculty of knowing when there is work to be done and do not have to be prompted to do it. These electricians may be said to have

    (A) initiative.
    (B) individuality.
    (C) virtue.
    (D) discrimination.

58. The number of threads per inch on a $\frac{1}{4}''$ diameter screw having American Standard coarse threads is most nearly

    (A) 20
    (B) 18
    (C) 14
    (D) 13

59. For general field or shop work, the proper tap drill size to use for a #6-32 machine screw is most nearly number

    (A) 50
    (B) 40
    (C) 36
    (D) 21

60. Graphical electrical symbols used on architectural plans are those recommended by the ASA. The abbreviation ASA refers to the

    (A) American Society of Architects.
    (B) American Standards Association.
    (C) Architectural Standards Association.
    (D) Architectural Standards of America.

61. Of the following, the best course of action to take if a motor bearing runs dangerously hot is to

    (A) cool it quickly with cold water; then rapidly decrease motor speed and oil the bearing freely.
    (B) oil the bearing freely and increase speed of motor.
    (C) decrease speed of motor until bearing cools sufficiently; then stop the motor and check for oil level and any damage to bearing.
    (D) add No. 40 SAE oil before increasing the load.

62. Ten graduations on the barrel of a micrometer indicate an opening, in inches, of most nearly

    (A) 0.010
    (B) 0.050
    (C) 0.250
    (D) 0.270

63. The type of motor that may be designed to run on both AC and DC is the

    (A) shunt motor.
    (B) repulsion motor.
    (C) compound motor.
    (D) series motor.

64. Assume that the cost of a certain wiring installation is broken down as follows: materials, $1,200; labor, $800; and rental of equipment, $400. The percentage of the total cost of the job that can be charged to labor is most nearly

    (A) 12.3
    (B) 33.3
    (C) 40.0
    (D) 66.6

65. Assume that it takes four apprentice electricians six days to do a certain job. Working at the same rate of speed, the number of days it will take three apprentices to do the same job is

    (A) six.
    (B) seven.
    (C) eight.
    (D) nine.

66. Assume that a 120-volt, 25-Hz magnetic coil is to be rewound to operate properly on 60 Hz at the same voltage. If the coil at 25 Hz has 1,000 turns, at 60 Hz, the number of turns should be most nearly

    (A) 2,400
    (B) 1,200
    (C) 416
    (D) 208

67. A coil having 50 turns of No. 14 wire as compared with a coil of the same diameter but having only 25 turns of No. 14 wire has

    (A) a smaller inductance.
    (B) a larger inductance.
    (C) the same inductance.
    (D) the same impedance.

Questions 68–80 are to be answered in accordance with the requirements of the National Electrical Code.

NOTES:

1. Unless otherwise stated, the word "Code" refers to the National Electrical Code

2. Questions are to be answered assuming normal procedures, as given in the Code. Do not use exceptions that are granted by special permission.

68. For elevator control wiring, conductors of $\frac{1}{64}$ insulation may be used. The number of such conductors that may be installed in a conduit should be such that the sum of the cross-sectional area of all the conductors expressed as a percentage of the interior cross-sectional area of the conduit should NOT exceed

    (A) 20 percent.
    (B) 30 percent.
    (C) 40 percent.
    (D) 60 percent.

69. Assume that the internal diameter of a 2-inch conduit is 2.067 inches. The interior cross-sectional area, in square inches, of this conduit is most nearly

    (A) 3.36
    (B) 4.79
    (C) 7.38
    (D) 9.90

70. No. 2 type R conductors in vertical raceways must be supported at intervals not greater than

    (A) 50 feet.
    (B) 60 feet.
    (C) 80 feet.
    (D) 100 feet.

71. A unit of an electrical system, other than a conductor, that is intended to carry but not consume electrical energy is called a(n)

    (A) device.
    (B) circuit.
    (C) appliance.
    (D) equipment.

72. Three No. 4 AWG rubber-covered type R conductors require a conduit having a diameter, in inches, of not less than

    (A) $\frac{1}{2}$

    (B) $\frac{3}{4}$

    (C) 1

    (D) $1\frac{1}{4}$

73. For control conductors between motors and controllers, the maximum number of No. 10 type R conductors that may be put into a $1\frac{1}{4}''$ conduit or tubing is

    (A) 10
    (B) 13
    (C) 15
    (D) 17

74. The type of wire commonly used for switchboard wiring is classified by type letter or letters

    (A) TF.
    (B) CF.
    (C) TA.
    (D) R.

75. Wires in conduit (approved as to insulation and location) are required to have stranded conductors if they are

    (A) No. 8 or larger.
    (B) No. 6 or larger.
    (C) No. 6 or smaller.
    (D) No. 8 or smaller.

76. Bends of rigid conduit should be so made that the conduit will not be injured. Where rubber conductors are used, the radius of the curve of the inner edge of any field bend should be not less than

    (A) 15 times the internal diameter of the conduit.
    (B) 10 times the internal diameter of the conduit.
    (C) 6 times the internal diameter of the conduit.
    (D) 4 times the internal diameter of the conduit.

77. In Class I hazardous locations, when a conduit leads from a hazardous location to a nonhazardous location, the conduit should be sealed off with a sealing compound that is not affected by the surrounding atmosphere and has a melting point of not less than

    (A) 200°F.
    (B) 150°F.
    (C) 100°F.
    (D) 75°F.

78. Feeders should be of such size that the voltage drop up to the final distribution point should not exceed

    (A) 6 percent.

    (B) $4\frac{1}{2}$ percent.

    (C) 3 percent.

    (D) $2\frac{1}{2}$ percent.

79. For not more than three conductors in raceway (based on room temperature of 30°C or 86°F), the current-carrying capacity in amperes of No. 10 type-R insulated aluminum conductor is

    (A) 10
    (B) 15
    (C) 25
    (D) 35

80. The maximum number of No. 12 wires terminating in a $1\frac{1}{2}''\times3\frac{1}{4}''$ octagonal junction box should be

    (A) 20
    (B) 15
    (C) 10
    (D) 5

ANSWER KEY

1.	B	17.	B	33.	C	49.	C	65.	C
2.	B	18.	D	34.	D	50.	C	66.	C
3.	B	19.	C	35.	A	51.	A	67.	B
4.	A	20.	A	36.	D	52.	A	68.	C
5.	B	21.	D	37.	B	53.	B	69.	A
6.	A	22.	B	38.	C	54.	B	70.	D
7.	C	23.	C	39.	B	55.	B	71.	A
8.	D	24.	D	40.	C	56.	B	72.	D
9.	B	25.	C	41.	A	57.	A	73.	B
10.	D	26.	D	42.	C	58.	A	74.	C
11.	C	27.	D	43.	C	59.	C	75.	B
12.	A	28.	A	44.	C	60.	B	76.	C
13.	A	29.	A	45.	C	61.	C	77.	A
14.	D	30.	D	46.	D	62.	C	78.	D
15.	A	31.	C	47.	A	63.	D	79.	C
16.	B	32.	D	48.	B	64.	B	80.	D

PREVIOUS EXAM 4—ELECTRICIAN

DIRECTIONS: Each question has four suggested answers, lettered (A), (B), (C), and (D). Decide which is the best answer and underline it. You may check your answers with the answer key that appears at the end of the test. Do not do so until you have completed the entire test.

TIME ALLOWED: 3 HOURS

1. In order to operate satisfactorily in parallel, two single-phase transformers must have

   (A) equal turn ratios, equal resistance drops, equal voltage ratings, and be connected so as to have opposite polarity.
   (B) equal turn ratios, equal impedance drops, equal kVa ratings, and be connected so as to have the same polarity.
   (C) equal turn ratios, equal impedance drops, equal voltage ratings, and be connected so as to have the same polarity.
   (D) equal turn ratios, equal resistance drops, equal kVa ratings, and be connected so as to have opposite polarity.

2. Of the following, the primary advantage of the wound-rotor induction motor over the standard (i.e., NEMA Design A) squirrel-cage induction motor is that the wound-rotor induction motor has a

   (A) higher starting current and a low power factor.
   (B) lower starting torque and a unity power factor.
   (C) higher starting torque and a lower starting current.
   (D) lower starting torque and a higher starting current.

3. The synchronous speed of a 60-Hz AC induction motor that has 8 poles is most nearly

   (A) 800 rpm.
   (B) 900 rpm.
   (C) 1,200 rpm.
   (D) 1,800 rpm.

4. As the load on a synchronous motor increases, its speed

   (A) remains constant until full load is reached and then decreases linearly as the load is increased further.
   (B) decreases slowly as the load increases.
   (C) remains constant until the "pull-out torque" is exceeded, causing the motor to stop.
   (D) decreases until the "pull-out torque" is exceeded, causing the motor to stop.

5. In the conventional synchronous motor, direct current is applied to the

   (A) stator at standstill.
   (B) rotor at standstill.
   (C) stator when the motor speed approximates synchronous speed.
   (D) rotor when the motor speed approximates synchronous speed.

6. The AC motor that would be used when only constant speed is required is the

   (A) synchronous motor.
   (B) high-slip, squirrel-cage motor.
   (C) high-torque, squirrel-cage motor.
   (D) wound-rotor motor.

7. The minimum number of commutator brushes required in a wave winding is

   (A) four.
   (B) two.
   (C) dependent on the armature coil.
   (D) dependent on the number of commutator segments.

8. In a simplex lap winding, there are as many paths through the armature as there are

   (A) commutator segments.
   (B) armature coils.
   (C) poles.
   (D) armature slots.

9. A half-wave rectifier has a ripple frequency that is

   (A) half that of the full-wave rectifier.
   (B) twice that of the full-wave rectifier.
   (C) equal to that of the full-wave rectifier.
   (D) one quarter that of the full-wave rectifier.

10. Blocking capacitors are used for the purpose of

    (A) passing AC and DC.
    (B) passing DC.
    (C) blocking AC.
    (D) blocking DC.

11. A battery that has an emf of two volts and an internal resistance of 0.2 ohm causes a current of one ampere to flow through a load. The terminal voltage of the battery under these conditions is

    (A) 0.2
    (B) 0.4
    (C) 1.8
    (D) 2.2

12. Resistances of 12 ohms, 6 ohms, and 4 ohms are connected in parallel with each other. The total resistance, in ohms, of the combination is

    (A) 22
    (B) 7.2
    (C) 2.0
    (D) 0.5

13. In American Wire Gage, any wire has double the cross-sectional area of any other wire whose gage number is

    (A) 2 greater than the first wire.
    (B) 3 greater than the first wire.
    (C) 6 lower than the first wire.
    (D) 6 greater than the first wire.

14. As the temperature increases, the

    (A) electrical resistances of both carbon and copper increase.
    (B) electrical resistance of carbon increases and the electrical resistance of copper decreases.
    (C) electrical resistances of both carbon and copper decreases.
    (D) electrical resistance of carbon decreases and the electrical resistance of copper increases.

15. The total capacitance, in microfarads, in a two-microfarad capacitor connected in series with a three-microfarad capacitor is

    (A) 1.2
    (B) 2
    (C) 3.2
    (D) 5

16. Two wattmeters are properly connected to read the load on a balanced 3-phase, 3-wire system. One of the wattmeters reads zero. The power factor of the load is

    (A) 1.73
    (B) 0.866
    (C) 0.5
    (D) 0

17. Assume that you have a coil of 2,000 feet of a certain size of bare copper wire that weighs one pound and has a resistance of 64 ohms and a coil of 1,000 feet of a different size of bare copper wire that also weighs one pound. The resistance, in ohms, of the second coil of wire is most nearly

    (A) 8
    (B) 16
    (C) 32
    (D) 64

18. If the allowable current density for copper bus bars is 1,000 amperes per square inch, the current-carrying capacity, in amperes, of a circular copper bar having a diameter of 2 inches is most nearly

    (A) 1,050
    (B) 2,320
    (C) 3,140
    (D) 4,260

19. A 10-hp motor is supplying power to a machine by means of a belt drive. If the motor runs at 900 rpm and the diameters of the pulley are 8 inches for the motor and 20 inches for the machine, the speed of the machine is most nearly

    (A) 2,250 rpm.
    (B) 1,800 rpm.
    (C) 360 rpm.
    (D) 40 rpm.

20. Of the following metals, the one that has the lowest resistivity at 20°C is

    (A) aluminum.
    (B) nickel.
    (C) tungsten.
    (D) soft steel.

21. The root-mean-square value, in volts, of a sine wave with a peak voltage of 100 volts is

    (A) 141.4
    (B) 70.7
    (C) 63.6
    (D) 50.0

22. Of the following, the one that is a unit of inductance is the

    (A) joule.
    (B) henry.
    (C) hertz.
    (D) ampere.

23. Assume that four inductors, each of a different value, are connected in parallel. The total inductance of the combination is

    (A) smaller than that of the smallest inductance.
    (B) greater than that of the greatest inductance.
    (C) equal to the average inductance.
    (D) equal to the reciprocal of the average inductance.

24. If two identical coils, each having an inductance of 1 henry, are tightly coupled and connected in series with fields aiding, the combined inductance, in henrys, is

    (A) greater than 2.
    (B) slightly less than 2.
    (C) slightly less than 1.
    (D) almost 0.

25. A circuit consists of a 0.5-microhenry coil connected in series with a combination of two 0.2-microhenry coils connected in parallel. The total inductance of this circuit, in microhenrys, is most nearly

    (A) 0.9
    (B) 0.6
    (C) 0.2
    (D) 0.1

26. In the conventional 4-point starting box for DC motors, the hold-up coil is of

    (A) high resistance and is connected directly across the line.
    (B) low resistance and is connected in series with the shunt field.
    (C) high resistance and is connected in series with the armature.
    (D) low resistance and is connected directly across the line.

27. Of the following, improving the commutation of a DC generator is most often done by means of

    (A) a compensator.
    (B) interpoles.
    (C) an equalizer.
    (D) a series rheostat in series with the equalizer.

28. Of the following, the type of motor that may be designed to run on both AC and DC is the

    (A) shunt motor.
    (B) repulsion motor.
    (C) compound motor.
    (D) series motor.

29. Assume that a 10-hp DC shunt motor has a counter-emf of 225 volts at full load, an armature resistance of 0.2 ohms, and a supply voltage of 230 volts. Under these conditions, its armature current, in amperes, is most nearly

    (A) 2.5
    (B) 25.0
    (C) 45.0
    (D) 91.1

30. Compensator starters for polyphase squirrel-cage motors are basically

    (A) autotransformers.
    (B) delta-wye switches.
    (C) QMQB across-the-line switches.
    (D) resistance banks.

31. Design C squirrel-cage induction motors have a

    (A) high torque and a low-starting current.
    (B) normal torque and a low-starting current.
    (C) normal torque and a normal-starting current.
    (D) low torque and a low-starting current.

32. Which of the following statements is NOT a valid evaluation of the advantages of using autotransformers?

    (A) They have a high efficiency.
    (B) They have better voltage regulation than two-coil transformers of the same rating.
    (C) They are less expensive than two-coil transformers.
    (D) They are safe for stepping down high voltage.

33. In an induction motor, the slip varies with the load. Doubling the load will cause the slip to

    (A) double.
    (B) halve.
    (C) increase slightly.
    (D) decrease slightly.

34. An 8-pole, 60-Hz induction motor that runs at 800 rpm has a slip of most nearly

    (A) 5.6 percent.
    (B) 8.9 percent.
    (C) 11.1 percent.
    (D) 12.5 percent.

35. Assume that the lead has become disconnected from one of the slip rings of a 3-phase, wound-rotor induction motor. Under these conditions, the motor

    (A) cannot run at all.
    (B) can run at exactly half speed when not loaded.
    (C) can be started with full load and run at full speed.
    (D) can be started at full load and run at two thirds of its normal speed.

36. Assume that a certain DC motor and a certain DC generator both operate so that in each case, the commutator turns in the clockwise direction as viewed when facing the commutator end. Neither machine has interpoles but both have movable brush rigging. To improve commutation in both machines when the load is increased, one should move the brushes

    (A) clockwise in both the motor and the generator.
    (B) counterclockwise in both the motor and the generator.
    (C) clockwise in the motor and counterclockwise in the generator.
    (D) counterclockwise in the motor and clockwise in the generator.

37. The tool that is used to align vitrified tile conduit in multiple ducts is a

    (A) mandrel.
    (B) reamer.
    (C) hickey.
    (D) rod.

38. Of the following, the best fastener to use in a hollow wall is the

    (A) expansion bolt.
    (B) carriage bolt.
    (C) machine bolt and nut.
    (D) toggle bolt.

39. Of the following, the tool that should be used for turning conduit is a

    (A) chain wrench.
    (B) crescent wrench.
    (C) monkey wrench.
    (D) hook spanner.

40. A method commonly used for testing armatures for short circuits and open circuits is the

    (A) segment-to-segment test.
    (B) Varley loop test.
    (C) Murray loop test.
    (D) Wien-Maxwell method.

41. A capacitor used for power-factor connection is connected to the line in

    (A) series with a machine drawing leading current.
    (B) series with a machine drawing lagging current.
    (C) parallel with a machine drawing leading current.
    (D) parallel with a machine drawing lagging current.

42. Of the following hacksaw blades, the one that should be used for best results in cutting thinwall tubing is one having

    (A) 14 teeth per inch.
    (B) 18 teeth per inch.
    (C) 24 teeth per inch.
    (D) 32 teeth per inch.

43. When pulling wire through conduit, sometimes one conductor crosses another, resulting in a hump that will wedge in the conduit. Of the following substances, the best one to use to make pulling easier is

    (A) powdered soapstone.
    (B) powdered carbon.
    (C) resin.
    (D) oil.

44. The horsepower ratings of motors are based on an observable safe temperature rise above ambient temperature. The ambient temperature is taken as

    (A) 60° C.
    (B) 55° C.
    (C) 50° C.
    (D) 40° C.

45. Three single-phase transformers having ratios of 10:1 are connected with their primaries in wye and their secondaries in delta. If the low-voltage windings are used as the primaries, and the line voltage on the primary side is 208 volts, then the phase voltage on the secondary side is, in volts,

    (A) 3,600
    (B) 2,080
    (C) 1,200
    (D) 690

46. Oil is used in many large transformers to

    (A) cool and insulate the transformer.
    (B) lubricate the core.
    (C) lubricate the coils.
    (D) prevent breakdown due to friction.

47. Of the following, the main reason for damping an electrical indicating instrument is to prevent

    (A) excessive oscillation of the needle.
    (B) the instrument from being damaged if it is dropped.
    (C) the instrument from getting too dry.
    (D) the needle from going off scale.

48. Of the following, flashing or excessive arcing from brush to brush in a motor is caused by

    (A) a high voltage on the line.
    (B) the brushes being too hard.
    (C) the brush pressure being too great.
    (D) the brushes being set at the improper angle for the direction of rotation.

49. Of the following groups of lamps, the one that is best for testing a 460/265-volt supply is a group of

    (A) four 120-volt lamps in series.
    (B) four 120-volt lamps in parallel.
    (C) two 120-volt lamps in parallel.
    (D) two 120-volt lamps in series.

50. Of the following, the best way to clean a dirty motor commutator is to rub it with

    (A) emery cloth.
    (B) sandpaper.
    (C) fine steel wool.
    (D) powdered soapstone.

51. Of the following, the one that is the proper maintenance procedure to be followed when the liquid level in a lead-acid storage battery is too low is to

    (A) pour out all of the old solution and replace it with new solution.
    (B) add enough double-strength solution to bring the level up to normal.
    (C) add only distilled water until the level is normal.
    (D) add weak solution to bring the level back up to normal.

52. Assume that a DC ammeter having a resistance of 2.0 ohms and a 0-100 scale has a full-scale reading when the meter current is .01 amperes. The resistance of the shunt that should be used with the ammeter so that it will read 10 amperes full-scale is, in ohms, most nearly

    (A) 0.0004
    (B) 0.001
    (C) 0.002
    (D) 0.02

53. The internal diameter of $\frac{3}{4}$-inch electrical conduit, in inches, is most nearly

    (A) 0.824
    (B) 0.804
    (C) 0.753
    (D) 0.690

54. The one of the following inspection and maintenance procedures that should be carried out on motors every six months, according to various authorities such as the *Electrician's Handbook, Westinghouse's Preventive Maintenance*, etc., is

    (A) check the oil level in the bearings.
    (B) make sure that the brushes ride freely in the holders, and replace any that are more than half worn.
    (C) examine the shaft to see that it is free of oil and grease from the bearings.
    (D) see that the oil rings turn in the shaft.

55. Of the following, the one that is NOT a type of file is a

    (A) mill.
    (B) flat.
    (C) tubular.
    (D) half round.

56. The set of a hacksaw blade refers to how much the teeth are pushed out in opposite directions from the side of the blade. Of the following, the one that is NOT a type of set is

    (A) an alternate set.
    (B) a lap set.
    (C) a raker set.
    (D) a wave set.

57. A transformer having its terminals marked in the standard method so that H_1 and H_2 represent its high voltage terminals and X_1 and X_2 represent its low voltage leads will have subtractive polarity if

    (A) H_1 and X_2 are adjacent.
    (B) H_2 and X_2 are placed diagonally.
    (C) H_1 and X_1 are placed diagonally.
    (D) H_1 and X_1 are adjacent.

58. The DC component of the harmonic composition of the output of a half-wave rectifier tube is

    (A) $\frac{2}{\pi}$ times the peak of the alternating voltage applied to the rectifier tube.
    (B) 2π times the peak of the alternating voltage applied to the rectifier tube.
    (C) π times the peak of the alternating voltage applied to the rectifier tube.
    (D) $\frac{1}{\pi}$ times the peak of the alternating voltage applied to the rectifier tube.

59. A widely used device is the SCR semiconductor. Of the following, the initials SCR stand for

(A) Signal Current Relay.
(B) Solid Circuit Relay.
(C) Semi Conductor Resonator.
(D) Silicon Controlled Rectifier.

60. An ammeter connected to the secondary of an energized metering transformer requires repairs. Before disconnecting the instrument, the electrician should

(A) open the secondary circuit.
(B) short-circuit the transformer secondary terminals.
(C) short-circuit the transformer primary terminals.
(D) remove the transformer secondary fuses.

61. A Class A extinguisher should be used for fires in

(A) potassium, magnesium, zinc, and sodium.
(B) electrical wiring.
(C) oil and gasoline.
(D) wood, paper, and textiles.

62. In the figure below, a test for transformer polarity is made on a transformer rated 2,400-240 volts, by applying a voltage $V_1 = 120$ volts to the high voltage terminals H_1 and H_2 and measuring the voltage between terminals H_2 and X_2. If the transformer is of subtractive polarity, the voltmeter will read approximately

(A) 132 volts.
(B) 12 volts.
(C) 108 volts.
(D) 0 volts.

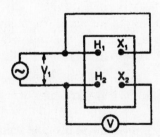

63. Of the following, the one that is NOT a safe practice when lifting heavy objects is

(A) keep the back as nearly upright as possible.
(B) if the object feels too heavy, keep lifting until you get help.
(C) spread the feet apart.
(D) use the arm and leg muscles.

64. When placing an extension ladder against a wall, the distance between the foot of the ladder and the wall should be

(A) always less than 2 feet.
(B) always more than 2 feet.
(C) $\frac{1}{4}$ the length of the extended ladder.
(D) $\frac{1}{8}$ the length of the extended ladder.

65. Continuity of an electrical circuit can conveniently be determined in the field by means of a(n)

(A) smoke test.
(B) bell and battery set.
(C) ammeter.
(D) Wheatstone bridge.

66. The speed of a motor can be measured by means of a

(A) potentiometer.
(B) megger.
(C) tachometer.
(D) thermocouple.

67. A blind hickey is used

(A) to cap a spare conduit.
(B) in lieu of a fixture stud.
(C) in lieu of a fixture extension.
(D) to hang a lighting fixture on a gas outlet.

68. If the voltage of a 3-phase, squirrel-cage induction motor is reduced to 90 percent of its rating, the power factor

(A) increases slightly.
(B) is unchanged.
(C) decreases slightly.
(D) decreases 10 points.

69. To reverse the direction of rotation of a wound-rotor, 3-phase induction motor,

(A) interchange all line wires.
(B) interchange all rotor connections.
(C) interchange any 2 rotor connections.
(D) interchange any 2 line wires.

70. An Erickson coupling is used

(A) to join sections of EMT.
(B) to connect EMT to flexible conduit.
(C) to connect two sections of rigid conduit when one section cannot be turned.
(D) as a substitute for all thread.

ANSWER KEY

1. C	15. A	29. B	43. A	57. D
2. C	16. C	30. A	44. D	58. D
3. B	17. B	31. A	45. C	59. D
4. C	18. C	32. D	46. A	60. B
5. D	19. C	33. A	47. A	61. D
6. A	20. A	34. C	48. A	62. C
7. B	21. B	35. B	49. A	63. D
8. C	22. B	36. D	50. B	64. C
9. A	23. A	37. A	51. C	65. B
10. D	24. A	38. D	52. C	66. C
11. C	25. B	39. A	53. A	67. D
12. C	26. A	40. A	54. B	68. A
13. B	27. B	41. D	55. C	69. D
14. D	28. D	42. D	56. B	70. C

PREVIOUS EXAM 5—ELECTRICIAN

> **DIRECTIONS:** Each question has four suggested answers, lettered (A), (B), (C), and (D). Decide which is the best answer and underline it. You may check your answers with the answer key that appears at the end of the test. Do not do so until you have completed the entire test.

TIME ALLOWED: 3 HOURS

NOTE: Whenever the term "The Code" appears in this test, it means the National Electrical Code.

1. Two copper conductors have the same length, but the cross-section of one is twice that of the other. If the resistance of the one having a cross-section of twice the other is 10 ohms, the resistance of the other conductor, in ohms, is

   (A) 5
   (B) 10
   (C) 20
   (D) 30

2. Assuming that copper weighs 0.32 lbs. per cubic inch, the weight, in lbs., of a bus bar 10' long and having a cross-section of $2'' \times \frac{1}{2}''$ is

   (A) 120
   (B) 32
   (C) 3.2
   (D) 38.4

3. In a 2-phase, 3-wire system, the voltage between the common wire and either of the other two wires is 200 volts. The voltage between these other two wires is then approximately

   (A) 200 volts.
   (B) 283 volts.
   (C) 141 volts.
   (D) 100 volts.

4. Three 30-ohm resistances are connected in delta across a 208-volt, 3-phase circuit. The line current, in amperes, is approximately

   (A) 6.93
   (B) 13.86
   (C) 120
   (D) 12

5. A storage battery consists of three lead cells connected in series. On open circuit, the emf of the battery is 6.4 volts. When it delivers a current of 80 amperes, its terminal voltage drops to 4.80 volts. Its internal resistance, in ohms, is approximately

   (A) 0.01
   (B) 0.02
   (C) 0.03
   (D) 0.04

6. In reference to question 5, the terminal voltage, in volts, when the battery delivers 50 amperes is approximately

   (A) 5.9
   (B) 5.4
   (C) 4.9
   (D) 4.4

7. In order to magnetize a steel bar, a magnetomotive force of 1,000-ampere turns is necessary. The voltage that must be applied to a coil of 100 turns and 10 ohms resistance is

   (A) 1
   (B) 10
   (C) 100
   (D) 1000

8. Rosin is preferable to acid as a flux for soldering wire because rosin is

   (A) a nonconductor.
   (B) a dry powder.
   (C) a better conductor.
   (D) noncorrosive.

9. If in tracing through an armature winding all of the conductors are encountered before coming back to the starting point, there is but one closure and the winding is

   (A) doubly reentrant.
   (B) singly reentrant.
   (C) triply reentrant.
   (D) quintuply reentrant.

10. A power-factor meter is connected to a single-phase, 2-wire circuit by means of

    (A) 2 wires.
    (B) 3 wires.
    (C) 4 wires.
    (D) 5 wires.

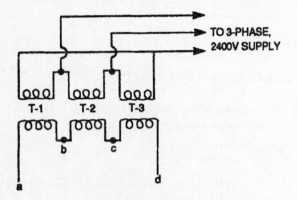

Figure 11

11. Figure 11 represents a transformer bank composed of 3 single-phase transformers, each having a ratio of transformation equal to 20:1. The primary is already connected to the voltage supply, as shown in the diagram, while the secondary side is only "partly connected."

    It is desired to connect the secondary of this transformer bank in delta. Before connecting *a* to *d*, the combination of voltages should correspond to which of the following?

    (A) Vab = 120, Vbc = 120, Vcd = 120 and Vad = 0
    (B) Vab = 120, Vbc = 120, Vcd = 120 and Vad = 120
    (C) Vab = 120, Vbc = 120, Vcd = 120 and Vad = 208
    (D) Vab = 208, Vbc = 208, Vcd = 208 and Vad = 0

12. With reference to Figure 11, assume that the combination of voltages read as follows: Vab = 120 volts, Vbc = 120 volts, Vcd = 120 volts, Vad = 240 volts, and Vbd = 208 volts. Before connecting a to *d* for *a* delta connection,

    (A) do nothing since the transformer bank is already phased out.
    (B) secondary winding of T-1 should be reversed by interchanging its leads.
    (C) secondary winding of T-2 should be reversed by interchanging its leads.
    (D) secondary winding of T-3 should be reversed by interchanging its leads.

13. The torque of a shunt motor varies as

    (A) the armature current.
    (B) the square of the armature current.
    (C) the cube of the armature current.
    (D) the cube of the field current.

14. The armature of a synchronous converter has

    (A) 3 slip-rings for the AC and 2 slip-rings for the DC.
    (B) 4 slip-rings, 2 for the AC and 2 for the DC.
    (C) a commutator and slip-rings.
    (D) no slip-rings.

15. An electrical device that transmits rotation from a driving to a driven member without mechanical contact—with stepless adjustable control and with almost instantaneous response—is the

    (A) eddy current coupling.
    (B) universal coupling.
    (C) planetary coupling.
    (D) coupling transformer.

16. According to the Code, in order that armored cable will not be injured, the radius of the curve of the inner edge of any bend must be not less than

    (A) 3 times the diameter of the cable.
    (B) 5 times the diameter of the cable.
    (C) 7 times the diameter of the cable.
    (D) 10 times the diameter of the cable.

17. In accordance with the Code, circuit breakers for motor branch circuit protection shall have continous current ratings not less than

    (A) 110 percent of the full-load current of the motor.
    (B) 115 percent of the full-load current of the motor.
    (C) 120 percent of the full-load current of the motor.
    (D) 125 percent of the full-load current of the motor.

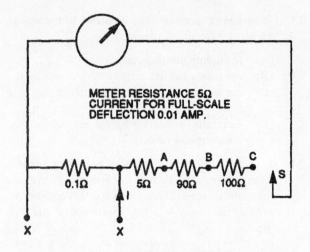

Figure 18

18. Figure 18 represents the circuit of a multirange ammeter. X – X is connected in series with an electric circuit for the purpose of measuring the current in that circuit. When slider S is connected to point B, the current I, in amperes, that will cause the meter to read full-scale is approximately

   (A) 30
   (B) 20
   (C) 10
   (D) 1

19. In reference to Figure 18, when slider "S" is connected to point "C," the current I, in amperes, that will cause the meter to read full-scale is approximately

   (A) 30
   (B) 20
   (C) 10
   (D) 1

20. The Code states that feeders over 40′ in length supplying two branch circuits shall NOT be smaller than

   (A) 2 No. 14 AWG.
   (B) 2 No. 12 AWG.
   (C) 2 No. 10 AWG.
   (D) 2 No. 8 AWG.

21. Speed control by a method that requires two wound-rotor induction motors with their rotors rigidly connected together is called speed control by

   (A) change of poles.
   (B) field control.
   (C) concatenation.
   (D) voltage control.

22. Before connecting an alternator to the bus bars and in parallel with other alternators, it is necessary that its voltage and frequency be the same as that of the bus bars but that

   (A) the rotor revolve at synchronous speed.
   (B) the voltage be in phase opposition as well.
   (C) its power factor be not less than unity.
   (D) its power factor be greater than unity.

23. A belt is used to drive a 3-kW DC generator by a 5-hp, 3-phase induction motor. Adjustments for proper belt tension, with the generator running at full load, can be made with the aid of a

   (A) 50-lb. weight as wide as the belt.
   (B) voltmeter and an ammeter.
   (C) power-factor meter.
   (D) 3-phase wattmeter.

24. The cold resistance of a 120-volt, 100-watt tungsten incandescent lamp is

   (A) greater than its hot resistance.
   (B) smaller than its hot resistance.
   (C) approximately 100 ohms.
   (D) equal to its hot resistance.

25. The correct value of the resistance of a field coil can be measured by using

   (A) a Schering bridge.
   (B) an ammeter and a voltmeter.
   (C) a Kelvin double bridge.
   (D) a Maxwell bridge.

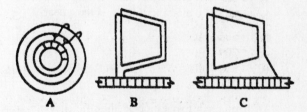

Figure 26

26. The three windings shown in Figure 26 belong respectively to the

   (A) ring, lap, and wave types of closed-coil windings.
   (B) ring, lap, and wave types of open-coil windings.
   (C) ring, lap, and wave types of reverse-coil windings.
   (D) ring, lap, and wave types of cumulative-coil windings.

27. Simplex lap windings have as many armature circuits as there are

 (A) commutator bars.
 (B) number of coils.
 (C) number of active conductors.
 (D) poles.

28. The power factor of a single-phase, alternating current motor may be found by using which one of the following sets of AC instruments?

 (A) One voltmeter and one phase-rotation meter
 (B) One voltmeter and one ammeter
 (C) One voltmeter, one ammeter, and one wattmeter
 (D) One voltmeter, one ammeter, and one watthour meter

29. When connecting wattmeters to AC motor circuits consuming large amounts of current, it is necessary to use

 (A) current transformers.
 (B) potential transformers.
 (C) power shunts.
 (D) isolation transformers.

30. A feeder consisting of a positive and a negative wire supplies a motor load. The feeder is connected to bus bars having a constant potential of 230 volts. The feeder is 500 feet long and consists of two 250,000 circular-mil conductors. The maximum load on the feeder is 170 amperes. Assume that the resistance of 1,000 feet of this cable is 0.0431 ohm. The voltage, at the motor terminals, is most nearly

 (A) 201 volts.
 (B) 209 volts.
 (C) 213 volts.
 (D) 217 volts.

31. With reference to question 30, the efficiency of transmission, in percent, is most nearly

 (A) 83 percent.
 (B) 87 percent.
 (C) 91 percent.
 (D) 97 percent.

32. With reference to AC motors, in addition to overload, many other things cause fuses to blow. The fuse will blow if, in starting an AC motor, the operator throws the starting switch of the compensator to the running position

 (A) too slowly.
 (B) too quickly.
 (C) with main switch in open position.
 (D) with main switch in close position.

33. A change in speed of a DC motor of 10 percent to 15 percent can usually be made by

 (A) rewinding the armature.
 (B) rewinding the field.
 (C) decreasing the number of turns in the field coils.
 (D) increasing or decreasing the gap between the armature and field.

34. In order to check the number of poles in a 3-phase, wound-rotor induction motor, it is necessary to check the no-load speed. The no-load speed is obtained by running the motor with load disconnected and with the

 (A) rotor resistance short-circuited.
 (B) rotor resistance all in.
 (C) rotor resistance half in.
 (D) rotor resistance one third in.

35. A group of industrial oil burners is equipped with several electric preheaters that can be used singly or in combination to heat the No. 6 oil for the burners. Electric preheater "A" alone can heat a certain quantity of oil from 70° to 160° in 15 minutes and preheater "B" alone can do the job in 30 minutes. If both preheaters are used together, they will do the job in

 (A) 12 minutes.
 (B) 11 minutes.
 (C) 10 minutes.
 (D) 9 minutes.

36. With reference to armature windings, in a wave winding, regardless of the number of poles, only

 (A) two brushes are necessary.
 (B) four brushes are necessary.
 (C) six brushes are necessary.
 (D) eight brushes are necessary.

37. The minimum number of overload devices required for a 3-phase AC motor connected to a 120/208 volt, 3-phase, 4-wire system is

 (A) 1
 (B) 2
 (C) 3
 (D) 4

Questions 38 and 39 are to be answered in accordance with the information given below.

To get equivalent delta from wye	To get equivalent wye from delta

$$A = \frac{ab + bc + ac}{a}$$ $$a = \frac{BC}{A + B + C}$$

$$B = \frac{ab + bc + ac}{b}$$ $$b = \frac{AC}{A + B + C}$$

$$C = \frac{ab + bc + ac}{c}$$ $$c = \frac{AB}{A + B + C}$$

The above formulas indicate the relationship between equivalent wye and delta networks.

38. If in a delta the branches are resistors such that $A = 5$ ohms, $B = 10$ ohms, and $C = 10$ ohms, the resistor of branch "a" of the equivalent wye is

(A) 5 ohms.
(B) 10 ohms.
(C) 2 ohms.
(D) 4 ohms.

39. In question 38 above, the resistor of branch "b" of the equivalent wye is

(A) 10 ohms.
(B) 4 ohms.
(C) 2 ohms.
(D) 5 ohms.

Questions 40 and 41 should be answered in accordance with the paragraph below.

Insulation resistance tests are best made with a direct-reading megger. These tests can also be made with a high-resistance voltmeter and a source of DC supply. Assume that a direct-reading instrument is not available but you have on hand a 100-volt voltmeter having a sensitivity of 5,000 ohms per volt and a 100-volt battery. The battery is connected in series with the voltmeter. One free battery lead is connected to the wire whose insulation resistance is to be measured and the other free lead to the grounded conduit. With this hookup, the voltmeter reads 50 volts.

40. The insulation resistance, in ohms, of the above conductor is

(A) 500
(B) 5,000
(C) 250,000
(D) 500,000

41. The resistance, in ohms, of the above mentioned voltmeter is

(A) 500
(B) 5,000
(C) 250,000
(D) 500,000

42. An ammeter and voltmeter are connected through instrument transformers to measure kVa of a balanced 3-phase load connected to a 2,400-volt, 3-phase, 3-wire system. The PT is rated 2,400/120 volts, and the CT is rated 200/5 amperes. If the ammeter reads 4 amperes and the voltmeter 100 volts, the load, in kVa, is approximately

(A) 0.4
(B) 6.8
(C) 320
(D) 555

43. A note on a lighting plan states, "All fluorescent fixtures shall be symmetrically spaced and oriented so that the major axis of the fixture is parallel to the major axis of the room." For a room 20′ long by 16′ wide with four 4-foot fixtures, the desired arrangement is fixtures parallel with and centered

(A) 4′ from 20′ wall, 5′ from 16′ wall.
(B) 5′ from 20′ wall, 4′ from 16′ wall.
(C) 4′ from 16′ wall, 5′ from 20′ wall.
(D) 5′ from 16′ wall, 4′ from 20′ wall.

44. According to the National Electrical Code, an externally operable switch may be used as the starter for a motor of not over 2 hp (and not over 300 volts), provided it has a rating of at least

(A) 2 times the stalled rotor current of the motor.
(B) 2 times the full-load current of the motor.
(C) 115 percent of the full-load current of the motor.
(D) 150 percent of the stalled rotor current of the motor.

45. According to the National Electrical Code, a single disconnecting means may serve a group of motors, provided

(A) all motors are $\frac{1}{2}$ hp or less.
(B) all motors are within a short distance from each other.
(C) all motors are located within a single room and within sight of the disconnecting means.
(D) one half of the motors are located within a single room and within sight of the disconnecting means.

46. In a 3-phase system with three identical loads connected in delta, if the line voltage is 4,160 volts, the line to neutral voltage is

    (A) indeterminate.
    (B) 7,200 volts.
    (C) 2,400 volts.
    (D) 2,000 volts.

47. If the current in each line is 100 amperes, the currents in each of the individual loads is (under the conditions as set forth in question 46)

    (A) indeterminate.
    (B) 57.7 amperes.
    (C) 173 amperes.
    (D) 50.0 amperes.

48. In a 3-phase system with three identical loads connected in wye, if the line to neutral voltage is 115 volts, the line voltage is

    (A) indeterminate.
    (B) 208 volts.
    (C) 200 volts.
    (D) 220 volts.

49. A room is 20 feet wide and is to be provided with 4 rows of lighting outlets symmetrically spaced. The distance from the wall to the center line of the first fixture row will be

    (A) 5′ 0″
    (B) 10′ 0″
    (C) 7′ 6″
    (D) 2′ 6″

50. A fixture mounting height of 9′ 6″ is specified for a room with a ceiling height of 12′ 0″, utilizing fixtures with a height of 6″. The size of stem required is most nearly

    (A) 3′ 0″
    (B) 2′ 6″
    (C) 2′ 0″
    (D) 1′ 6″

51. Specifications for a project require that 40W, T-12, RS/CW lamps be installed in a given group of fixtures. The type of lamp required is

    (A) 40 watt, type 12, reflector spot, clear white, incandescent.
    (B) 40 watt, single pin, relay start, code white, fluorescent.
    (C) 40 watt, bi-pin, rapid start, cool white, fluorescent.
    (D) type 12, medium base, recessed spot, clear white, incandescent.

52. In accordance with the Code, all wiring is to be installed so that when completed the system will be free from shorts or grounds. A circuit installation of No. 12 wire with all safety devices in place, but lampholders, receptacles, fixtures, and/or appliances not connected shall have a resistance between conductors and between all conductors and ground not less than

    (A) 10,000 ohms.
    (B) 100,000 ohms.
    (C) 250,000 ohms.
    (D) 1,000,000 ohms.

53. The Code states that wires, cables, and cords of all kinds except weatherproof wire shall have a

    (A) distinctive marking so that the maker may be readily identified.
    (B) tag showing the minimum working voltage for which the wire was tested or approved.
    (C) tag showing the maximum current passed through the conductor under test.
    (D) tag showing the ultimate tensile strength.

54. The Code states that conductors supplying an individual motor shall have a minimum carrying capacity of

    (A) 110 percent of the motor full-load current.
    (B) 120 percent of the motor full-load current.
    (C) 125 percent of the motor full-load current.
    (D) 135 percent of the motor full-load current.

55. For not more than three conductors in raceway "based on a room temperature of 86°F," the allowable current-carrying capacity, in amperes, of a No. 12, AWG type-R conductor is

    (A) 15
    (B) 20
    (C) 30
    (D) 40

56. In accordance with the Code, the number of No. 14 AWG type-R conductors running through or terminating in a $1\frac{1}{2}″ \times 3\frac{1}{4}″$ octagonal outlet or junction box should NOT be greater than

    (A) 5
    (B) 6
    (C) 7
    (D) 8

57. The part of a circuit that melts when the current abnormally exceeds the allowable carrying capacity of the conductor is called a(n)

    (A) circuit breaker.
    (B) thermo cutout.
    (C) overload trip.
    (D) fuse.

58. Defects in wiring that permit current to jump from one wire to another before the intended path has been completed are called

    (A) grounds.
    (B) shorts.
    (C) opens.
    (D) breaks.

59. In accordance with the Code, a grounding conductor for a direct-current system shall have a current-carrying capacity not less than that of the largest conductor supplied by the system and in no case less than that of

    (A) No. 12 copper wire.
    (B) No. 10 copper wire.
    (C) No. 8 copper wire.
    (D) No. 6 copper wire.

60. In accordance with the Code, the grounding connection for interior metal raceways and armored cable shall be made at a point

    (A) not greater than 5 feet from the source of supply.
    (B) not greater than 10 feet from the source of supply.
    (C) as far as possible from the source of supply.
    (D) as near as practicable to the source of supply.

61. In accordance with the Code, motors

    (A) may be operated in series multiple.
    (B) may be operated in multiple series.
    (C) shall not be operated in series multiple.
    (D) shall not be operated in multiple.

62. Boxes and fittings intended for outdoor use should be of

    (A) weatherproof type.
    (B) stamped steel of not less than No. 16 standard gage.
    (C) stamped steel plated with cadmium.
    (D) ample strength and rigidity.

63. Two $\frac{1}{4}$-hp motors, under the protection of a single set of overcurrent devices and with or without other current-consuming devices in the current, are considered as being sufficiently protected if the rating or setting of the overcurrent device does not exceed

    (A) 15 amperes at 250 volts.
    (B) 15 amperes at 125 volts.
    (C) 30 amperes at 125 volts.
    (D) 30 amperes at 250 volts.

64. In a balanced 3-phase, wye-connected load, the

    (A) line to neutral voltage equals the line voltage.
    (B) line to neutral voltage equals the line voltage multiplied by the square root of 3.
    (C) line voltage equals the line to neutral voltage divided by the square root of 3.
    (D) line voltage equals the line to neutral voltage multiplied by the square root of 3.

65. The output of a 6-pole DC generator is 360 amperes at 240 volts. If its armature is simplex lap-wound, the current per path, in amperes, through the armature is

    (A) 52.5
    (B) 60
    (C) 105
    (D) 210

66. In reference to question 65, the voltage per path, in volts, is

    (A) 120
    (B) 420
    (C) 60
    (D) 240

67. In reference to question 65, the kilowatt rating of the machine is approximately

    (A) 86
    (B) 50
    (C) 14
    (D) 7

68. Specifications for a project require the use of indirect type of lighting fixtures. The one of the following types that will meet this requirement is

    (A) RCM dome fixture.
    (B) concentric ring fixture with silverbowl lamp.
    (C) downlight with par 38 spot.
    (D) opal glass bowl.

69. An industrial plant utilizes acetone as a solvent in one area. All wiring in this area must be

(A) vaportight.
(B) watertight.
(C) explosion proof.
(D) of normal construction.

70. In an area where explosion-proof wiring is required, each conduit entering an enclosure containing apparatus that may produce arcs, sparks, or high temperatures shall be provided with

(A) insulating bushings.
(B) a cable terminator.
(C) an approved sealing compound.
(D) double locknuts.

ANSWER KEY

1. C	15. A	29. A	43. A	57. D
2. D	16. B	30. D	44. B	58. B
3. B	17. B	31. D	45. C	59. C
4. D	18. C	32. B	46. A	60. D
5. B	19. B	33. D	47. B	61. C
6. B	20. C	34. A	48. C	62. A
7. C	21. C	35. C	49. D	63. B
8. D	22. B	36. A	50. C	64. D
9. B	23. D	37. B	51. C	65. B
10. B and C	24. B	38. D	52. D	66. D
11. A	25. B	39. C	53. A	67. A
12. D	26. A	40. D	54. C	68. B
13. A	27. D	41. D	55. B	69. C
14. C	28. C	42. C	56. A	70. C

APPENDIX

Content for Future Exams

THE ELECTRICIAN AND FIBER OPTICS

Electricians are now called upon not only to string wire in buildings but also to pull coaxial cable and fiber-optics cables into existing buildings as well as new construction. At the present time, the electrician examinations do not cover the area of fiber optics. We include information here to inform you about the basics of fiber optics in the event that this is added to the exam in the future.

The National Electrical Code has established standards for the cable and its installation. Knowing something about the cables, splices, and installation distinguishes the electrician who is "up to date" from the one who is just a wire puller. Even residential building now requires cable to be installed for computers, fast access to the Internet, and central control systems for heating, air conditioning, and lighting.

Damage to the cable can result in a complete or partial loss of the transmitted signal. Due care should be taken in installation to prevent nails or screws from damaging the cable coating. The angle of the bend or turn in the installation of the cable can contribute to losses in signal. Coupling the fiber-optic cable to devices and making sure there is a minimum of loss associated with the connection means a lot of practice and some very expensive tools and equipment.

A look at some of the difficulties with splices and the treatment of the fiber cable and the light conductors that are in it will give you a better idea as to how much attention to detail the cable needs as compared to pulling wire through 2 by 4's and walls and floors.

FIBER OPTICS SPLICING

There are two methods of splicing fiber optics: fusion and mechanical.

Fusion splices have less fresnel refraction when they are complete and, therefore, less loss than mechanical splices. The way a fusion splicer works is after the two fiber ends to be spliced are inserted into the splice housing, the splicer cleaves the ends, butts them together, and thermally fuses the ends together. One of the most popular models of the splicer is made by Fujikura.

Fresnel refraction is a loss of signal in a fiber cable because of a splice or a crack in the glass of the fiber. The splice or crack causes a type of reflection, called a fresnel reflection. This causes the light to scatter in different directions, rather than "focus" its way down the fiber. The term can also refer to a terrestrial radio signal off of an object, such as a building, hill, or body of water from its fresnel zone. Fresnel reflections can cause a reduction in signal strength or total loss of the signal altogether.

MECHANICAL FIBER-OPTIC SPLICE

The mechanical fiber-optic splice is an alternative type of splice. It is also called fusion splicing. Fusion splicing equipment is very expensive. A typical splicer may cost $40,000. Mechanical splices come as a kit, which connectorizes the ends of the fibers. A tool kit is required for mechanical splicing. It consists of a microscope, polishing puck, cleavers, epoxy, and polishing compound. They cost about $1,200. An oven used to "hot cure" the epoxy is also available. With a mechanical splice, you cleave or cut the end of the fiber as square and smooth as possible, then epoxy the fiber end to the connector. The epoxy takes about 12 hours to cure without an oven and about 20 minutes with an oven. After the epoxy has cured, the tip of the connector (which should be flush with the end of the fiber optic) is polished by holding it with a device called a puck (it is shaped like a hockey puck). The puck holds the fiber connector while it is gently rubbed against a pad coated with polishing compound. When the polishing is done, the connector is ready to be mated with another connector and the splice is complete. Mechanical splice kits cost about $15 per splice and are available in SC- and ST-style connectors.

CONNECTORS

There are three types of connectors used in the field: FT, SC, and ST.

FT connector—a metallic, screw-on fiber-optic connector.

SC connector—a square-shaped snap-on fiber-optic plastic connector. SC connectors come in single or dual. This is the latest model used for connecting fibers.

ST connector (*Straight Tip connector*)—an older type of fiber-optic connector. The newer type is the SC connector, which is constructed of plastic instead of metal.

Western Electric fiber cable is shown in Figure A. This cable package has 12 ribbons of 12 close-packed coated fibers. These 144 fibers are then wrapped in paper, encased in a polyethylene jacket and a Kevlar-type braid that is surrounded by steel wires embedded in a plastic protective sheath. There even exists a mass splice for aligning all 144 individual fibers when cables longer than 1 km are needed.

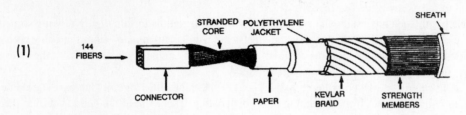

(1)

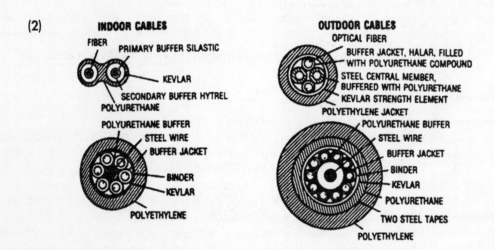

(2)

Figure A. (1) Western Electric fiber cable. (2) Indoor and outdoor cables for fiber optics.

Alignment of the fibers when splicing is critical to an installation. There are at least five different sources of light loss and therefore signal strength (see Figure B).

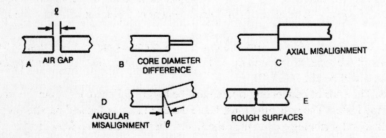

Figure B. Optical signal loss sources.

Air gap. Air gap losses include *reflectance* and loss due to diverging light rays (Figure C). Each glass-to-air interface can result in a 4 percent loss. The loss between air and GaAs sources and detectors, however, are more like 32 percent. Diverging rays can miss the core altogether or fall outside of the cone of acceptance of the receiving fiber (Figure D).

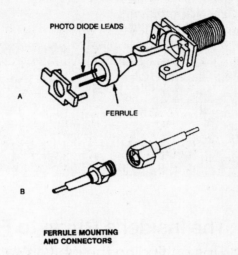

Figure C. A–Reflective coupler and B–Transmissive star coupler and light reflection.

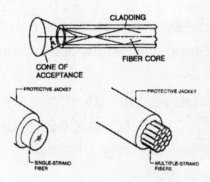

Figure D. The cone of acceptance.

Core diameter difference. This loss is unity (0 dB) if the receiving fiber (or other device) is larger than the source. However, this can result in large mode-dispersion in the fiber waveguide.

Axial misalignment. This is also called *lateral* or *radial* displacement. If the displacement is as much as 15 percent of the smaller core diameter, the loss will be about 1 dB. Displacement of 5 percent will keep the loss below the 0.3 dB level.

Angular misalignment. Losses here utilize a formula that is very complex and is a function of the numerical aperture (NA), the reflective index of the separating medium, and of course the angle theta (θ). For typical fibers with NA = 0.5 and O = 2 degrees, the loss will be about 0.5 dB.

End-surface roughness. The ends of connecting fibers must be highly polished, less than 0.5 micrometer grit (μm), in order to avoid scattering losses. The polishing must leave the end faces as flat and parallel as possible. The best way is to use a sapphire or diamond scribbing tool to nick the fibers, then pull until the fiber snaps.

NATIONAL ELECTRICAL CODE AND FIBER OPTICS

The Code covers the treatment of fiber-optic cables and raceways in Article 770. The cables are classified as nonconductive, conductive, and hybrid. Article 770 covers the use of Fiber Optical Cables and Raceways in association with conventional metallic-conductor circuits. Nonconductive optical fiber cables are permitted to be installed in the same raceway and enclosures as metallic-conductors circuits where the functions of the two different types of cables are associated with the same equipment, operation, or process. The article limits its coverage to joint installations of electrical cable and optical fiber cable.

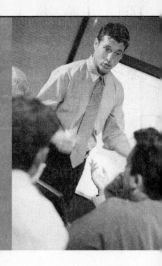